Elke Krasny
Living with an Infected Planet

X-Texts on Culture and Society

Editorial

The supposed »end of history« long ago revealed itself to be much more an end to certainties. More than ever, we are not only faced with the question of »Generation X«. Beyond this kind of popular figures, academia is also challenged to make a contribution to a sophisticated analysis of the time. The series **X-TEXTS** takes on this task, and provides a forum for thinking *with and against time*. The essays gathered together here decipher our present moment, resisting simplifying formulas and oracles. They combine sensitive observations with incisive analysis, presenting both in a conveniently, readable form.

Elke Krasny (PhD) is a professor for Art and Education at the Akademie der bildenden Künste Wien. Her scholarship addresses ecological and social justice in the global present with a focus on the politics of interdependencies and the emergence of a twenty-first century care feminism.

Elke Krasny
Living with an Infected Planet
COVID-19, Feminism, and the Global Frontline of Care

[transcript]

Supported by the Open Access Publication Fund of the Academy of Fine Arts Vienna

A...kademie der
bildenden Künste
Wien

Bibliographic information published by the Deutsche Nationalbibliothek
The Deutsche Nationalbibliothek lists this publication in the Deutsche Nationalbibliografie; detailed bibliographic data are available in the Internet at http://dnb.d-nb.de

This work is licensed under the Creative Commons Attribution-NonCommercial-NoDerivatives 4.0 (BY-NC-ND) which means that the text may be used for non-commercial purposes, provided credit is given to the author. For details go to
https://creativecommons.org/licenses/by-nc-nd/4.0/
To create an adaptation, translation, or derivative of the original work and for commercial use, further permission is required and can be obtained by contacting rights@transcript-publishing.com
Creative Commons license terms for re-use do not apply to any content (such as graphs, figures, photos, excerpts, etc.) not original to the Open Access publication and further permission may be required from the rights holder. The obligation to research and clear permission lies solely with the party re-using the material.

First published in 2023 by transcript Verlag, Bielefeld
© Elke Krasny

Cover layout: Alexander Ach Schuh – achschuh.com
Cover illustration: Marga RH: Hasta que la dignidad se haga costumbre (Until Dignity Becomes a Habit), 2020
Proofreading: Alexandra Cox, Dortmund
Printed by Majuskel Medienproduktion GmbH, Wetzlar
Print-ISBN 978-3-8376-5915-3
PDF-ISBN 978-3-8394-5915-7
https://doi.org/10.14361/9783839459157
ISSN of series: 2364-6616
eISSN of series: 2747-3775

Printed on permanent acid-free text paper.

Contents

Acknowledgements 7

Introduction: Worry and Hope 11

Chapter 1: We Are at War 25

Chapter 2: Serving at the Frontlines 61

Chapter 3: Feminist Recovery 109

Conclusion: We Care Therefore We Are 167

Bibliography 171

Notes 187

Acknowledgements

Writing a book is held to be solitary, and it is, or rather, it can be. At the same time writing is always writing in relation and in webs of care and support, which make sharing and generating ways of living and knowing with the planet possible. I want to acknowledge the generosity and work of all the people who make such writing possible

Special thanks to my family, with all family members offering different kinds of support, care, encouragement, thought, feedback, and ideas. I want to thank Alexander Schuh for designing the cover and Yamna Krasny, Yona Schuh, and Yaron Schuh for believing that books have a life in the real world.

I want to thank my colleagues and students at the Academy of Fine Arts Vienna, in particular my PhD students, whose work is dedicated to novel and challenging feminist thinking. I am thankful to Johan F. Hartle, Rector of the Academy of Fine Arts Vienna, for inviting me to contribute an essay to the Academy's series of corona essays, which led me to thinking about the global international care order.

I want to thank Lara Perry for feminist friendship and unwavering commitment to understanding how feminist organizing and scholarship can inspire emancipatory change. I want to thank Angelika Fitz for her inspiring optimism and for working together on planetary perspectives of care. I am grateful for sharing open-ended thoughts and doubts with Elke Gaugele, such sharing in feminist intellectual solidarity is the best. Pandemic walks with Alexa Färber, Christiane Feuerstein, and Ruby Sircar provided time for treasured conversations. I am very grateful to Emma Dowling, Riikka Prattes, and Olga Shparaga for feminist scholarly companionship and discussions dedicated to care. I am particularly thankful for the work of Joan Tronto and her inspiring and critical thinking on care.

I want to thank all the people who have, in the last two years, invited me to share thoughts on care, feminism, and what it means to live with an infected planet. Their interest in care feminism makes that thinking means to be in relation. I want to thank some of them in person here: I want to thank Aisling O'Carroll for inviting me to contribute to a special issue of *Site Magazine* and to think in real time about a response to the virus outbreak and for introducing me to the work of Carol Anne Hilton and her ideas on indigenomics. I want to thank Mijo Miquel Bartual for encouraging me to write a contribution for the peer-reviewed journal *Escritua y Imagen*. I want to thank Lisa Stuckey for inviting me to speak about care in relation to infrastructure at the first Freiburg Biennale and telling me that she had seen infrastructural dimensions in my thinking all along. I want to thank Sofia Wiberg and Stina Nyberg for curating the symposium *A thinking practice* that made people come together carefully in pandemic times and for inviting me to speak about care, feminism, and Covid-19. I want to thank Andros Zins-Brown for asking a complex question about care in relation to violence, or put differently, if violence can become a form of care when thinking about Black Lives Matters physically dismantling and taking down monuments to supremacy. This brought me to thinking even more than before about care as a form of state violence and how such care violence is enacted through interlocking regimes of imposed and forcible care, care negligence, and care extractivism. I want to thank Joulia Strauss for feminist friendship and the insistence that care feminism should be brought to the garden in Athens, where Plato met with students more than 2000 years ago, as part of her long-term project Avtonomi Akadimia. I want to particularly thank Athena Athanasiou, Angela Dimitrakaki, and Iris Lykourioti for contributing to the care feminism workshop and for sharing their thoughts on the complex challenges of care in times of crisis and war. I want to thank Maddalena Fragnito and Zoe Romano for most inspiring public and private conversations about matters of care in Milano. I want to thank Urška Jurman for inviting me to speak at the Maribor EKO 8 Eko Triennale and for her initiative to start the working group Ecologies of Care. Ecologies of Care, Simona Vidmar, Yasmin Vodopivec, Breda Kolar, Eszter Erdosi, Vida Rucli, Gabi Scardi, Nicola Feiks, Inês Moreira, Nada Schroer, Alessandra Pomarico, Joulia Strauss, Rosario Talevi, Raluca Voinea, Inga Lace and Daria Bocharnikova, provide inspiration and hope. I want to thank Lindsay Harkema, Women in Practice, for attending an online lecture on care and architecture I delivered at the Spitzer School of Architecture, New York, and for subsequently initiating together the working group Environments of Care. Environments of Care, Bryony Roberts, Isabelle Doucet, Ven Paldano, Sumayya Vally, Licia Soldavini, Mascha Fehse, Sonya Gimon, Shona Beechey, Huda Tayob, Justine Djernes, Emmy Laura Perez Fjalland, and Marianne Krogh.

To Karin Werner, the publisher at transcript, and Annika Linnemann, the managing editor at transcript, I offer my thanks for their confident endorsements of the importance of the subject. The readers of the manuscript, Jenna Ashton, Lara Perry, Alessandra Pomarico, and Henriette Steiner, gave generous and constructive feedback. I am thankful for their feminist intellectual solidarity and their support. I am grateful to Alexandra Cox for her thorough work on the manuscript. I want to thank feminist activist Marga RH for allowing me to use the illustration for the cover. I first saw the illustration Until Dignity Becomes a Habit by Marga RH when it was used for the invitation to the Feminist Recovery Plan Project. A Feminist Recovery Plan for Covid-19 and Beyond: Learning from Grassroots Activism hosted at the University of Warwick. This illustration provides feminist hope.

Introduction: Worry and Hope

Worrying about what would become the central concerns addressed in *Living with an Infected Planet. Covid-19, Feminism and the Global Frontline of Care* set in in March 2020. Thinking about writing what became this book began on March 13, 2020. That was the date on which António Guterres, the secretary-general of the United Nations, "the world's largest universal multilateral international organization", informed all the human beings who inhabit their shared planet together that "we must declare war on the virus".[1] Just two days before, the World Health Organization, the United Nation's agency which has the task to "direct and coordinate the world's response to health emergencies", had declared the outbreak of a new strain of coronavirus, Severe Acute Respiratory Syndrome Coronavirus 2—SARS-CoV-2, the cause of coronavirus disease 2019, known as Covid-19—a pandemic.[2] Like millions and millions and millions of other human beings around the world, I most intently followed the news on the global health catastrophe, listening to reports and watching images of ambulances rushing the infected to hospitals only to end up in long queues and find themselves unable to deliver those in most urgent need of oxygen to the intensive care units. There was news on the surging numbers of people dying from infection. The news circulated images of healthcare workers, nurses, and doctors, in their gowns, goggles, gloves, and face shields, working with utmost dedication under enormous stresses and strains. The news showed images of dead Covid-19 patients in the hallways of hospitals, of Covid-19 dead piling up in funeral homes and on burial grounds that were operating around the clock, while friends and family were not allowed to be with their infected kin, with the dying or the dead, so that the spread of the deadly virus could be slowed down. Worry consumed me as I followed the news on the pandemic in March 2020 and sought to comprehend what it means to be living with an infected planet. While the pandemic realities were reason enough for utmost worry, what worried me even more was that the response to the pandemic catastrophe by the world's largest universal, multilateral, international organization was fundamentally based on the idea of war. The international political response to the global health emergency, with its aim to ensure the formation of a global frontline of care, relied on terms and imaginaries of war.

António Guterres stated that the "only war we should be waging is the war against COVID-19".[3] Political oratory bound care to war in order to define the duty to care as a social obligation through the ethos of militarized solidarity. My interest is on how public, political, and social imaginaries are constituted, and made material, by way of words and metaphors. Susan Sontag's book-length critical essay *Illness as Metaphor*, first published in 1978, identified a specific historical moment in which war and disease were metaphorically joined together. Sontag states that the "military metaphor in medicine first came into wide use in the 1880s" when "bacteria were said to 'invade' or 'infiltrate'".[4] Given that there is this long history of a traffic between illness and war, disease and the military, I am interested in the implications these metaphorical relations have for care. War and disease are even linked in statistical comparison.

> There are dozens of calculations showing the cost equivalent in fighter jets or nukes, which governments apparently can afford, compared with the costs to develop, produce and stockpile the lifesaving medical goods we need.[5]

Political oratory uses words or metaphors in order to work ideologically and strategically with specific associations that words have acquired. Human rights activist and writer on human rights, conflict, and peace Alex de Waal spoke of the importance of words and metaphors in pandemic times and stated that "it is imperative we attend to the language and metaphors that shape our thinking."[6] What, then, does it mean in cultural, social, spiritual, affective, and emotional terms that the response to the pandemic health catastrophe was not articulated in a vocabulary of care, but in the terminology of war? War is a key imaginary in the histories and value systems of masculinist patriarchy and militarized nationalism. The realities of war are stimulants and drivers of colonial capitalist economies. War reproduces and fuels patriarchy and capitalism. How does one respond to having been made part of, and implicated, in a war effort against the virus when one wants to contribute to care, in particular to an alternative importance, value, and understanding of care beyond, or outside, the violent regimes of economic extraction, politics of domination, and epistemic silencing? This book represents an humble attempt at a response to the implications of the hegemonic response to the needs of care in pandemic times. This includes engagement with the specific feminist response to Covid-19 at the level of feminist-policy making articulated through the notion of recovery.

As a cultural feminist theorist, whose analytical interests "follow words around", as Sara Ahmed inspirationally put it, and examine "ways of seeing", as John Berger critically advised, I began to follow words in political speeches, press briefings, and policy documents and to look at ways of seeing care workers transformed into frontline workers under the pandemic gaze as they appeared on the cover image of a globally distributed magazine, or in a popularized painting by a very well-known artist.[7] The visual rhetoric of pandemic portraits in documentary photography, and the accompanying narrative, affirmed and celebrated the masculinist and militaristic rhetoric of public political oratory. I was worried about the fact that the *political response to the pandemic* turned the so-called metaphor of war into a political concept for global solidarity, which resulted in militarized care essentialism. What is equally, if perhaps even more, worrying is the metaphorical normalization of war terminology, as war and its imaginaries also penetrate legal and economic policy in times of non-war. The definition of the *frontline worker* is a central example of the normalization of the idea, and ideology, of war in economic state policy and economic realities. Worry led me to search for a distinct *feminist response* to the pandemic, in particular, a *feminist response to this hegemonic political response* that relied on the imaginary of war for mobilization at the *global frontline of care*. This led me to study *feminist recovery plans* that were drawn up and written in the early months of the pandemic lockdown situation in 2020, when political war rhetoric was permeating the global public sphere. Learning about and studying *feminist recovery plans* gave me *feminist hope*. *Feminist worry* and *feminist hope* motivate and drive this book.

Working with the concept of "keywords", first introduced by Marxist critic Raymond Williams in 1976 and defined by him "as significant binding words in certain activities and their interpretation" and as "strong, difficult and persuasive words in everyday usage", I understand *war*, *frontline*, and *feminist recovery* as most significant words that articulated politics and policy in relation to care after the World Health Organization had declared the virus outbreak a pandemic in mid-March of 2020.[8] Structured in three chapters, "We Are at War", "Serving at the Frontlines" and "Feminist Recovery", this book follows the words *war*, *frontline*, and *feminist recovery* around as they matter to care and provides a feminist cultural analysis of their meanings and implications. Words and metaphors are used to articulate imaginaries. The power of words and metaphors to form associations and to deliver up imaginaries is harnessed by hegemonic politics and put to use for violent ideologies. At the same time, this specific power of words and metaphors is used for emancipatory struggle and feminist resistance. As words and metaphors are shared articulation, able to be put to use for very different purposes at the level of political articulation, it is most important to attend analytically to the material-making of the meaning they hold in the response to living with an infected planet. The political pandemic vocabulary of war and the frontline spread quickly and globally. Approaching from a feminist cultural analysis perspective this vocabulary and the deep semantic implications of the meanings held by its words, terms, and metaphors requires close attention to the epistemic, affective, and social implications, and impact, that words have as they circulate in public realm of politics and policy. Key to my motivation here is the interest in the traffic among words, images, meaning, imaginaries, and ontologies as they connect the crisis to metaphors and realities of war and disease. Words and metaphors are central to constituting and spreading meaning. "Metaphors [...] are conceptual in nature. They are among our principal vehicles for understanding. And they play a central role in the construction of social and political reality."[9] Words, and metaphors, seep into cultural imaginings and visual imagery as they constitute social imaginaries and give shape to public ideas and public consciousness.

This book is concerned with the meanings and implications of the words war, frontline, and feminist recovery in public and social imaginaries in relation to care. Rather than working with a narrow definition of care, the understanding of care that underpins my approach is most expansive and includes all kinds of cares: labors, infrastructures, natural resources, knowledge, feelings, ethics. Care is, at once, corporeal, material, infrastructural, natural, environmental, ecological, epistemological, emotional, spiritual, and ethical. Perhaps most importantly, care, even if imperfect or unjust, starts from and practices the acknowledgement of interdependency in social, ecological, infrastructural, epistemic, and emotional terms. Feminist philosopher and public intellectual Judith Butler stated that "social interdependency characterizes life".[10] Following Butler, "the description of social bonds without which life is imperiled takes place at the level of a social ontology, to be understood more as a social imaginary than as a metaphysics of the social."[11] What, then, to make of the state of social bonds when politics and policy turn to imaginaries of war and the terminology of the frontline in order to ensure essential care? War imaginaries are harmful and destructive to social ontologies. Therefore, work toward a different understanding of care, based on both worry and hope, has to start with analysis of the political response to the pandemic, which is characterized by the erosion of public imaginaries of care and by militarized violence in frontline ontologies.

In *Dispossession: The Performative in the Political*, Judith Butler and feminist theorist and anthropologist Athena Athanasiou explore in conversation "what makes political responsiveness possible"[12]. They examine how political imaginaries are constituted. Athanasiou speaks of "opening up conceptual, discursive, affective, and political spaces for enlarging our economic and political imaginary."[13] In order to open up such spaces for alternative economic and political imaginaries of care, one also needs to understand what kind of imaginaries occupy such spaces. In particular, the space between the literal and the metaphorical, which is central to constituting public and social imaginaries, has been occupied by war and frontlines in pandemic times. The hegemony of capitalist economies was allied with the use of war imaginaries in public political oratory and policy made real in the policy term frontline work, which mandated the continuation of essential work and demanded that all essential workers continue working while all the non-essential work had to stop and people were required to shelter in place at home. The term frontline work clearly exposes the militarization of exploitative, extractive, and dangerous conditions of essential labor under the hegemony of capitalism, as it made clear how deeply the imaginaries of war had penetrated and defined policy frameworks and economic realities. Understanding critical feminist cultural analysis as relevant to feminist social theory and as a contribution to feminist activism and practice, my interest is on what a critical cultural analysis of the imaginaries of care, as they emerged in public articulations circulating on an international level and informing a global public sphere, tells us about our humanity and how we live in social and cultural terms with the conditions of ontological interconnectedness and interdependencies, which we can begin to understand at the level of our dependency on breathing. The analysis presented over the chapters of this book is seen as a modest contribution to a still largely unwritten history of political, economic, and epistemic cultural imaginaries and social ontologies relevant to understanding care. Such imaginaries will have to be critically unearthed and reconstituted from the long history of multiple silences around care.

Worried about the absence of public imaginaries of care and about the political use of the idea of war in order to ensure care led me to ask critical questions of my own work as a feminist cultural theorist and of the field of feminist cultural theory and feminist cultural analysis. Why have feminist approaches to cultural theory and analysis failed to more fully think with epistemologies of care and care as knowledge? Why has feminist cultural theory not contributed much more to an expanded, more nuanced, and richer vocabulary around care?

The contribution this book makes is the introduction of *feminist worry* and *feminist hope* as methods, which emerge from taking care as knowledge seriously. I will say more about feminist hope at the end of this introduction; for now, I will stay with worry. Worry has to do with care. Historical semantics and etymology connect care and worry through the Proto-West-Germanic root of karu, which is also related to the Old Norse kǫr, which means sickbed. The everyday experience of care, both care-giving and care-receiving, offers ample instruction on how care fills one with worry and requires one to respond to needs of care with worry. Feminist worry as an analytic includes worried listening, looking, reading, writing, and questioning. As a cultural theorist, I hold it to be my task and social obligation *to look at and listen to words and images*.[14] As a feminist cultural theorist, I am particularly interested in the space that opens up between the *literal meaning* and the *metaphorical meaning*. I see this space as a space of and for "political responsiveness", as a space for feminist political agency, and as a space to be used with care.[15] Words and metaphors are never independent, they come with meanings, histories, and associations attached to them. They have been to many places before one starts using them. Metaphors, in particular, are very agile. They move quite effortlessly between times as well as between real spaces and discursive spaces. Metaphors connect, while they separate: they separate a word from its literal meaning, by connecting it more deeply to this meaning in order to free up this meaning for transference onto other contexts, situations, objects, things, humans and so on and so forth. Use of metaphors has far-reaching implications in the contexts of social, political, material, cultural, religious, spiritual, ecological, and economic meaning-making. Expanding on the notion of keywords, one can think of keymetaphors as useful to the analysis of how politics, culture, and society relate to the meanings of words, in particular in situations of extremes. I understand metaphors to be conveyors of the deep meaning of language to the surface. Furthermore, the figurative use of words has to be understood as a specific form of language-based heritage, through which we can grasp important ontological, cosmological, and spiritual concepts through which relations between humans and their world are imagined. Metaphors reflect back to us, they tell us out loud how we imagine ourselves in relation to the world. Metaphors rely on understandability and on stretching understandability to the maximum, and, perhaps, even beyond, as they invite those, who hear, read, or see metaphors to add their own associations and comparisons. While one might think of metaphors as an explicitly, perhaps even exclusively, literary device, metaphors are, in fact, everywhere. We make use of metaphors in everyday language. Political oratory is quite purposefully, strategically, and ideologically filled with metaphors. Metaphors are held to be more persuasive than the bare literal meaning of words. They enhance the power of language as they invite affective and analytical responses. They make meanings hotter or colder, sharper or softer. Metaphors are articulations of structures of thought just as much as of structures of feeling. Metaphors cause us to relate to our realities and our imaginaries differently. I see this space that opens up between the literal and the metaphorical as a profoundly political space, as a space in which meaning can be shaped and reoriented, as a space from which influential public imaginaries can emerge. How this space between the literal and the metaphorical is put to use in the contexts of politics and policy requires feminist cultural analysis. At the same time, this space between the metaphorical and the literal is open to feminist political agency and collective action. *Looking at*, and *listening to*, words and images are not only seen as critical social obligations in feminist cultural theory, but also as distinct methods.

Approaching my study material of political speeches, press briefings, policy briefs, popular imagery, and feminist recovery plans with worry and with hope led me to ways of working that interrogate, interpret, and use the space between the literal and the metaphorical, based on the understanding that meaning-making is always material. Feminist historian of science Donna Haraway has challenged the separation between semiosis and materiality. She speaks of "material-semiotic nodes or knots" and "material-semiotic makings".[16] Therefore, metaphors cannot be separated from their material histories. Worried analysis includes the methods of *reading back* and *reinscribing*. This entails reading literal meanings back into the figurative use of metaphors in order to provide a critical feminist cultural analysis of how imaginaries and ontologies are interdependent and interrelated. Reading back builds on activist feminist epistemological traditions of Black feminist thought, in particular on social activist and scholar on race, class and feminism bell hooks' notion of "talking back".[17] Reading back means reading political keymetaphors, which are understood as the articulation of political will and public imaginaries from above, through their hegemonic and canonical meanings in order to provide critical interpretive approaches to the analysis of the materialization of power in meaning-making, for resistance and, ultimately, for developing other metaphors and other imaginaries. *Reinscribing* supports the method of reading back and places emphasis on the material realities captured in the literal dimension of words. Reading back and reinscribing are methodological tools for the critical analysis of how the materiality of metaphors operates as part of their ideological function.

Metaphors are constituted through the relations between the literal and the figurative. In political usage, war metaphors are used to manage a perceived societal problem. What is war a political metaphor for? When I asked family and friends for help to provide me with associations of war as metaphor in political public oratory, they drew up the following list for me: war stands for the army, manliness, honor, responsibility, heroism, patriotism, strong male bonds, strength, force, power, vigilance, resolve, unity, comradery, loyalty, defensibility, armament, being equipped for war, sacrifice, uniformity, obedience, and endurance, but also mass death, ethnic cleansing, extinction of life and nature, war crimes, violence, destruction, nationalism, fundamentalism, killing the enemy at all costs, sexual violence and mass rape, sacrificing the lives of soldiers, cannon fodder, ruination, mourning, suffering, pain, disease, terror, futility, disease, refugees, and displacement. While the political rhetoric comparing the pandemic to war mobilizes unity, endurance, obligation, commitment, and readiness for personal sacrifice and heroism, the mass death, suffering, pain and deadliness associated with war can also be linked to pandemic disease. My feminist examination is aimed at understanding the implications of the frontline. The inquiry is focused on how the emergence of pandemic frontline imaginaries changed the social ontologies of care. The duty to care was ideologically construed as a new form of militarized care essentialism. Like all other forms of sexism, these modern social ontologies and imaginaries of gendered care essentialism matter to state governance, capitalist economies, political thought, and the realities of women's lives. The militarization of care in pandemic times is placed, here, in relation to the modern formation of sexism, in order to foreground that the notions of mobilization and the frontline imaginaries served the purpose of re-gendering the image of care as a male virtue and masculinist heroism, while, at the same time, perpetuating its feminized material and economic realities. Taken together, reading back and reinscribing insist that material realities cannot be decoupled from the metaphorical use of terms. I understand it as an ethical commitment and a social obligation of worried analysis, and feminist cultural theory in general, to work for a better understanding of the ideological effects that the literal meanings of words, and the changing material realities stored within them, produce when these words are used metaphorically as political ideas. At the same time, I see analysis not only as a way of responding to circumstances, to what is already given, using the tools of critical cultural theory, but as a contribution in order to be responsive to what is yet to come. Therefore, my hope is that such a focus on the importance of words and imagery can be useful to future feminist work on words and imagery that inspire public imaginaries of care, of which there is a chronic lack.

This book does not present a history of the pandemic during its first months of lockdown in March and April 2020, but an unfolding of matters and concerns around imaginaries and realities of care that were thrown into stark relief because of the pandemic. There exists a large body of research, in particular social science research, on gendered, racialized, and classed dimensions of care, labor, health, and poverty as well as care injustices and care discrimination. What this book brings to the understanding of care, defined by political theorist and care ethicist Joan Tronto and educational scholar Berenice Fisher as "everything we do to maintain, continue, and repair our world so that we may live in it as well as possible", is the political idea of imaginaries of care and the epistemological view on care as a distinct way of generating knowledge.[18] The legacies of Western philosophy and political thought are characterized by the understanding of the human being as ζῷον πολιτικόν.[19] In historical hindsight, one can see today that this history is marked by the absence of a political thought tradition that conceives of the human being as a caring being. Furthermore, there is an also an absence of political thought traditions in the imaginaries of care that would understand the human "species activity" of care as one of many activities of care engaged in by a multitude of species.[20] I see this lack of public care imaginaries, which includes the still widely assumed human exceptionalism and human-centered speciesism, in care, and the absence of multispecies care, as cultural, ethical, and spiritual poverty around care. This became acute in the militarized care essentialism and the expectation of care heroism that emerged through the political response of declaring war under the aim of ensuring care. This poverty of imaginaries of care is part of the profound crisis of care.

The "crisis of care" that has long been diagnosed by critical feminist thinkers, as for example by Marxist political scientist Nancy Fraser, has been described as a gendered, classed, and racialized crisis of labor and infrastructures.[21] This crisis of care, which is commonly understood to result from the violence of economic extraction as well as infrastructural injustice and discrimination, is, at the same time, a crisis of imaginaries of care. The historical invisibilization and silencing of care cannot be understood through the violence of politics and economies only, but has to be more fully recognized as a form of lasting epistemic violence that largely excluded care as knowledge from Western traditions of thought. Care as knowledge is always embodied, always corporeal. This understanding of knowledge is useful to seeing that the violent separation of body from mind, human from nature, was epistemological warfare. Let me think about breathing for a moment. Breathing is vital. Breathing is essential for human life. Thinking of the breathing of human bodies-and-minds is a fundamental way of understanding the utmost violence of such separatist traditions of thought. The Covid-19 pandemic was a global lesson of care in breathing and shared air. As it was understood that the "novel coronavirus can spread through the air" and the Covid-19 infection is airborne, it became clear that human breathing presented a potentially deadly threat to others and to oneself. [22] Humans had to learn how to protect themselves and others from being exposed to the easy spread of the virus from an infected person's nose or mouth through the air. The risk of infection required that human beings fully acknowledge that being in the world is embodied and fundamentally depends on air and breathing. Breathing is not a choice. If one wants to continue living, one has to breathe. Humans cannot choose not to breathe. When our breath stops, our life ends. Breathing is a matter of life and death. Breathing, on the most fundamental level, connects humans with one another and with the planet as a whole in interdependency and vulnerability. Protecting others from one's own breath and protecting oneself from the breath of others, in order to avoid infection, became a global task and responsibility. Breathing became an act of care for oneself and others. More than before the outbreak of the virus, breathing, with humans on average breathing in and out 22,000 times a day, had to be socially acknowledged as a concern of interdependencies and vulnerabilities, as a concern of interconnectedness in life and in death. Breathing, which during the pandemic so deeply connected human beings to the threats of infection, illness, and death, is chosen here to raise awareness of how deeply and complexly human beings are interconnected in their interdependencies with one another, with their environments, their infrastructures and technologies, and the planet as a whole. At that very moment in March 2020, when fundamentally confronted with the shared responsibility toward living and dying, and becoming more deeply aware than before that one's breathing in could carry the infection into one's own body and that one's breathing out could cause someone else to be infected, fall ill, or even die, it was most troubling and unsettling to learn that it was expected from us, the human inhabitants of planet Earth, to wage a global war against the virus.

While the first two chapters of this book use the method of *feminist worry* in order to analyze how imaginaries of war are connected to *frontline ontologies* that subjugate the production of care to a militarist masculinist ethos of heroism and sacrifice and militarized care essentialism, which comes out of a long history of essentializing care that I trace back to mammalian epistemologies and its gendered essentialization, the third chapter introduces the method of *feminist hope* and studies *feminist recovery plans*. The feminist response to Covid-19, and to the hegemonic political and economic ways of dealing with the pandemic, in no way, of course, limits itself to feminist policy. There is now an abundance of feminist research on the pandemic and, in particular, many sociological and political science studies on the conditions of caring labor and healthcare in the pandemic.

In the context of this book, the feminist policy documents of *feminist recovery plans* were chosen as study material, as my interest is on how public imaginaries around care were being articulated in response to the pandemic crisis of care. Feminist policy provided a distinct political response not only to Covid-19, but also to the failures of and the violence in the hegemonic political and economic response. Feminist policy emerged as a distinct practice of public pandemic articulation, in which economic and political imaginaries were enlarged and in which care was actively redefined. That feminist recovery plans were being thought and written was hope-inspiring. The proposals of these feminist recovery plans were aligned with my own understanding that it was necessary to imagine and organize a new "international global care order" to resist and overcome hegemonic politics and economies of care.[23] Feeling hope made me understand that feminist hope is also a distinct method that emerges out of care as knowledge, in particular ways of knowing care in relation to recovery.

Feminist hope as a methodological approach and theoretical perspective, much like *feminist worry*, emerges from understanding care as knowledge that counteracts epistemologies of mind/body and nature/culture separation and renders epistemic violence, including violence against care and violence of care, legible.[24] In particular, when dealing with care in processes of recovery, there is at once worry and hope. Worries arise on account of the uncertainties of recovery and the specific, and oftentimes changing, vulnerabilities of minds, bodies, and environments in the process of recovering from disease, loss, harm or violence. Hopes arise because of the very fact that the possibility of a recovery is assumed. While recovery can never be taken for granted, hope for recovery is also hope for futurity and for meaning-making for futures based on different economic and political imaginaries. Worry and hope as epistemologies of care pull us into obligations and responsiveness, understood here as social obligations and political responsiveness. This pull extends to the past, the present, and the future. Worry and hope connect human beings with their own situated moment as the two concepts extend to the afterlives of violent pasts and to the possible lives in transformative futures. In everyday language, recovery is associated with *getting better*, not with returning to normal. While feminist worry as a method is used to read hegemonic meanings, realities, material histories, and past associations back into words and metaphors used in political speech and policy, feminist hope as a method is used for turning to words and metaphors and for opening up the space between the literal and the metaphorical as part of the process of recovering from past associations and of prefiguring healing.

Writing this book in a state of worry, I sought, at the same time, to remain hopeful. How does one respond to the presence of war within political imaginaries of care? How does one not despair? Worry and hope were necessary in order to continue writing despite the too-large questions, the too-painful planetary realities. How can one find meaning in writing when one understands that the infected planet is the result of a Man-made condition?[25] The pandemic was caused by the environmental ruination known as the Anthropocene Epoch, which is the period of planet Earth's history that results from Man-made impact on the planet and is the condition all living and non-living beings find themselves coping with today. As massive urbanization, environmental ruination, deforestation, and rampant extraction move humans closer to viruses, the risks of zoonotic spillover—the transmission of pathogenic viruses from wild animals to humans—increases. How can one find it meaningful to share, through writing, a feminist cultural analysis of political pandemic keywords in relation to care, when grief and loss because of mass death due to a global health catastrophe are overwhelming? In May 2022, the World Health Organization reported estimates that "the full death toll associated directly or indirectly with the COVID-19 pandemic (described as "excess mortality") between 1 January 2020 and 31 December 2021 was approximately 14.9 million."[26] Perhaps, meaning in feminist writing can be found through sharing worries and hope in analytical observations and through the concerns and questions they raise which can, if ever, only be responded to collectively. Questions I am thinking of here include the following: How could it be that war was seen as curative? How could it be that the most urgent need for more care was secured through the notion of frontlines? Why was care made part of a war effort against the virus? How, in this situation of a global health catastrophe and acute awareness of interdependencies and intervulnerabilities, could the political response to the pandemic mobilize for war in order to ensure solidarity and duty under pandemic lockdown conditions? Why were care workers—historically feminized—ordered to be warriors and soldiers—historically masculinized—at the pandemic frontlines? How could it be that care was made hyper-visible through sacrifice and forced heroism? How could it be that there was such a poverty of political and public language around care? How had human beings maneuvered themselves into such a situation of acute lack of public imaginaries of care that the void created by this lack could be filled with imaginaries of war? How could it be that the violent modern ideology of individualism is still being perpetuated, when every breath that human beings took in pandemic times reminded them of their existence in embodied interdependency and interconnectedness? How could it be that human exceptionalism was still being upheld when human beings had learned that "human genomes can be found in only about 10 percent of all the cells" in their bodies, with the "other 90 percent of the cells [...] filled with the genomes of bacteria, fungi, protists, and such"?[27] How could it be that care, including healthcare, was still mostly conceived of through human-centered, even human-centric perspectives, when care is largely provided by non-humans, by air, water, or food? How could it be that the Man-made pandemic did not immediately result in a consequential rethinking of what it means to be living with an infected planet? Questions and concerns like these are huge, they can feel overwhelming, too much, too painful. Sharing such questions and concerns with others by way of writing is a feminist way of responding. Sharing questions that are too large for any one to be answered alone is feminist response. "Response, of course, grows with the capacity to respond, that is, responsibility."[28] Response grows with the capacity to share "response-ability".[29] Questions around public imaginaries of care can only be worked through collectively. The huge and painful questions raised here are shared in order to explain what motivated my humble attempt at contributing to a better understanding of how deeply human beings have failed in ethical and social terms, to develop a culture of care for living together with their planet. These questions are shared in feminist worry and in feminist hope that political responsiveness to care will become possible and that care as knowledge will enter into ways of thinking and feeling. Feminist worry and hope are not held to be simple or easy. Much rather, worry and hope complexly, ambivalently, and conflictingly respond to the given, to the conditions of living and dying with an infected planet. Feminist worry and feminist hope as methods emerge from epistemologies of care. Worry and hope are central to the emergence of a new *care feminism* and its political responsiveness and response-ability to living with an infected planet.

Chapter 1: We Are at War

"We must declare war on the virus."[1] Since March 13, 2020, we are at war. On that day, just two days after the WHO, the World Health Organization, had declared the outbreak of the novel Covid-19 virus a pandemic, António Guterres, who has been serving as the ninth Secretary-General of the United Nations since 2017, declared war on the virus. Speaking as UN chief, appealing to the 193 member states of the United Nations, and, at the same time, addressing the global public on the member states' behalf, Guterres explained what follows from the declaration of war on the virus:

> That means countries have a responsibility to gear up, step up and scale up. By implementing effective containment strategies. By activating and enhancing emergency response systems. By dramatically increasing testing capacity and care for patients. By readying hospitals, ensuring they have the space, supplies and needed personnel. And by developing life-saving medical interventions. And all of us have a responsibility, too. To follow medical advice and take simple, practical steps recommended by health authorities.[2]

The requirement that countries gear up, step up, and scale up is resonant with the pandemic imperative. War oratory like this is intended to unite. Its political message seeks to provide guidance and inspiration for governance, and at the same time it formulates an imperative to all the political leaders worldwide to join forces so their countries work together for finding concrete ways to solve the pandemic emergency. It seeks to enlist international cooperation for coordinated and purposeful responses to the crisis. The war imaginary is mobilized for creating national as well as international unity for a well-coordinated emergency effort. What the UN chief actually called for in his pandemic war speech on March 13, 2020, was unity and cooperation for the global provision of care. However, the UN chief did not call for a global care effort to ensure the public health measures he described. His speech relied on rhetorical mobilization for a global war effort against the virus. Public political speech seems to turn to militarist rhetoric to demonstrate resolve, to assure the public that a battle plan is in place and that all efforts will be put into applying this strategy. On March 23, just ten days after the declaration of war on the virus, the United Nations held a virtual press conference at the UN Headquarters in New York, which was shared live over the Internet. *UN News* reported: "UN chief calls for global ceasefire to focus on 'true fight for our lives. […] Our world faces a common enemy: the virus […] and it attacks all, relentlessly."[3] Rather than invoking global unity through imaginaries of vulnerability, care, or solidarity, his speech draws together realities of war and metaphors of war. Stating that the planet is under attack by one common enemy, he pleads for a temporary period of truce in order to focus on this one true fight for our lives. His oratory brings together the commonly understood metaphor of fighting a disease and the idea of a new global frontline between two parties at war: virus and humans. The subsequent part of his speech introduces a strange tension between the literal and the metaphorical meanings of war and disease. He makes it very plain: "The fury of the virus illustrates the folly of war."[4] Fury and folly make an interesting choice of words: both have long been connected to war accounts or critical diagnoses of war. Fury evokes the raging, violent, and intense, potentially highly destructive and deadly activity of the enemy. Folly, from the French word folie for madness, not only means foolishness, but can also denote costly mistakes with ruinous outcomes. To all parties at war in March 2020, Guterres appeals as follows: "End the sickness of war and fight the disease that is ravaging our world", he pleaded. "It starts by stopping the fighting everywhere. Now. That is what our human family needs, now more than ever."[5] Invoking the senselessness of war, presenting what the pathogenic virus does to humans as a war, ties in well with the UN chief's plea for a global truce and cessation of all ongoing war activities, which can also be understood to be ruinous and costly mistakes. The two-way traffic between war and disease becomes obvious. War is likened to disease and, at the same time, war and fighting are suggested as the best possible political and social response to disease. Viewing real wars to be a folly clears the space for the metaphorical use of the word war, which Guterres employs for the political mobilization of global unity in response to the threats posed by the virus. In order to begin a new war—the true fight for our lives—, all the old wars have to end. All real wars have to be put on hold if war is to appear as the desired common strategy for fighting the virus. If there is such a clear understanding that war is sick and sickens, why, then, turn to the imaginary of war as a response to global threat? Why does war hold such power over human consciousness and collective imagination?

Confronted with and increasingly worried by my observations that the international political response to the outbreak of the novel coronavirus and the global public health crisis was cast in terms of war—in particular by the United Nations, an organization for international peace—this chapter is concerned with why war seems to be the apt choice for political imaginaries that plead for unity and collaboration in times of planetary emergency. Feminist worry caused by masculinist imaginaries of war and their militaristic implications raises a number of painful questions about the fate of care. How can it be that the idea of a global war front presents the way forward for coordinated protection against the virus? Why was the pandemic imperative to care formulated as a declaration of war? What makes the imaginary of war so very persuasive and thus deemed to be most useful to political pandemic oratory addressing world leaders and the global public? How has international politics arrived at a point at which war has come to offer the ideal semantic representation of what states and governments should do to work together in global unity? Which histories and cultural imaginaries have led to a situation of such acute poverty of imaginaries that a war effort seems to serve best the call for caring measures to prevent the spread of infection, mass disease, and death? Answers to questions like these go beyond the remit of this book. They are used here as feminist tools to examine with heightened and painful awareness how the power of meanings and the meaning of power and the two-way traffic between war and disease converge in the strategic deployment of political metaphors. Metaphors are understood as central to the formation of cultural and social imaginaries impacting upon the realities they at once articulate and shape.

Journalists, commentators, philosophers, and theorists were quick to point out that the political response to the outbreak of the virus used a highly militarist rhetoric. They diagnosed that war was used as a political metaphor. Alex de Waal, for example, stated that war is not a "harmless metaphor" as it also evokes associations of the power of winning so "that leaders feel entitled to declare 'victory'".[6] While this lucidly draws attention to how politics feed on the imaginary of the potential of winning a war, declaring its end, and celebrating the victory, what motivates me goes beyond the exploit of war on the level of political rhetoric and is concerned with how, at an ontological and existential level, the terminology of war has most deeply penetrated everyday language and imaginaries and, at the same time, how there is a growing lack and erosion of language and imaginaries of care. I argue that metaphors, and figures of speech more broadly, contain at once histories of ideas as well as ecological, economic, emotional, material, social and political realities, and can help us understand, at the level of language, how thoroughly entangled ideas and realities are as they constantly feed into one another and are most intimately co-joined, as they permeate one another.

Reading slowly and closely some of the key examples of public political war oratory, as they were repeated over and over again in pandemic times, this chapter offers feminist cultural analytical reflections on war as a political metaphor as I take very seriously the "materiality of metaphor".[7] I ask what this mobilization of war in the name of care asks us to think about: What does this turn to war as a response to crisis tell us about humanity? How has this militarization of the mind taken command? Of what is the lack of language, and of political imaginaries for the response to mass threat to life, a deeper symptom? Why have we ended up with war as the best possible solution for protection against vulnerabilities? The purpose is to "listen carefully" to the language of war mobilized in times of extreme crisis and deadly threat and, at the same time, raise awareness of the necessarily "long attention span" for the histories, including the histories of ideas, stored in and transmitted through figures of speech, as they convey profound insights into the ways modern human subjectivity is thought to relate to itself, to others, to nature, and to the world.[8] The concern is why war has become so central to the formation of modern human subjectivity that its relation to the planet came to be understood as constant acts of warfare. Starting in the here and now with the worries, and the questions, caused by public political oratory in pandemic times, the chapter opens up to a much larger historical horizon and to dimensions of futurity as it asks how to think, and act, beyond imaginaries of war as a solution to living with and caring for an infected planet.

Just a few months before this appeal that "we must declare war" on the virus, Guterres had delivered his "Remarks at 2019 Climate Action Summit", which was held at the headquarters of the United Nations in New York in September of that year. This earlier speech can also be viewed as reliant on war rhetoric. Even though he does not actually use the term war, words, notions, and imaginaries connected to war permeate his speech. Seeking to inspire concrete climate action, Guterres fills his speech with powerful associations of attack and retaliation to address today's disaster realities and their devastation: "Nature is angry. And we fool ourselves if we think we can fool nature. Because nature always strikes back. And around the world nature is striking back with fury."⁹ His choice of words suggests that there is a war going on. One strikes back after one has been attacked. The chronological sequence of Guterres' narrative suggests the following: humans started a war against nature when they started their attacks on nature, and now nature is retaliating. In temporal terms, retaliation is a response to an action that has taken place in the past. In military terms, retaliation means responding to a military attack by launching a counter-attack. His speech makes it clear that nature did not start the war—humans did. As he calls out their war on nature, the UN chief then goes on to specifically identify the enemies of nature. They are those who subsidize a "dying fossil fuel industry", those "who build ever more coal plants that are choking our future", those "who reward pollution that kills millions with dirty air and makes it dangerous for people in cities around the world to sometimes even venture out of their homes."¹⁰ One might add to his list here that the enemies of nature are those who engage in land-grabbing and deforestation in order to set up large-scale plantations, which then make it dangerous for children in villages to venture out and play in hollow trees: these trees might have become the refuge for fruit bats, which have been driven away from their natural habitat that was cut down and now present a threat to humans as they are carriers of zoonotic viruses which, through the jump from animal to human, can result in epidemics or global pandemics.¹¹ The enemies of nature are the enemies of human life. Therefore, we have to ask ourselves on whom we actually must declare war when "we" are called upon to "declare war on the virus" knowing that the outbreak of the novel Covid-19 virus, like other virus outbreaks before and predicted future virus outbreaks, are in fact the result of a hegemonic way of human life created by the relentless attacks of "Man" on nature, which have long infected the planet as a whole.¹² These are difficult facts. Who are "we" actually declaring war on when faced with the fact that today's pandemic is produced by the very conditions that have been created by Man-made harm of nature. Furthermore, the way political oratory casts the relation between humans and nature in terms of war thinks of nature in anthropomorphic terms. Man attacks nature. Nature strikes back. Telling history like this exposes the anthropomorphism of nature. This is yet another expression of human supremacy, which is the root of such thinking that nature might relate with humans in the way humans relate with one another and with nature. At the center of all these relations we see the idea of war.

Political Imaginaries of War

The idea of war not only has profound political implications, but is also central to shaping understandings of the value systems of the economy and of society that are expressed in philosophical ideas, cultural creeds, and ethics. Even though the specific meanings of war invoked by the UN chief in his two speeches, one given at the beginning of the global Covid-19 pandemic and one given on the occasion of the International Climate Action Summit, are very different, they provide proof that the idea of war underpins public political oratory and its political imaginaries. Guterres' pandemic speech in early 2020 invokes meanings of war such as the formation of a closed front against the virus, military-style efficiency, and the employment of all efforts under the unified goal of defeating the disease. War is presented by the UN chief as a solution for organizing care to save human life under the deadly circumstance of the pandemic, as he calls on governments to cooperate in order to "ensure targeted support for the people and communities most affected by the disease."[13] Guterres' climate action speech invokes the notion of a war on nature with nature now retaliating against its enemy. War is rendered legible in this speech as the original Man-made attack on nature, in response to which nature is now striking back with fury. This war on nature constantly, relentlessly, and most violently attacks nature so it yields more of its resources, provides more raw materials, and offers more planting ground for a global economic system based on excessive profiteering. Since the beginnings of industrialization, this war has developed and refined its arsenal of weaponry put to use to colonize nature through rampant extractivism, which feeds the economy's growth based on the paradigms of over-production and over-consumption.

What appears to be a paradox, namely that war offers the imaginary to present the solution to as well as the cause behind the problem, is actually not a paradox. It shows how limited political imaginaries are. It shows that there apparently exists no other political approach outside of imaginaries of war. War is central to human-nature-virus relations. War is behind the system in crisis, but also drives the responses to it. War provided the ideas that led to ruination and destruction, putting planet Earth on the edge of the precipice. And now, there seems no other solution than to answer this war with war. War necessitates war. I propose referring to this process that makes war at once the root of the solution to the problem and the cause of the problem to start with as general warification. This general warification that entangles bodies, minds, and nature can be traced, I argue, through war figures of speech, especially in public political oratory in times of emergency. This reveals how the Man-made world relates to planet Earth through imaginaries of war. War figures of speech make abundantly obvious that the long-spanning legacies of modern warification dominate over other imaginaries, such as imaginaries of care and imaginaries of peace. As public political speech tells us that we find ourselves surrounded by enemies, whom we have to annihilate in order to live and survive, the dominant political world view hinders our ability to see, and relate to, the world otherwise. The domination of the idea of war over imagining our relation to the world keeps us from imagining living with our infected planet in a different way.

The Pandemic 'We': Unite in the Fight against the Invisible Enemy

Pandemic war oratory serves the creation of a pandemic 'we' standing in unity against the enemy. This 'we' is imagined as a united warfront against the virus. Very soon after the first international pandemic war speech was delivered by UN Secretary General on March 13, 2020, there was a turn to war by political leaders. Public pandemic address to nations turned into speeches of war. Only a few days after the speech by Guterres, Emmanuel Macron, who has served as the elected President of France since 2017, delivered his pandemic address to the French nation on March 16, 2020. His speech drew global attention and was widely commented on in international media. "We are at war," the French president informed his nation. While the UN Secretary General had urged that we need to declare war, the French President took that one step further and stated that his country was already at war. He had already ordered his country's land borders to be closed and all French people to stay at home. "The enemy is invisible and it requires our general mobilization," President Macron stated, safely assuming that he could leave out the name of the invisible enemy, as everybody would be able to fill it in by themselves.[14] In his speech, the virus was addressed as the enemy of all French people, and, therefore, became a national concern. The nation had to fight as one against the virus.

Ten days after President Macron delivered his war speech, on March 26, 2020, war and care are, again, most closely joined together at a global level in a speech to the most powerful world leaders, the G20. Tedros Adhanom Ghebreyesus, the Ethiopian biologist and public health researcher, who was elected by the World Health Assembly as Director-General of the World Health Organization in 2017, gave an address to the world leaders who had gathered virtually for the G20 Extraordinary Leaders' Summit on Covid-19 organized and hosted by the Kingdom of Saudi Arabia, which had assumed the G20 Presidency in December 2019.[15] Understanding that the World Health Organization holds the global authority to declare a disease a pandemic makes the fact that Tedros's address to the G20 world leaders framed the pandemic through the idea of war of particular interest. Tedros addressed the world leaders as follows:

> My brothers and sisters. We come together to confront the defining health crisis of our time. We are at war with a virus that threatens to tear us apart – if we let it. Today I have three requests for our esteemed leaders: First, fight. Fight hard. Fight like hell. Fight like your lives depend on it – because they do. [...] Second, unite. No country can solve this crisis alone. [...] Third, ignite. [...] ignite a global movement to ensure this never happens again.[16]

The pandemic is the defining health crisis of our time and this crisis is seen as a war that can only be solved through war efforts. With the nexus pandemic, health crisis, and war firmly established, it is of particular importance to keep in mind that declaring a pandemic, but also a declaration of war, are formal acts. A pandemic may already have been a pandemic before being declared to be one. A pandemic may still be ongoing but already have been declared to have come to an end. The declarations of beginnings and endings of pandemics do not necessarily correspond to the realities of a disease, but they do create political realities. The only organization globally with the authority to officially declare the beginning as well as the end of a pandemic is the World Health Organization. In awareness of the impact on the economy of declaring a pandemic, and of how countries are reliant on their own economies as well as on globalized economies, the appeal of the World Health Organization's highest ranking official to the G20, self-described on their website as the "premier world forum for international economic cooperation", carries particular weight.

Both the French President and the Director-General of the World Health Organization make use of the word war to stress, and politically justify, the necessity of the extraordinary measures required. War enlists everyone. In times of war, those who do not fight the common threat become a threat themselves, as they jeopardize the unity in fighting, as they endanger the unified front against the enemy. The French president imagines a 'national we' and national unity for the French war against the virus, while the Director-General of the World Health Organization—in his address to the world leaders of the multilateral G20 forum, whose member states include some of the largest economies globally—speaks to the possibility of a 'global we' and of necessary global unity in the war against the pandemic. This imagined global political 'we' in Tedros's speech is carefully crafted. He constructs and mobilizes this 'global we' by moving through different scales, through which he reminds individual world leaders of their obligation toward their countries as well as toward the global community. Tedros very carefully introduced two different threats posed by the pandemic: the threat to individual life and the threat of losing global unity. He stated that "we are at war with a virus that threatens to tear us apart."[17] As I read it, this statement not only allows for more than one interpretation, but is actually meant to be understood through different readings which are intended to complement one another. The Covid-19 virus exposes us to our physical and existential vulnerability. The virus can tear our lives away from us. Therefore, we have to fight to tear our lives away from deadly contagion and pandemic death. The outcome of existing global inequalities which define public health and access to medical infrastructures around the world is the very uneven distribution of the threat of having one's life torn away by the virus. The conditions under which people are able fight to tear their lives away from contagion and death are highly unequal. At the same time, Tedros's pronouncement can be read to mean that standing in unity against the virus can be torn apart by political leaders, can be torn apart by individuals who do not follow pandemic measures, and can be torn apart by pre-existing economic and social realities of inequality and injustice. The war effort is not shared equally. Not all of us can keep safe and stay in shelter. Not all of us are obliged to contribute to the war effort in the same way. Some are frontline workers, while others live in relative safety. This inequality tears us apart.

When people are torn apart in social, in political, and importantly, in economic terms, they are divided. This division is a threat to unity which tears apart the war effort and makes it impossible to defend all of us, to protect us against contagion, to provide us with tests and vaccines. The message of the opening speech of the General-Director of the World Health Assembly at the G20 Extraordinary Leaders' Summit is the following: the loss of unity presents the most serious threat to the war against the virus. In order for there to be unity, existing divisions that cannot be overcome need to be put aside. The logic of war is based on the idea that only unity can beat the enemy. If there is no unity, it is less likely the enemy will be defeated. If the war is not united, the virus will win and the human beings on planet Earth will suffer the loss of millions of lives, as humans were not able to organize politically and socially in such a way that disease and death were prevented. Those who will not have had access to the kinds of support that would have been necessary for them to fight the virus, to tear their lives away from Covid-19 death, will be counted as the casualties of this failed war against the virus. The futures of those who will have been failed by the war against the virus will have been torn from them, but also from planet Earth, to whose future they can no longer contribute. The threat of our being torn apart by this war against the virus is just as deadly as the deadly threat posed by the virus. The threat that the war will divide us will make many more people especially vulnerable to the virus and exponentially increase existing health inequalities that tear apart societies around the world.

Presenting his three requests to the assembled G20 world leaders, the Director-General of the World Health Organization makes an appeal for a global united war against the virus. Constructing his requests as pandemic imperatives, Tedros binds them together along the three different, yet inextricably interconnected scales of the individual, of countries and, finally, of a not-yet existing and yet to be formed future global movement. In his first request, he addresses the world leaders as individuals and asks them to fight as if fighting for their own lives. In his second request, which actually instructs the world leaders to unite, he does not address them as individuals at all; much rather, he now refers to the countries, and therefore metonymically to all the people, whom these political leaders not only represent, but also have an obligation toward. He makes it clear that no country alone can fight a pandemic. His third request invokes the future and demands a global movement to prevent further pandemics. He lays out a sequence of actions for this war effort which build upon one another and are necessary in order to defeat the enemy. This sequence is captured through the three imperatives: fight, unite, ignite. "Fight like your lives depend on it," the Director-General of the World Health Organization told the world leaders, reminding them of their own existence through their bodies, which are also under threat by the deadly virus. This addresses them as bodily beings and political leaders, vulnerable and in positions of wielding global power and responsible to millions of people. The political rationale behind the imperative is that if the world leaders imagine having to fight for their own lives, they will do a better political job in fighting for the lives of all human beings, and if all of them, individually, fight for their lives together, they will all fight for all. Metonymically, the bodies and lives of the world leaders stand in for the bodies and lives of all the people living in the countries which they represent. Metonymy in this political rhetoric turns the lives of the world leaders into a representation of all lives under the new pandemic realities. The lives of the world leaders are the part that represents the whole, for which the world leaders are to fight as if their lives depended on it. The second imperative, unite, moves from the scale of the individual to the scale of the country. As he tells the world leaders to unite, he speaks of their countries. When he states that "no country can solve this crisis alone" there is, again, metonymy at work. He actually asks of the countries these leaders represent, and therefore all the people living across these countries, to unite in war against the virus. His third imperative is to "ignite" a "global movement to ensure this never happens again". Even though the Director-General of the World Health Organization remains vague on how exactly this will be ensured, I read his third request as an imperative to work against deadly conditions created by anthropogenic climate change, as there is "growing evidence" of the interconnectedness of "infectious diseases, pandemics and climate hazards" as "many of the same human activities that are contributing to climate change are also contributing not only to the emergence of new diseases but also their spread."[18] There might be many more pandemics in the future, as the global economies, which are based on the twin paradigms of growth and extraction, cause humans to move ever closer to new viruses, which increases the risks of "spillover events".[19] The third request asks for the creation of conditions that will prevent future pandemics, as well as of conditions in which the world is no longer torn apart, as unity is needed to respond to the challenges, problems, emergencies, crises, and catastrophes that all concern the planet in its entirety. This third and last request actually moves away from the language of war to the language of movement, and hope for the possibility of working toward a different future.

More than twelve months into living with pandemic realities and pandemic death, the idea of war continued to define the response to the virus. "We are at war with the virus," António Guterres stated in his opening address for the 74th World Health Assembly in May 2021.[20] The annual meeting of the World Health Assembly, which is the decision-making body of the World Health Organization and therefore the most important health policy body globally, normally takes place in Geneva, Switzerland, but, because of the pandemic conditions, it was again held remotely, as had already been the case in 2020. Addressing the health ministers of the 194 member states, who, through the World Health Assembly, govern the World Health Organization, adopt resolutions, and decide on future global policy, Guterres "called for the application of wartime logic in the international battle against COVID-19."[21] By May 31, as the World Health Assembly closed, the delegations of the member states had agreed to come together again in a special session toward the end of the year, in November 2021, in order to work on a global agreement, on a new treaty on pandemic preparedness and response in order to strengthen global health security, as "COVID-19 and other major disease outbreaks, as well as continuing humanitarian situations, highlight the need for a stronger collective and coordinated approach to preparedness and response to health emergencies."[22]

The pandemic speeches by Guterres, Macron, and Tedros have been chosen as examples in order to draw attention to the global presence of political imaginaries of war since the outbreak of the global pandemic. Why do international leaders make war the basis of their political statements in public pandemic oratory? Why do they display such a strong political belief that war can be seen to provide the best framework for solutions in times of emergencies, crises, and catastrophes? Is there any political awareness of the constant spillover of political war oratory into everyday language? Is there political consideration being given to how this constant presence of war since the outbreak of the pandemic impacts on social and cultural imaginaries? Listening carefully, over and over again, to these pandemic war speeches and training my attention to the metaphorical and rhetorical use of language, what struck me most was the firm use of the indicative mood in this turn to war. "We must declare war on the virus." "We are at war." Cast no doubt: indicative mood, present tense. The indicative mood is used for facts, statements, and beliefs. Consequently, "We are at war" has to be understood as political statement, as a belief, and as a fact. War was not a doubt. What is even more depressing, a state of war was never doubted. Stating that they are at war against the virus seems to allow political leaders to demonstrate their resolve, their firm authority to resolve, that is, to find a solution to the crisis. They can show their utmost determination to end the pandemic. It is held by political analysts as well as in common everyday understanding that "war is largely about willpower".[23] There is no doubt that the deadly realities of a pandemic require resolve. Earnest decisions, which will decide over life and death, have to be taken. Also, time is of the essence: decisions have to be taken immediately. Actions are required, without hesitation. "In a fast-moving pandemic, the cost of *inaction* is counted in the grim mortality figures announced daily [...]."[24] The application of wartime logic is thus understood to be a political manifestation of willpower, of fast decision-making, and of the ability to control the course of actions. War stands for political resolve. Words closely associated with resolve aid understanding of the political imaginaries which are invoked by war. These words include determination, firmness, self-command, self-control, steadfastness, and purpose. If war is held to be the expression of all the attributes connected to resolve, then belief in the political statement that we are at war can be understood to embody the political will to command and the ability to decide on all the actions necessary. This leads to more questions that have to be raised here, asking about the relationship between this political invocation of war as demonstration of resolve and willpower and 'us', as 'we' are constantly being told that 'we' are at war. Why am I forced into war? Why do I have to be made to feel that I am following a war regime when caring about others, when following mask mandates, when respecting physical distancing rules, when testing for the virus, when getting vaccinated? Why do political leaders want people globally to share their belief, or rather their masculinist ideology, that war is the solution to emergency, crisis, and catastrophe? Why do political leaders present war in the indicative mood? Why do they speak of war as a fact? A fact is not a decision. A fact is not a choice. We cannot choose our facts. But decisions have to be taken, choices have to be made, because there are facts. Facts are resulting from decisions and choices. If it is assumed a fact that we are at war, then certain choices can be made, certain decisions can be taken, which, in other times, would not be possible. In times of war everything can and will be mobilized in order to defeat the enemy. If the notion of war allows political leaders to demonstrate their resolve and their will to control the situation, it also presents them with the political opportunity to ask of 'us' that we share this resolve and partake in their willpower so that all actions that are asked of us, that are required on our part so the war can be won, will be carried out by us. In pandemic political oratory, the invocation of war serves the forcible creation of a 'we'. War as the utmost embodiment of political resolve is imagined to best serve the formation of unity in the collective will to fight together against a common enemy. The idea of war thus wills a 'we', which is based on the identification of a common enemy. Willpower, at once the will to use one's power and to be in control of one's power, is closely linked to the political idea of war.

Prussian general Carl von Clausewitz, in his book *On War*, a military theory of war published posthumously by his wife Marie von Brühl and a philosophical treatise and military strategy at once, offers the following definition of willpower: "[...] willpower, as we know, is always an element in and a product of strength."[25] Following this logic, willpower is crucial to the collective strength on which wartime efforts rely, but this willpower is also generated through strength, meaning that those political leaders who display their resolve through the statement "we are at war" have such strength in them. The strength of political leadership, therefore, is the precondition for the mobilization of collective strength which is required for war. Will is central to the definition Clausewitz has given of war: "War is thus an act of force to compel our enemy to do our will."²⁶ In order for this collective force to come together, 'our' enemy has to be identified as the commonly agreed upon enemy and 'our' will has to be bent into a will so collective that it actually willingly conjoins with the act of force. Political pandemic resolve mobilizes collective willpower, which is the basis for the collective strength of a 'we' crucially needed in times of war. We can see here the politically as well as philosophically produced nexus between war, resolve, willpower, strength, and force, which were historically forged by the links among the ideology of patriarchy, the formation of the modern independent subject, and the general warification of life on the planet.

Effects of War and the State of Exception

The politics of choosing words of war in pandemic political oratory was widely noticed.

Many, including political commentators, columnists, journalists, bloggers, critical theorists, and scholars, were quick to draw attention to the centrality of war in the global political response to the virus. Words can make us appear as "soldiers in a war", as international relations scholar Constanza Musu has observed.²⁷ Alex de Waal has written that by "zoonosis from metaphor to policy, 'fighting' coronavirus may, in the worst case, bring troops onto our streets and security surveillance into our personal lives."²⁸ The omnipresence of war rhetoric did, in fact, lead to very real new societal frictions and conflicts, as people questioned the pandemic measures imposed—and justified—in the name of war. Opposing camps formed around issues like the mask mandate or vaccination requirements. This gave rise to the formation of new fronts and confrontations, which could be understood as wars over Covid-19 measures resulting in deeply divided societies. In the following I will look at some examples of the effects of the use of war as metaphor.

On March 21, 2020, Simon Tisdall, writing for the Guardian, titled "Lay off those war metaphors, world leaders. You could be the next casualty."²⁹ On April 11, 2020, Lawrence Freedman, a scholar of war studies, wrote a piece for the Statesman in which he made observations on the ubiquity of the war metaphors, with Xi Jinping speaking of a "people's war" and Donald Trump presenting himself as "wartime president" and referring to the corona virus as "the Chinese virus."³⁰ Writing for the *Conversation*, Constanza Musu titled that "War metaphors used for Covid-19 are compelling, but also dangerous".³¹ One of the indicated reasons for why war imaginary is at once compelling and dangerous is that it suggests that there is a strategy in place, that people know what to do. At the same time, the war metaphor provides for identification not only of what has to be done, but also of who has to do it and who can be faulted in the event of failure.

The war-time imagery is compelling. It identifies an enemy (the virus), a strategy ('flatten the curve', but also 'save the economy'), the front-line warriors (health-care personnel), the home-front (people isolating at home), traitors and deserters (people breaking the social distancing rules).[32]

War not only offers the possibility to present political resolve and determination, but it also subordinates life in general to the war effort. Musu points out that, with all of us understood to be "soldiers" in a war, "politicians call for obedience rather than awareness and appeal to our patriotism, not to our solidarity."[33] This draws attention to the political as well as the ethical consequences of mobilizing societies in the name of war. The warification of Covid-19 effectively led to the justification of authoritarian rule and even to heightening ethno-nationalism, as nation states went about protecting and caring first and foremost for their own. It also led to violently pitting people against one another along new enemy lines formed through Covid belief systems. Enemy lines include coronavirus rule breakers, anti-lockdown marchers, Covid-deniers, anti-vaccine protesters as well as test or vaccine refuseniks. They also include people who, even though they are in general agreement with Covid-19 measures, are in opposition to what is portrayed as infringement or violation of freedom. These new causes of stark disagreement, conflict, and even violent confrontations mark daily life under pandemic conditions and also present a new cause of conflicts among family members, kin, and friends. These new lines of conflict create realities on the ground that heighten vulnerability to exposure to viral infections, with people refusing to get vaccinated, not covering nose or mouth with their masks in public transport, or with people staging so-called Covid parties or participating in Covid demonstrations that advertise their refusal to adhere to rules necessary for protecting one another from contagion.

The fact that measures for protection against viral infection and the social actions needed for keeping one another as safe as possible have been politically constructed through imaginaries of war used to legitimize the imposition of states of emergency, also known as states of exception or martial law, led to very justified critiques of the effects of such constant warification. Simultaneously, people on the right, including positions on the extreme right, began to invoke freedom to push against measures imposed by the state in order to mobilize against state politics, in general, as well as against specific governments. Advocating for freedom and fundamental rights was, therefore, coopted by those on the right, whose political ideologies are never liberating or emancipatory. At the same time, arguments made by them began to sound very much like arguments made by people at the opposing end of the political spectrum. Therefore, paradoxical new alignments and oppositions arose, as individuals and groups in societies were split over pandemic measures. Would the response to such measures, which restricted freedom of movement or freedom of assembly, have been different if international organizations and political leaders had advocated for global unity in the name of care? Would people have been less divided if measures imposed had been introduced as a pandemic state of caring solidarity rather than as a militarized state of exception? We will, of course, never know. Such questions are hypothetical, but they are not rhetorical. They tell us how limited global political imaginaries actually are when it comes to calling for mutuality in care and how humans have practiced habits and routines of trust in accepting restrictions to protect themselves and others.

One much-referenced example of the philosophical responses to pandemic politics, the arguments of which can be aligned with the arguments that drive Covid denialism and so-called Covid demonstrations held against measures imposed by states, are opinion pieces, essays, and interviews by Italian philosopher Giorgio Agamben. Shortly after the outbreak of the novel coronavirus, Agamben began to publish his politico-philosophical comments on the political response to Covid-19 in Italy. These pieces can be found at *Una Voce di Agamben*, hosted on a website run by his Italian publisher Quodlibet. Agamben collected pandemic interventions that have been collated in the book titled *Where Are We Now? The Epidemic as Politics*.[34] The philosopher, known for his important work on the concept of bare life and his theorization of thanatocracy, sharply criticized the state of exception, the measures of surveillance, containment, physical distancing, and lockdown. Agamben's analysis of the state of exception is based on its theorization by political philosopher and jurist Carl Schmitt, a prominent member of Germany's Nazi party. In his 1922 *Political Theology: Four Chapters on the Concept of Sovereignty*, Schmitt writes: "Sovereign is he who decides on the exceptional case."[35] Such sovereignty is characterized by the power over taking decisions, even decisions that are outside the law. In a situation of "extreme peril" or emergency, states turn to the state of exception for their rule. According to Schmitt, the "exception reveals most clearly the essence of the state's authority. The decision parts here from the legal norm, and (to formulate it paradoxically) authority proves that to produce law it need not be based on law."[36] The German original is even more ambiguous with the expression "nicht Recht zu haben braucht", which has two different meanings. As in the translation quoted here, the meaning can be that for the state to act this "need not be based on law", but at the same time this can also mean that the state "need not be right" to do so, can actually and factually be in the wrong. Therefore, the German original inseparably joins legal implications to epistemic, moral, and ethical dimensions. States can be wrong about there being a state of extreme threat or peril, yet, nonetheless, they still have the right to impose a state of exception. In the specific situation of the Covid-19 pandemic, this became relevant to the philosophical and political arguments against measures of prevention and protection. Covid-19 denialism and public protests against responses to the Covid-19 pandemic denied that the virus presented a deadly threat, and therefore called for the rejection of measures such as physical distancing and the wearing of masks, and later, when vaccines had been developed, called for a rejection of vaccination.

Early on, Agamben viewed lockdown and the mask mandate as a form of new pandemic state despotism. His diagnoses thus lent philosophical legitimacy to the protests of those who called into question both the threat of the virus and governments' imposition of measures, and to their refusal to follow the rules while they recklessly and carelessly denied that we are interdependent for protection against infection. Diagnosing a dictatorship of techno-medical-authoritarianism, he wrote:

> We can use the term 'biosecurity' to describe the government apparatus that consists of this new religion of health, conjoined with the state power and its state of exception – an apparatus that is probably the most efficient of its kind that Western history has ever known. Experience has in fact shown that, once a threat to health is in place, people are willing to accept limitations on their freedom that they would never heretofore have considered enduring – not even during the two world wars, nor under totalitarian dictatorships.[37]

Unfolding the banner of freedom and the rhetorical philosophical claim to occupy the position of truth by calling medicine a new form of "religion"—that is, something one cannot be forced to believe—is a philosophy of carelessness.[38] While the argument is valid that the political goal of public health can be abused to legitimize governments' turn to authoritarianism, turning against measures for mutual care and protection presents a very real threat to human life and has to be understood as a philosophy of warring carelessness.

Reactions to the restrictions on civil liberties took a very sinister turn in the formation of a new political movement against national responses to the pandemic that united many different positions across the political spectrum who, before, would never have joined forces with one another. In Germany, for example, there arose an "anti-establishment movement" that draws together people of very different, even contradictory, political beliefs and thus leads to the unexpected alliance of followers of the far-right, conspiracy-theorists, people voting for the left, but also Green voters.[39] Observing these developments in Germany since their first culmination that even led to storming the Reichstag building in Berlin on August 29, 2020, the UK-based political website *openDemocracy* titled: "How Germany became ground zero for the COVID infodemic".[40] According to the World Health Organization, an infodemic

> is too much information including false or misleading information in digital and physical environments during a disease outbreak. It causes confusion and risk-taking behaviors that can harm health. It also leads to mistrust in health authorities and undermines the public health response.[41]

Viewed from the perspective of a declaration of war on the virus and the call for unity in a war effort, such an infodemic nourished by conspiracy theories and by freedom hyperbole has to be understood as a form of counter-attack or insurgency. Agamben's philosophical critique of the state of exception in pandemic times, and popular protests against Covid-19 measures under the banner of reclaiming individual freedoms are trapped in a toxic, violent, and deadly cycle of warification. As philosophy scholar Carlo Salzani critically observed in his piece on "Covid-19 and State of Exception: Medicine, Politics and the Epidemic State", Agamben's critique of the epidemic as politics supplies no ideas either for "new forms of resistance", which Agamben himself called for, or for a different model of the state in times of peril and in times of non-peril.[42] Salzari writes:

> What this resistance will consist in cannot be defined or described a priori, but if there is one thing that the 2020 pandemic has taught us, it is that this new political strategy cannot be reduced to an all-too-common and essentially anarcho-libertarian focus on individual freedoms (to which also Agamben's project ultimately amounts) but will have to be a positive collective project towards the common good.[43]

My assumption of a critical perspective on the imaginaries of war which, here, underpin the legal idea of the state of exception leads to my diagnosis that political analysis per Agamben and the rampant spread of misinformation through the emergent alignments among fascist supremacists, conspiracy fundamentalists, but also critical minds along the left and the green political spectrum, along with other political beliefs based on hyper-individualism, are responses that fully embrace the logic of war. The physical realities aligned with this logic are large-scale protests in which people actively break lockdown rules by not respecting social distancing and by not wearing masks. Such an understanding of freedom becomes carelessness: freed from the response-ability to respect each other's vulnerability and the obligation to protect one another from infection.[44] Overarching characteristics of the anti-lockdown movement, as well as the anti-vax movement, are hyper-individualism and border-less freedom that disregard the realities of interdependency and vulnerability to one another. When freedom trumps vulnerability, individualism becomes warfare. Being care-free, that is, being free to not care, has to be understood as a view of the subject to be without obligations to others and to have the right to exercise, autonomously and independently, one's own freedom. Such a conception of a care-free subject is dangerously close to a care-less subject that disregards and willfully ignores interdependencies in vulnerability. Carelessness and warification make explicit the acute poverty of political imaginaries beyond war and the state of exception, and points to a much deeper and fundamental political crisis owed to the historical lack of having developed political imaginaries based on freedom in interdependency and mutuality of care.

At the same time, it is, of course, crucial to understand the very real danger of states turning authoritarian in pandemic times and abusing the state of exception. Critical political responses with that very aim included close monitoring and reporting on the use of the state of exception by different supranational and intergovernmental organizations, non-governmental organizations, and bottom-up individual-based activism. Human rights organizations, such as Human Rights Watch, immediately criticized that the far-right ethno-nationalist Hungarian president Viktor Orbán "used the pandemic to seize unlimited power."[45] A day after the report on Human Rights Watch, on March 24, 2020, the Council of Europe Secretary General Marija Pejčinović Burić wrote an official letter to Viktor Orbán to offer "expertise and assistance" to ensure that "democracy, rule of law and human rights" will be safeguarded in Hungary.[46] The Council of Europe Secretary General clearly differentiated between legitimately taking "drastic measures" to protect public health and restricting "a number of individual rights and liberties enshrined in constitutions and in the European Convention on Human Rights" and the situation in Hungary, which presented the threat of an "indefinite and uncontrolled state of emergency" which "cannot guarantee that the basic principles of democracy will be observed and that the emergency measures restricting fundamental human rights are strictly proportionate to the threat which they are supposed to counter."[47] International non-governmental and civic organizations closely monitoring and tracking the impact of Covid-19 measures on public political life, civic space, civil society, basic freedoms, and human rights include, among others: the *Covid-19 Civic Freedom Tracker* set up by the International Center for Not-For-Profit Law and the European Center for Not-For-Profit Law; the *Global Monitor of Covid-19's impact on Democracy and Human Rights* by IDEA, the intergovernmental organization International Institute for Democracy and Electoral Assistance; *Tracking the Global Response to Covid-19* by Privacy International, the UK-registered charity dedicated to promoting the human right to privacy; *#Tracker_19* by Reporters Without Borders, a Paris-based non-profit and non-governmental organization that promotes and defends freedom of information.[48] Their work is crucial, and constructive, to understanding how civic life was impacted on by Covid-19 conditions. This work also invites reflection on the fact that governments did not immediately set up provision for new digital civic spaces or think of other possibilities for public political participation in times of a pandemic, when physical distancing makes it difficult to gather in public space. There has not been any news on states offering free broadband internet to all those living in their territories or on states envisioning the digital realm anew as public space together with their citizenry.

The state of exception re-defines the ways in which people are able to act as political beings. What we do not see in philosophical responses like those provided by Agamben and in public protests against governments and their response to the pandemic are caring ways forward. Such philosophy and such protests are warring and violent and offer no alternative political ideas as to how states, governments, or municipalities can better ensure civil liberties in pandemic times. Calling for unlimited rights to freedom fails the fundamental right to care for oneself and others, which has to be understood as mutually inseparable. Such philosophical opinion-making does not provide constructive thought on how to enact differently a new pandemic "space of appearance", which, in the sense of political philosopher Hannah Arendt, is understood as "the reality of the world [...] guaranteed by the presence of others".[49] When our close presence can become a threat to others, when their close presence can become a threat to us—in short, when we are a threat to one another, co-presence is not an expression of freedom but an expression of threat, danger, and risk. This requires novel pandemic approaches to thinking of presence and appearance through forms of distance as caring in the name of mutual protection. What is needed are new forms of civic space and public thought outside of frames of warification and violence, supported by a new political philosophy in favor of public imaginaries, and articulations, of care. Politics has not been built on public imaginaries of care. Historically, political oratory has not supported the development of such public imaginaries of care. The pandemic proclamation of the state of exception tied to the political metaphor of war led, as we have seen, to continued and even deepening warification of the mind.

War and Illness: Political Metaphors in Crisis

War and illness have a shared history of serving as metaphors. While all metaphors have political implications, which can be studied by turning to the critical framework of the politics of metaphors, war and illness-based metaphors have a special role in political rhetoric. Used to influence public opinion and to shape political imaginaries, metaphors in political oratory are used as powerful rhetorical means to compel global publics or national electorates to view social, economic, environmental, or historical realities as well as the political response to them in a very specific way. Metaphors in political oratory appeal both to reason and to emotion. Periods of crises, in particular, lead to the increased use of political metaphors. "Punitive notions of disease have a long history," as Susan Sontag remarked in *Illness as Metaphor*.[50] Equally, curative notions of war or combat have a long history. And both disease and war, as they are deeply connected to notions of threats posed by invaders or enemies, have been central in the arsenal of metaphors used in the political rhetoric of warfare. US American presidents have mobilized war as political metaphor, presenting war as a political solution to societal crises or problems. In his First State of the Union Address US President Lyndon B. Johnson proclaimed that "this administration today, here and now, declares unconditional war on poverty in America."[51] Since then, the militaristic rhetoric of declarations of war against crises and disease has played an important role in public political speech. One may think, here, of the prominent example of the 'fight' or the 'crusade' against cancer.[52] Yet the metaphorical political traffic between war and disease at the intersections of governance, policy, public health, and science are much older. When physician Robert Koch, government advisor at the Imperial Health Office in Germany, worked on measures to contain the cholera outbreak in Hamburg, he "characterized the cholera vibrio as an 'invader'".⁵³ At the same time, articulations of the connections between diseases, politics, and the military extend beyond figures of speech. In particular, with the beginnings of a broader notion of security during the last decade of the twentieth century, as for example in the 1994 Human Development Report, disease was understood to form part of security.⁵⁴ Within this changing political understanding of epidemics and this expanded understanding of threats to security that began to "regard microbes as threats to the security of states and to the international order", war metaphors remain the dominant historical narrative. Frank M. Snowden, for example, stated that the World Health Organization took major steps in the 1990s to prepare "for the ongoing siege by microbial pathogens".⁵⁵

In a 1989 essay published in the journal *History and Memory*, historian Omer Bartov states the following on the "reality and the heroic image in war":

> War is essentially a military confrontation between two armed groups or organizations of men; yet at the same time, war seems to present an image of heroic individuals upon whose supreme qualities its outcome depends. Whereas the former image denotes an impersonal mass, the latter implies the centrality of personal valor.⁵⁶

The political rhetoric for a common war against the virus strongly mobilizes around individuals upon whom the outcome depends. Following this logic, winning the war and defeating the virus depends on the frontline. War provides the frame through which the common good of pandemic care is viewed, and the pandemic imperative is articulated as an ethics of unity against the common enemy. The global frontline of care, which is the focus of the next chapter, is cast as a heroic effort in the pandemic war. Disregarding completely the historical and contemporary gender realities of war, war casts a heroic image of the exploited, exhausted, and feminized care workforce, speaking to the supreme qualities expected of the workforce and its personal valor on which others depend for their life and survival. Care workers are viewed as pandemic war heroes. The metaphor of war makes care work a national and global war duty and subjugates care to war. Fighting the virus renders it evident that some have to fight harder in this war than others, and that those in need of essential care are in fact fully dependent upon those who are seen as the ones who will fight the fight with them, who will fight the fight for them. The realities of war speak of interdependency, reliability, and the extreme vulnerability of life to death. At the same time, the use of war as metaphor overwrites vulnerability with necessary sacrifice and the myth of heroism. The cunning of the political use of the metaphor of war for the pandemic situation is the mobilization of the term's heroic imaginaries, while simultaneously it renders the realities of the state of exception, also known as martial law, inevitable, as humans are faced with a war waged against them by deadly pathogenic microbes.

Feminist Worry: War and Care

As a feminist, as a pacifist, as a realist who still tells herself every morning that it is possible to believe in the potentiality of hope, and as a mother of two sons who were found unfit for the army and celebrated the day this was determined during the obligatory military draft process for men in Austria, where we live, I was worried to the extreme about this general turn to war in pandemic times. War is based on the logics of annihilation and extinction. War causes trauma, grief, and pain. War realities are death-making realities. As a feminist theorist and an educator, I propose feminist worry as a lens through which to view humans in relation to their response to the world. *Feminist worry is personal and political.* It is an activity of relating to knowing and understanding. Worry has a specific relation to temporality, we worry about what might happen. Worry has a specific relation to others, as we worry for them. What interests me in proposing feminist worry as a method useful to critical cultural analysis are the close etymological and semantic connections with care, curiosity, and cure. Historian, artist, and theorist of visual cultures Jill H. Casid writes that "care derives, according to the OED [*Oxford English Dictionary*], from the common Germanic and Old English caru for trouble and grief."[57] Drawing on Casid, art historian and educator Carla Macchiavello writes that such "deep concern and sorrow" can "be manifested as providing aid to someone and sometimes even a cure [...] and an emphatic response to others' troubles leading to action."[58] Understanding that the etymological roots of curiosity are closely linked to caru, worry, I read the following by Donna Haraway as an invitation for feminist worry: "Caring means becoming subject to the unsettling obligation of curiosity, which requires knowing more at the end of the day than at the beginning."[59] Worrying about something and worrying about others also means knowing more and differently at the end of the day. At once epistemological and ethical, feminist worry thus leads to wanting to know and to care, otherwise and differently. Cultural theorist and political philosopher Erin Manning observed that "care carries a weight, a responsibility. It is both worry and attunement to. It is caru – anxiety, sorrow, grief. It is karo – lament – and kara

– trouble."⁶⁰ Ethics, the desire to know, and epistemology, curing and healing and the labors of care all converge in feminist worry. Approaching the political metaphor of war with feminist worry requires not only the grief caused by engagement with "hegemonic thought", in which "the metaphor of war has acquired a solid place", but also opening up painful and troubling questions that have to do with how being human is understood in terms of political oratory and the realities of politics.⁶¹

Over the period of writing this book, there were continuous updates on the counts of Covid-19 cases and deaths worldwide. In August 2021, close to 4,5 million people had lost their lives to the virus. About a year later, in July 2022, "Nearly 15 million people around the world have died from the impact of COVID directly or indirectly during the first two years of the pandemic. That is the estimate from a new report by the World Health Organization. It is also nearly three times higher than governments have reported publicly so far."⁶² How can war, which always means killing and mass death, provide the best possible political answer when life is in peril and millions of people are dying because of the pandemic? How can anyone think of war as a cure when faced with pandemic mass death? How can it be that war is seen as a solution to disease and helpful for the prevention of death? What about the gendered and racialized dimensions of this political mobilization for war? What does the use of the war metaphor tell us about the long-spanning legacies of the warring mind and warification as a way of relating to ourselves, to others, and to the world?

War has, of course, long been a feminist concern, or a feminist worry, as I have proposed to call it. Large parts of historical as well as of contemporary feminist and women's movements can be understood as peace movements. Feminist aims in these struggles have, of course, not been unified. While some strands of feminist and women's movements are dedicated to permanent peace seeking to end all wars by "addressing the root causes of violence with a feminist lens", others have been fighting for the inclusion of women in the army, from which women had been historically excluded.⁶³ Historically, war has been gendered masculine. The war/masculinity bind has shaped the historical stages of patriarchy as patriarchy transformed by and through the paradigms and realities of coloniality based on the violent domination and exploitation of humans and nature as resources in the name of profit. War renders masculinity toxic. As licensed therapist and clinical psychologist Andrew Smiler explains in the book *Is Masculinity Toxic?* that men have been defined through the exercising of social dominance, which has given rise to what the author defines as "masculinity ideology".⁶⁴ This masculinity ideology is firmly tied to the ideas around the military and the belief system of war. Even today, masculinity is widely imagined through "the military model".[65] Every historical reality and every philosophical theory of politics can be understood to contain a perspective of war and, at the same time, to be characterized by the deep meaning of the idea of war. The military is seen to be a service of and to the nation state, and military service, which is obligatory for the male population in many countries around the world, forms part of the modern institution of citizenship. In his theory of citizenship developed after World War II, sociologist T. H. Marshall elaborates in his social philosophy of citizenship how citizenship structures the social relations and rights and obligations between individuals and the state. These obligations include "paying taxes, insurance contributions and military service".[66] Joan Tronto remarks in her observations on Marshall's theorization of welfare that, in the second half of the twentieth century, the ideal of citizenship was no longer based on the model of the "soldier" but on the model of the "worker".[67] Neither the soldier nor the worker stays at home. The soldier goes to war and the worker goes to work. All others are homemakers, who stay behind at home, where their task is to take care of all those who depend upon it.

In the formation of Western genealogies of ideas and political consciousness, this divide between the so-called public, concerned with the interests and purposes of community and state, and the so-called private, focused on the basic physical needs and routines of everyday care in the life of individuals, can be traced back to Aristotle's philosophy of politics and of the state. Hannah Arendt's *The Human Condition* is at once an elaboration on and extension of Aristotelian lines of thought. Everything to do with basic human needs, all matters of physical survival, were considered not to be of the state, not to be of public importance, but left to be organized privately. Historically, all those whose laboring bodies were responsible for providing life and sustenance, who, in the Greek polis, included "women", but also "slaves, servants and others", were "considered a threat to public life".[68] The legacies of this division, which is central to Western thought, of course long predate modernity but have gained ultra-prominence with the separate spheres model since the beginning of the industrialized period. The care/dependence bind is the social and material expression of the separate spheres model with its private-public divide, through which, quite paradoxically, all those upon whose labor others were fully dependent for their bodily existence were cast as dependents, whereas those whom they sustained through their care were considered independent. Independence guaranteed access to public life. Dependence, on the other hand, meant exclusion from active participation in the dimensions of public life, of which one of the most prominent legal expressions is the status of citizenship, which is characterized by the entanglements and conflicts that run through the provision of essential care and sustenance, dependence, power, and independence. These phenomena resulted in social realities in which those marked by their gender, their sexuality, their ethnicity, their race, their social status, class, or caste were essentialized as necessarily having to perform this work, whereas those who were free to choose not to perform this work were seen as more powerful and superior. Those who were made to perform the essential work of sustenance and care were largely excluded from public office, from the vote, from military service, and from access to paid labor. The knowledge of those who had to worry about everyday human needs and physical and emotional concerns—those who were, therefore, closest to care, curiosity and cure—were excluded from the public realm of politics. Conversely, this means that politics has profoundly suffered from this lack of worry that only comes with the deep knowledge of care, sustenance, and everything to do with everyday life and survival.

In historical terms, "war" has been understood as central to the "birth [sic!] of the nation state".[69] The death system of war is a keymetaphor in the political imaginaries of the formation of the nation state. Politically, war is understood as an act of birth. The political imaginaries of war shaped the political realities of how nation states were formed. Wars need militaries and armies. War is fully entrenched in the making of the modern institutions of the nation state, their tax systems, their bureaucracies, and their exclusionary notions of citizenship. War is also connected to modern public health as the "military model of public health became hegemonic".[70] These systems of state hierarchies and state dependencies, states as dependent upon militaries, tax payers, and public bureaucracies are marked by the notion of separate spheres. Those who contribute to protecting the state and keeping it running were considered to visibly contribute to the purpose of the nation state's public interest, whereas those who take care of all the things which are not part of this public machinery remained invisible in the private territories of care. Yet in times of war it becomes more apparent than ever that care is essential and that those who perform the labors of keeping life alive are of utmost importance to those who serve the nation state's public interest. Those going to war fully and entirely depend upon all those who take care of the military's care needs, who take care of the wounded, sick, and tired soldiers, who take care of the hinterland with civilians under attack and suffering physical, mental, emotional exhaustion and massive pain.

Historically, powerful states expressed their hegemony to the world through military superiority and strength. It was never part of public and political imaginaries that powerful states can express such hegemony to the world through care superiority, through strength produced by better care. For the military power they needed in order to ensure territorial independence, self-determination, protection, and security, nation states relied on those who worked toward those ends in unity, obedience, and discipline. The realities and atrocities of war make it abundantly clear that the bodies of soldiers are at extreme risk and exposed to their own vulnerability, to the very real war threats of injury, disease, and death. Therefore, the physical, material, and ecological dimensions of war are linked to the physical, material, and ecological dimensions of care provided under the conditions of war. The most depressing and most revealing term cannon fodder makes it very clear that the lives of soldiers are at risk in times of war, that they are expected to sacrifice their lives, to fight, get injured, or even die for their nations. At the same time, nations are tasked to take care of their soldiers in times of war. Those who are at war are in extreme need of care. The history of war has been written as the public history of nation states. But the provision of care, including the very specific expectations concerning how care is thought of, produced, and maintained under the conditions of war, has largely been wiped from historical record. With much feminist attention focused on the gendered, sexualized, and racialized dimensions of the hegemony of the separate spheres model and on analyzing the implications of this model on men's and women's lives, and also on the theoretical understanding of masculinities and femininities in philosophical, political, and social concepts of subject formation, the equally crucial dichotomy—namely, the military-civilian dichotomy—has remained largely overlooked in its importance to the economies, politics, and ethics of care. We have to extend the notions of the separate spheres and the public-private dichotomy to dimensions of the military-civilian dichotomy if we are to gain a more complex perspective on the gendered entanglements of the politics of war and care as they intersect the public, the private, the military, and the civilian dimensions of social life.

This deep-running, yet not fully grasped, interconnectedness between war and care is central to why the idea of war and militarist rhetoric are used in public appeals to the global community of nations around the world in times of global emergency. That said, there has been much feminist scholarly work to recover the histories of war as part of women's history, and as central to women's lives globally. Feminist scholars across many disciplines including history, anthropology, sociology, political philosophy, political economy or international relations studies have examined the gendered dimensions of war and the different impact war has on defining masculinities and femininities, on men's lives and women's lives. Yet the feminist focus on war has not fully located war in the historical formation of social expectations, norms, obligations, duties, and responsibility that concern the provision of care. The ideas that inform the ethos of war have not informed the study of the ideas and the ethos of care.

Even though it is well understood that, for example, "one of the jobs most transformed by war was that of the nurse", feminist perspectives have not viewed the realities and the imaginaries of war as most influential to the understanding of care in historical and theoretical terms.[71] War produces care in very specific ways. The warification of care, the obligations for sacrifice as well as the endurance of violence, have to be much better understood as part of the long-spanning expectations of, and pressures on, care. Theories of care have to take care out of the home and follow care into the war, into the battlefield, into what is called the home front. Overcoming the effects of the structure of public/private and military/civilian dichotomies on the ways in which realities are studied and theorized has to be continuously recast as central feminist worry in scholarship. Again, language and the deep meaning transported through words and metaphors as a specific form of public philosophy under the umbrella of historical semantics offer excellent starting points for taking feminist worry into the field of study. The term home front captures and expresses the deep connection between war and care. This coinage originated during World War I and, according to the Merriam Webster dictionary, refers to "the people who stay in a country and work while the country's soldiers are fighting in a war in a foreign country." Women's contributions to the home front during World War I did not go unrecognized. The Wikipedia entry on the "home front during World War I" even goes so far as to state that women's "sacrifices" were recognized "with the vote during or shortly after the war, including the United States, Britain, Canada (except Quebec), Denmark, Austria, the Netherlands, Germany, Sweden and Ireland."[72] This is fully in line with the state logic that all those who, like soldiers, leave their homes and wage war for their countries are included in full citizenship and all aspects of public life. If women's suffrage is understood as the recognition by their states of women's central importance to the home front and their sacrifices during World War I, then granting women the vote is incorporated into an androcentric and state-centric historical narrative and viewed as an outcome of women having received a reward for their contribution to men's history of waging war, rather than as an outcome of the women's movement fighting for the vote. Following the realities of care beyond the domestic realm to which perspectives on care are often confined and expanding the understanding of care as having been shaped by the histories of war is helpful to understanding that care was not only the reason for exclusion from politics proper and subjected to economic exploitation, but is also a component part of the public interests and the public purpose of the state. Locating the realities of care in war, which is always an attack on life and nature, expands the philosophical understanding and theoretical perspectives of care.

The violence of war gives rise to extreme needs of care, both in times of war as well as in the aftermath of war. Violence heightens the risk of being made vulnerable and wounded. Violence increases the need for care. Violence is bound to vulnerability, and the use of "violence against the enemy is part and parcel of every militarist system."[73] The perpetration of violence exploits the existential human condition of vulnerability and "injurability".[74] Judith Butler has written widely on vulnerability and injurability as they matter to existential precariousness. Butler argues that humans are "all subject to one another, vulnerable to destruction by the other, and in need of protection through multilateral and global agreements based on a recognition of shared precariousness."[75] What we all need protection from, being exposed to the vulnerabilization of life and its mortality through the violence wrought by war, is, paradoxically, what war and the logic of militarization rest on. Also, the realities of the violence committed in the name of war increase tremendously the need for care. This is the "common human vulnerability"[76] which, for Butler, presents the ontological condition for a politics in common, and in my view for an ethics of care. Politics needs to be based on an acceptance of shared human vulnerability, and out of this, the political structures and material infrastructures necessary to caring for and protecting livability as a common good must be built. Butler's insight into the ontological condition of vulnerability and injurability is in fact exploited through the politics and realities of war, which are based on the possibility of the injurability of the enemy and even the complete annihilation of the enemy. As we are vulnerable to one another we are at risk of being injured by the other and of injuring the other. Butler writes that "we each have the power to destroy and to be destroyed."[77] Therefore, there is need for protection from this power of destruction.

Joan Tronto has written about dimensions of the state and of the institution of citizenship, which is legally enshrined through the nation state, in relation to protection and to care. Her argument is that protection has historically been gendered as a male obligation and care as a female duty. From this it follows that protection was understood on many, but not on all, levels as a public obligation, while care, on the other hand, was understand on many, but not all levels as a private duty. "Protection of the body politic from its enemies, external and internal, has always been part of the responsibility of citizenship."[78] The premise of citizenship is the promise of protection. The promise of protection rests on the realities of the militarization of this protection delivered through the army and the police. The nation state has created these historical institutions of the army and the police for the protection of its citizenry against external and internal enemies. Protection and care are understood by Tronto to shape two central dimensions of the public and private dichotomy, which, as I argued earlier, has to be understood as the dichotomy between the military and the civilian.

According to Tronto, to be part of delivering protection offered a pass from care, not only effectively separating protection and care from each other along the lines of class, gender, race, sexuality, and status of protection, but also, in a strange way, obliterating the fact that those who are obliged to protect are much more in need of care than others, in need of urgent and intensive care as they are exposed to their injurability and the capability of being destroyed by those seen as external or internal enemies. In reading together Butler's thought on ethics, which proceeds from ontological vulnerability, and Tronto's thought on care, which is based on the ontological dependence upon care, we can begin to expand further ethical thought. Finding themselves open to vulnerability and therefore at risk of being injured, those who are there to fulfil the public service of protecting the state and its citizenry are, in fact, very often being made vulnerable and are consequently in need of extreme care. We therefore have to study the relations between those who protect and those who care as relations that were shaped in such a way that they were perceived to be of uneven dependence, with those tasked with protection held to be more important and more powerful than those tasked with care. Yet, as has become most abundantly clear, they cannot be without each other, as all humans are reliant upon care in even more fundamental ways than upon protection. Care is tied to the realities of the body. Our bodies cannot live and survive without care for sustenance and basic needs. Without air, water, food, or sleep, bodies die. The need for care is part of the human condition. Without care, no human life.

Protection from external or internal enemies is needed by our bodies, but it is not a need that originates from our bodies, but a need produced by political and social conditions imposed upon our bodies. As political decisions and social processes continue to define realities through ideas based on the paradigm of enmity, histories, and of nations, the lives of their citizenry and the landscapes in their territories are being defined through structures that create internal and external enemies. Protection and violence have to be understood as most closely related. Acts of protection are often closely bound up with acts of violence committed by the police or by the military in the name of protection. Thus, protection, paradoxically, results in the normalization of violence and the militarization and securitization of everyday life. Therefore, amid our exposure to the risks of deadly violence and infection because of the climate catastrophe and the pandemic catastrophe, new political imaginaries are very much needed for organizing ways of taking care of protection, to be better protected against the old kinds of protection that have made us more vulnerable to our vulnerability and have exposed us to intrinsic and endemic violence.

As a *feminist worrier* I raise the following questions in order to prompt reflection on the problems posed by the normalization of violence through militarized imaginaries and realities in protection. What if those who are there to protect turn their violence against those upon whose care they are dependent? What if those who provide much-needed care to those who protect are being forced to do so? What if those who care cannot protect themselves while they care? What if those who care cannot care for themselves, because they are burdened with and completely exhausted by the care for others? What if the relations between protection and care are rendered vulnerable and violent?

The understandings of both the philosophical ideas and the historical realities of what is understood as protection and what is understood as care have to be located within these structures of enmity as they underpin war and the process of general warification. Political philosopher and public intellectual Achille Mbembe published extensively on enmity. Following his thought, we can see how protection from internal and external enemies, which I have shown not to be a primary bodily need but a socially produced need, has taken on ontological dimensions in what I propose to call today's world disorder. Mbembe writes:

> In this depressive period within the psychic life of nations, the need, or rather the drive, for an enemy is no longer purely a social need. It corresponds to a quasi-anal need for ontology. In the context of the mimetic rivalry exacer-

bated by the 'war on terror', having an enemy at one's disposal (preferably in a spectacular fashion) has become an obligatory stage in the constitution of the subject and its entry into the symbolic order of our times.[79]

The need for protection, then, results from this entirely Man-produced ontology of enmity that gives rise to external or internal enemies. Care is now even more ontologically needed precisely because of this Man-produced ontology of enmity that structures societies. Therefore, dependence upon bodily care results from the conditions of bodies under the societal regime of general warification. Today, under climate change realities, the relation between care and protection has become much more complicated, with the air polluted, water poisoned, food pumped with hormones and chemicals, and sleep eroded because of 24/7 efficiency, environmental degradation or homelessness.[80] We also have to raise the question of who the enemy we are declaring war on actually is when we refer to the virus as the enemy. War, enmity, independence, and dependence are inextricably bound up with one another. Nestled inside of them are protection and care as they are defined in philosophical terms as well as shaped by real world conditions precisely through the ways in which their relation to violence and vulnerability is imagined and, ultimately, cared for.

Warification of the Modern Mind: Man-Made Planetary Death

How, then, have we arrived at this warification of the modern mind, which today confronts us with the omnipresence of war as a key political metaphor for the production of care, upon which life essentially depends? "Enlightenment Man", to use feminist multi-species anthropologist Anna Tsing's coinage, who served as the universal model of the modern subject, fully relied on joining together the two central notions of independence and domination.[81] In political terms, this was achieved, or maintained, by the political mobilization of the threat of war and violence. The history of this subject has come to dominate the history of our infected planet. As we have seen, care is absolutely necessary to life and survival. This dependency upon care of course gets in the way of being and feeling truly independent. One can never be independent from one's own care needs. In order to create independence, care had to be thought through structures and organized through real world conditions in such a way that "living" and "nonliving" beings who were not considered to hold the universal subject position corporeally embodied by Enlightenment Man were made to care for His independence.[82] Feminist anthropologist Elizabeth Povinelli has raised awareness of the enduring legacies of Western thought built on "how Aristotle distinguished between living and nonliving things".[83] This distinction was crucial to the scale of hierarchies that came to define politics and economies governing independence in relation to care. While the focus of feminist and race-critical scholarship was largely on the sexist and racist dimensions of care hierarchies, including both the exploitation of those who had to care and their lack of access to care or the exploitation of their bodies for medical and health care experimentation, the environmental dimensions of this scale of hierarchies as they are most intricately connected to social dimensions are only more recently being examined in the context of feminist and race critical climate scholarship, Anthropocene studies, and political ecology. Recognition of the notion that care is provided by living and nonliving beings is crucial to an expanded understanding of the formation of modern violence against care.[84] This violence includes extraction and exploitation and has political, economic, and epistemic dimensions.

Silencing dependency on care was a precondition for independence. All those living and nonliving beings indispensable or considered necessary for Enlightenment Man's care were historically subjugated to the idea of their own incapacity for independence and of their natural capacity to care. At the same time, if all those living and nonliving beings tasked with providing the care indispensable to independence had resisted, revolted, or gone on strike, then this independence would have been made impossible. Thus, through its very dependence upon care, independence is open to being wounded. Enlightenment Man's independence relied on naturalizing and essentializing those who perform the labors of care and on holding them to be inferior. He also engaged in inventing political forms of permanent warfare to continue this subjugation and oppression and to affirm His own dominance. Exclusion from politics, governance, and access to the economy and education are the expressions of this politics of dominance and subjugation. This ultimately results in a deep structure of enmity. Independence and domination can thus be viewed as constitutive to Enlightenment Man's permanent war on those who (have to) care. Independence is potentially under threat, as indispensable care might not be made available; and all those living and nonliving beings providing this care can be understood as potential enemies to independence. Therefore, this structure of power, which is always already imbalanced and completely and utterly unequal, relies on the fact that those who are independent present the threat of violence to those are taking care of their needs which make them dependent. Independence, then, can only be upheld through permanent domination over those who could always become enemies. The course of history was largely defined by the violent consequences of the human exceptionalism of Enlightenment Man, which made Man independent from care and from nature as both care and nature were transformed to serve the needs of Man. White supremacy, coloniality, and patriarchy resulted in the domination over all those humans who were not Enlightenment Man and were thus considered not to have progressed far beyond the status of nature.

Warification is entrenched in the deep structure of the philosophical ideas and political processes which made Enlightenment Man the universal model of what it means to be a fully human subject. Two very different feminist thinkers, the anthropologist Anna Tsing and the philosopher and environmental historian Carolyn Merchant, have provided important analyses and insights helpful to understanding the profound structural and material impacts of the ideas connected to Enlightenment Man's quest for domination and supremacy as a form of permanent war. They both introduce notions deeply connected to violence and destruction, with Anna Tsing introducing the notion of Enlightenment Man stalking the Earth and Carolyn Merchant titling her 1980 book *The Death of Nature*.[85] The pursuit of prey, as captured in the notion of stalking, and killing and murder, as associated with violent death, are closely associated with war and contributed to my understanding of colonial patriarchal modernity as a process of ongoing warification. In her 2015 lecture "A Feminist Approach to the Anthropocene: Earth Stalked by Man", Anna Tsing explains how Man took the place of God. "Man, the Enlightenment figure, arose in dialogue with God. He inherited God's universalism."[86] Enlightenment Man took the place that had been occupied by God as creator or God sending wars to punish humans. During the period of the Enlightenment, the planet began to be more fully understood to exist on the terms created by Enlightenment Man and seen to be there to serve the interests and, ultimately, the care needs of Men. Carolyn Merchant traces relations to the planet of nurturing and of domination. In her groundbreaking book *Death of Nature. Women, Ecology and the Scientific Revolution*, one of the first studies in Western philosophy to trace the political, social, and economic structures that led to seeing nature and women as sources for extraction and exploitation, she uncovers nurturing and domination as the two fundamentally different and opposing perspectives through which humans have conceived of their relationship with planet Earth. Throughout, I use the word care to speak of life-making and life sustaining activities that not only sustain and maintain human life, but living and nonliving beings on the planet in general. I understand Merchant's use and understanding of the term nurture to be very close to my understanding of what care is and what care enables. Metaphors are, as stated earlier, conveyors of deep meaning. Merchant uses the word metaphor to describe the centrality of the two paradigms of nurturing and domination that have profoundly shaped the ways in which humans relate to the earth until the beginnings of the formation of the modern mind and the modern subject with the scientific revolution and the Enlightenment era. Merchant writes:

> Both the nurturing and domination metaphors had existed in philosophy, religion and literature. The idea of dominion over the earth existed in Greek philosophy and Christian religion; that of the nurturing earth, in Greek philosophy and other pagan philosophies. But, as the economy became modernized and the Scientific Revolution proceeded, the dominion metaphor spread beyond the religious sphere and assumed ascendancy in the social and political spheres as well.[87]

Metaphors are articulations of human cosmologies, ontologies, spiritualities, philosophies, and systems of value. Therefore, the meaning of metaphors allows us to trace in historical terms how meaning evolves over very long timespans. We may want to think of metaphors as tools of memory, as they constantly remind us how we make sense of the world. In historical hindsight, we come to understand today's pandemic, climate change, and the destruction of the environment to have been caused by the birth of modern Enlightenment Man and the beginnings of the long and violent "death of nature".[88] Domination and carelessness have resulted in a war on nature, the consequences of which we are living through now on our infected planet marked by the long-term ecological, material, and social destruction caused by the fact that Man's domination transformed humanity into a geological force that is causing ruination and mass death. The term Anthropocene was first proposed by atmospheric chemist Paul J. Crutzen and biologist Eugene F. Stoermer in the year 2000. They suggested the term "Anthropocene" as a designation for a new Earth age, to express the fact that Man has become a planetary force and that Man-made changes have taken on geophysical proportions which are disastrously affecting the future existence of the entire planet.[89]

In 2016, the interdisciplinary Anthropocene Working Group, which is part of the International Commission on Stratigraphy and was established in 2009 by their Subcommission on Quaternary Stratigraphy, voted that the Anthropocene is a new geological epoch. Over the last twenty years since the introduction of the term Anthropocene, the ways in which humans view themselves in relation to the planet they inhabit have profoundly changed. Humans have come to understand themselves as a geological force, and, at the same time, as a cause of planetary catastrophe, mass extinction, and ecocide. The warification of modern consciousness based on structures of domination and extraction led to a war against planet Earth, which has not ended yet. Extinctions, loss of biodiversity, and deforestation, the brutal and deadly effects of the Man-made world on the planet are leading to the increased spread of diseases from animals to humans on this "frontier of human expansion".[90] War leads to death.

There is currently no peaceful modern way of living with and in nature. If living with the planet Earth is to be understood as defined by the total sum of the conditions of possibilities for living, then why are we at war with these conditions, why are we at war with the very possibilities for living? If, as political scientist and theorist of ethics Ella Myers has stated, "political life is inevitably inhabited by an ethos", then it is crucial to think about the reasons why so much of political life, which is to be understood as inextricably interconnected and interdependent with the total sum of eco-material, eco-social, geo-biological, and bio-material conditions of possibilities for living, is hinged on what I propose to call an ethos of war.[91] The larger questions that have driven this chapter are concerned with the political and social dimensions of a pervasive ethos of war that bears heavily on the ways in which humans imagine, and value, their being-in-relation with one another and with the planet. War generates and legitimizes death. War is an ideology of death. Asking how to understand better how we have arrived at an ideology of death as the best possible response to millions of lives at risk, this chapter has linked the response to the current pandemic to fundamental questions of the making of the modern subject, Enlightenment Man, which has given birth to the slow and painful process called death of nature with its anthropogenic climate catastrophe, the ongoing sixth mass extinction, and now pandemicide. Now, with the planet infected with Man-made war, new imaginaries for planetary care and cure are most urgently needed. The emergence of new forms of care feminism in response to the pandemic and the planetary need for care is the focus of this book's third and last chapter.

Chapter 2: Serving at the Frontlines

With the global outbreak of the coronavirus, the rapid spread of infection, and rising numbers of Covid-19 deaths in spring 2020, governments around the world were swift to take policy measures. They introduced mandates and laws to prevent the spread of the deadly virus, which caused mass infection and rising numbers of people dying from the Covid-19 disease. Lockdown measures, previously unimaginable during times of peace, included shelter-in-place and stay-at-home orders. Businesses, shops, daycare facilities, kindergartens, schools and universities, restaurants, museums, cinemas, theatres, and airports closed. Pandemic emergency measures included curfews and led to travel restrictions or travel bans.[1] Measures to reduce the time people come into contact with one another and restrict, or deny, access to public spaces were aimed at slowing down the spread of the deadly virus and flattening the curve. Entire continents, such as Australia, or countries, like Japan, imposed travel bans and closed their borders to protect their population. At the very same time, governments were under obligation to ensure the continuity of essential critical infrastructure and its operation. Governments defined what counts as essential critical infrastructure and activated regulatory and legal frameworks, ordering the workforce needed for maintenance of essential critical infrastructure to continue working and not shelter in place. Frontline workforce was the official policy term used for these essential workers. While one group of people was ordered to shelter in place, the other group, the frontline workers, was not allowed to stay at home and see to their own safety: they were obliged to leave their homes and continue working. The frontline workforce was made responsible for ensuring the continued and unbroken provision of infrastructures and of care, elements which are essential to human life and survival. All those decreed mandates, laws, and policies went into safeguarding care. This chapter examines the language of war with its militarized imaginaries at the level of pandemic frontline ontologies of care. It juxtaposes the politics of invisibilizing care expressed through the term standstill with the hyper-visibilization of care effected through the term 'frontline' and concomitant expectations of sacrifice and heroism.

On April 3, 2020, when many countries were in their first full lockdown, Kristalina Georgieva, a Bulgarian economist, who since 2019 has been the managing director of the International Monetary Fund, spoke at the World Health Organization Press Briefing. Georgieva stated the following: "Never in the history of the IMF, we have witnessed the world economy coming to a standstill. [...] It is way worse than the global financial crisis."[2] This diagnosis, which was communicated through the captivating figurative language of the world economy in standstill, was most widely circulated in the global public sphere. The standstill of the world economy was reported by international news outlets around the world, such as the *Financial Times* or the *Deccan Chronicle*.[3] Global commentators, representatives of international organizations, and journalists were quick to pick up on the notion of standstill to capture the exceptional situation of the lockdown in its entirety: "Life as we know it has come to a standstill."[4] Some commentators even went so far as to describe the entire year of 2020 as "the year the earth stood still" on account of completely deserted squares, airports devoid of people, and vacant urban centers.[5] The word standstill has a wide affective reach and a high metaphorical density. Standstill captures a condition of crisis, where movement has become impossible. Standstill invokes feelings of the state of being stuck and a sense of dread and impossibility, especially if such a standstill is not of one's own choosing but has been imposed upon people, as was the case with pandemic lockdown restrictions. What is of interest is that the diagnosis of the world economy at a standstill betrays a very narrow understanding of what counts as economy and what does not.

Frontline and Standstill

The pandemic crisis required an immediate political response. Pandemic rules and regulations along with situation reports were communicated in public political speeches, global press briefings, and in measures taken to communicate policies as swiftly and widely as possible. In this context of politicians addressing the public, international organizations holding press briefings, and public administrations communicating public pandemic policy and legal frameworks, a new political vocabulary emerged. This pandemic political vocabulary relied heavily on the use of specific terms in order to articulate the response to crisis and its diagnosis and management. Frontline and standstill were used as political figures of speech in response to the pandemic crisis. As these two words spread swiftly and widely and thus came to be included in what Raymond Williams called a "shared body of words and meanings" when he elaborated his concept of keywords, I kept asking myself with growing worry what kind of political ideas surrounding care, and consequently what kind of public imaginaries, were articulated by these notions of frontline work and the world economy coming to a standstill, while everything had to be done to ensure that all the caring labors, all the essential tasks were, in fact, being continued.[6] The realities of the pandemic required the workforce in entire sectors, such as the health care sector, the care sector in general, or the essential retail business, to name just a few here, to continue working. The work of those in the paid care sector as well as of unpaid care providers became longer, harder, and physically, emotionally, mentally and spiritually much more challenging. Many of the frontline workers who were obliged to continue working under lockdown conditions were exposed to higher risks of infection, were confronted with Covid-19 mass death, and had to deal with high levels of stresses including pandemic grief, fear and anxiety. Their work went into overdrive, as demands, pressures, risks and dangers increased. The physical, mental, and emotional health of the care workforce was under threat. Yet their labors, and the threats that their continued working under pandemic conditions posed to their own health and wellbeing, are conspicuously absent from the diagnosis of the standstill of the world economy. For these reasons, the political use of the words frontline and standstill stirred my feminist curiosity, but even more my deep feminist worry.

What worried me is that, viewed from a perspective informed by decades of feminist activism and critical scholarship, it did not even come as a surprise to me that the International Monetary Fund pronounced the diagnosis of the standstill of the world economy. As a feminist, one could even go so far as to say that the use of the metaphor of standstill to describe the situation of the world economy under lockdown conditions only confirmed, out loud, the structural devaluation and extraction of care under capitalism: considered unproductive, care simply does not count; such is the extent of economic violence against care in globalized capitalism. Analysis of the gendered, classed, and racialized dimensions of the extraction and exploitation of caring labors from female bodies and minds was central to the emergence of modern feminism in the nineteenth century. Since then, labors of care have informed central feminist organizational policies aimed at transforming the structural conditions of the political and economic systems that had established a political economy of care as extractable and exploitable. Transnational and local feminist activism and international feminist politics today continue to organize around caring labors.[7] Feminist activists, policy makers, and scholars and researchers have analyzed and collected data on the classist, sexist, and racist dimensions of the systemic exploitation and extraction of care. How this relentless extraction of care from women's bodies and the devaluation of care in the hegemonic economy went hand in hand with a cultural invisibilization and social silencing of care remains less well understood. How the lack of public imaginaries of care induced by the hegemonic economic system has impacted on the ways in which care is thought of and felt socially needs further inquiry and study. The analysis here contributes to such an inquiry by examining the political vocabulary and its cultural effects on public imaginaries of care. Placing the metaphor of the standstill as diagnosis of the world economy against the realities of unpaid and paid care work under lockdown conditions renders legible who and whose work are silenced by this metaphor. All those who were obliged to perform the essential work of care were hardly in standstill. Quite the contrary: they were required to work more, and harder. UN Women observed that "Care Work" meant "Increased Burdens for Women" in the pandemic.

> Paid care workers in the health sector have faced increased workloads [...]. The burden of unpaid care and domestic work, which already fell disproportionately on women before the pandemic, has increased dramatically during the pandemic, and data shows that women are continuing to shoulder an unequal portion. Working parents, and mothers in particular, have had to juggle paid work with full-time childcare in the wake of school and daycare closures. The burdens of caring for sick family members and collecting fuel and water, among other tasks that tend to fall disproportionately on women, have also increased during COVID.[8]

The diagnosis of standstill is absolutely brutal when placed against the realities and the enormous amount of demanding, stressful, and exhausting labor required of all those who provide this essential work. There is ample reason for feminist worry because of the political and epistemic ignoring of care implied in this standstill diagnosis. What had me worry even more was the use of the term frontline to safeguard the continuity of essential caring labors, which, at the same time, were completely invisibilized and silenced by the metaphor of standstill. While standstill perpetuates the structural devaluation of care, the frontline brings war into care. Viewed together, standstill and frontline produce the present-day formation of patriarchal ideology through the convergence of the silencing and the militarization of care. The specific politics of pandemic care extractivism argued through necessity and responsibility is the product of taken-for-grantedness and forced mobilization. This can be seen not only as pertinent to the economy, public health, and policy, but it also has cultural, ethical, epistemological, emotional, and spiritual implications.

How Metaphors Can Be Made Accountable

What follows unfolds a worried feminist analysis, in fact a very worried feminist analysis, of the meaning of the pandemic political keymetaphors standstill and frontline, with the major part of this chapter dedicated to the implications of making use of the frontline as a political idea and as policy framework: which was not only propagated through words, but also through the emergence of a new popular visuality depicting armies of essential workers or hero nurses at the pandemic frontlines. My worried analysis in this chapter proceeds through the methods of reading back and reinscribing literal meanings of the two words standstill and frontline into their figurative use as political metaphors. Literal meanings are understood primarily through material realities and contexts, rather than through historical semantics and etymology. Reading back such material realities and contexts into figures of speech takes seriously the power that metaphors unfold as political ideas. How power relations, and gendered, classed, racialized social norms, and perspectives on nature, the environment, and resources are articulated by metaphors, how metaphors speak to a relational ethics of bodies, minds, and environments in complex interdependencies is rendered legible through the attentive and slow reading of keymetaphors and into how their meaning-making unfolded in public imaginaries, social ontologies, and material realities. Metaphors powerfully draw imaginary, social, and material worlds of meaning together. This makes metaphors so very effective as political ideas. They are imaginary, social, and material at once, and, at the same time, they are claimed to be only figurative and therefore are held less accountable to their meaning than words in their non-figurative use. Here, I seek to raise awareness of how metaphors can be made accountable to the power implications of their meanings. A single metaphor can be associated with wide semantic contexts, which the political use of metaphor strategically brings into play. In the case of standstill and frontline, these wider semantic contexts are movement and war. How, then, to understand better the ethical and social implications of the semantic webs of movement and war which were articulated by standstill and frontline, the terms that expressed the political response to the pandemic? And how to comprehend the way this response defined the political economy of care in these conditions of crisis? How to relate to these two keymetaphors ethically and critically? How to produce an analytical narrative that makes the hegemonic use of metaphors accountable to their power of meaning-making? The word standstill draws attention to the existence of a central economic vocabulary comprising distinct economic imaginaries that derive from terms of movement. The word frontline raises awareness that there exists, also, an economic vocabulary with its associated economic imaginaries that come from the use of terms of war and the military. Economy, then, can be understood through movement and through war. An inquiry into terms of movement and war as central to the history of political economy, and to popular everyday economic imaginaries as well, goes far beyond this chapter and this book. Here, my intention is to deliver some observations that show how standstill and frontline are connected to a larger field ripe for worried analysis. Historically, the term progress, literally defined as movement toward a desired state, has been used to articulate one of the core ideas of modern capitalism.

Today, the term fast capitalism perfectly captures the acceleration and speed-centricity of globalized capitalism in its neoliberal version, which relentlessly requires bodies, resources, and things to move as dictated by the economy. Movement in response to economic conditions also includes the forced movements of economic migration or displacement due to climate catastrophe, ecological ruination, and massive accumulation of debt. In *Capital*, his foundational analysis of political economy as materialist theory, Karl Marx developed a specific analytical language based on terms of movement and on terms of war. Marx turned to signification through metaphors. He deployed metaphors as analytical tools beyond the boundaries of distinct scientific disciplines. Metaphors, even when primarily used for the purpose of analysis, never lose their other dimensions, their connections to realities and their affective effects. Metaphors constitute imaginaries, as they allow readers, or listeners, to open up their thoughts to associations with realities, materialities, ideologies, and politics. Metaphors in Marx serve the dual purpose of anchoring the analysis in scientific objectivity and of making analysis part of political aims. Wanting his analysis to be on a par with the scientific objectivity held to be the domain of modern natural sciences, Marx states at the very beginning of volume one of *Capital* that the purpose of his analysis is to "lay bare the economic law of motion of modern society."[9] Motion describes the physical properties of movement. An object's state of motion is defined by its speed and direction of movement. Speed and direction are firmly established as key imaginaries of the capitalist economy. Marx's use of the word motion underlined his claim to scientific relevancy and objective analysis, as law of motion is a direct reference to Newton's law of motion, and it made terms of movement central to political economy. At the same time, Marx's writings provide ample evidence that his scientific analysis of the economic law of motion led him to express the social condition created by the capitalist economy using the terminology of war. The capitalist organization of time and the subordination of work to capitalist time is diagnosed by Marx as a form of civil war: "The establishment of a normal working day is therefore the product of a protracted and more or less concealed civil war between the capitalist class and the working class."[10] Armies, barracks, soldiers, or non-commissioned officers—that is, officers who have been granted the authority to supervise enlisted soldiers by commissioned officers who, in turn, have received their authority from a sovereign power—all figure in Marx's analysis of the condition of the working class:

> The technical subordination of the worker to the uniform motion of the instruments of labour…gives rise to a barrack-like discipline…dividing the workers into manual labourers and overseers, into private soldiers and the N.C.O.s of an industrial army.[11]

Marx analyzes history under capitalism as a class struggle, which his analysis expresses in terms of war. The vocabulary of war, enmity, and fighting has become central to viewing the economy. Metaphors of war are used in economic theories, scholarly writing in economic studies, and business and economic journalism as well as in everyday parlance: the market is a battlefield; competitors attack one another; companies plan the hostile takeover of other companies. In the economy, some win, some lose, yet others are forever defeated. The frontline is not the only term that views the economy as war. Quite the contrary: the frontline is one word in a whole vocabulary that conceives of the economy as perpetual war.

In this chapter I approach the frontline through its literal meanings. These are connected to the material realities of the military and of armies, with conditions of the battlefield and patriarchal definitions of masculinist values of endurance, commitment, honor, and heroism. I read these literal meanings back into the term frontline used as a political metaphor and a policy term. The frontline penetrated essential work and care, on the military's organizational and managerial model based on command hierarchies and strict compliance with orders; the masculinist moral code of honor built on sacrifice and fighting to the death was also followed. Militarized understandings of hierarchy, heroism, and morality, therefore, are deeply inscribed into the metaphorical use of the word frontline. The realities of the frontline in times of war are defined by atrocities, violence, and woundedness. Historical images of frontlines show the disastrous effects of combat violence through wounded bodies, harmed environments, damaged infrastructures, and a general condition of death-making. The frontline, which is a highly mobilized space, a space made out of fighting bodies and their weapons organized for battle, is associated with loss. Every frontline in military battle leaves behind dead, wounded, injured, or mentally and physically harmed bodies. Every frontline in military battle leaves behind wounded environments with the earth, the water, and the air defined by toxic residue, abandoned weapons, and the lasting aftermath of destruction. The metaphor of the frontline as a political idea of care is an ideology of violence. It proclaims out loud that care is based on a regime of war. While it was emphasized that war in pandemic political oratory was used as a metaphor, frontline is a policy term. In the context of policy and economy, the frontline, even though—of course—it still has the semantic properties of a metaphor, is, strictly speaking, not used figuratively, but literally. Understanding this transformation of the word frontline from a military war term into a term that is part of the specialized vocabulary of policy and economy allows me to show that the frontline not only articulates the lastingness of a deep culture of war within the economy, but was used urgently and acutely for the purpose of the pandemic mobilization of care as a war effort. Mobilizing the pandemic frontline of care as part of the pandemic war effort leads to viewing and organizing care through a regime of violence. The frontline is a most worrying political metaphor and policy term. From the perspectives of feminist cultural analysis, political keymetaphors have to be examined as a distinct and important part of the history of political ideas and of collective public imaginaries. Because they join the power of meaning to emotions and feeling, metaphors are a very specific tool of communicating ideologies without making an explicit claim to a distinct ideology. The frontline as metaphor conveys the ideology of war-fighting and militarization with its masculinist value system. The frontline made the war against the virus a global reality and connected care to the ideas, realities, and social imaginaries of war. "In times of war, men [...] are expected to be able to be transformed into people willing to go through the torture and terror of soldiering, war-fighting, and killing."[12] In pandemic crisis, all care workers, all essential workers, are expected to be able to be transformed into people willing to fight the virus. Political scientist and feminist war studies scholar Laura Sjoberg, who has analyzed the militarization of masculinities and femininities, observes that "war-fighting requires, then, the military control of masculinity/ies (and by extension, men) asking them to behave as *men*—as soldiers, protectors, and providers—not only for their family or their city or their town but for state and nation, at the risk of all else, including death."[13] Analogously, the virus-fighting requires the political control of essential care, with care workers asked to behave as soldiers, protectors, and, ultimately heroes at the risk of all else, including death.

Worried Analysis

Using here the methodology of worried analysis as a specific feminist approach, my central concern throughout this chapter is how the use of military metaphor of the frontline as a political idea for care is, in fact, an expression of the militarization of care and of a new ideology of violent care extractivism, in which care is seen as military duty. In order to understand better what the frontline means with its shift to seeing care as virus-fighting and its militarization of care in pandemic crisis, the first section focuses on today's militarized care essentialism. I understand militarized care essentialism to be an expression of the most recent transformation of patriarchy and its political economy of care, which is connected to the modern idea of care essentialism as it was shaped by Enlightenment epistemologies and their production of caring femininity and warring masculinity. These epistemologies were central to the historical establishment of the gendered divisions of care and war and, ultimately, the reason behind how modern patriarchy and colonial racial capitalism invisibilized, silenced, and devalued care and, at the same time, led to the persistence of inequality through the extraction and vulnerabilization of care.

Worried analysis takes time. Worried analysis is persistence in uneasiness. It is a continued effort to raise awareness of the space of meaning between the figurative and the literal, in which material realities and social imaginaries have to be understood as co-constitutive. The use of metaphors in politics and policy, in particular the use of metaphors of war and the military, is a distinct form of how patriarchy takes command (sic!). The ongoing process of patriarchialization is shaped through the establishment and use of keymetaphors, of which the pandemic politics of turning to war and the frontline is an expression. Worried analysis takes time to feel and to think. Here, it takes the form of slow and attentive readings that examine the selected examples with the commitment to feeling-thinking, "sentipensar", the immense violence and pain caused by the inscription of war into care.[14] From introducing militarized care essentialism, the chapter's second section moves on to a close reading of the contradictions between the so-called economic standstill and the essential continuity of care, which were rendered legible in the joint press briefing of the World Health Organization and the International Monetary Fund. Along the way, the second section analyzes how the central term of the frontline was surrounded by other terms of war, such as attack or siege, in order to show how the imaginaries of war were unfolded not through one single term, but through a whole new pandemic political vocabulary. The third section examines how the rhetoric of the frontline led to realities of the militarized mobilization of care, using as an example India's *Covid Warriors*. Concurrently with the political use of the frontline, a new pandemic visuality emerged in documentary photography and painting. The chapter's fourth section examines key examples of this frontline visuality and introduces the pandemic gaze as an analytical tool to examine how the pandemic frontline ontologies were articulated visually. The reading of visual examples expands the analysis of the frontline as metaphor in political oratory and policy to the use of the frontline in pandemic "keyimages".[15] Building on the well-established critical feminist, anti-imperial, and decolonial analytic of the gaze as a way of scrutinizing hegemonic ways of seeing, this chapter introduces the pandemic gaze as an analytic to examine pandemic ways of seeing care.[16] The dichotomy between the economy in standstill, with people sheltering in place, and the essential critical workforce at the pandemic frontlines was rendered legible as a relation of seeing and being seen. A politics of 'we' as global class opposition between the "caring classes" and those who are not part of the caring classes was visually established through the pandemic gaze and its politics of vision.[17] Those at the global frontline were captured in documentary photographs, drawing, painting, and portraiture and rendered visible to those not at the frontlines. The pandemic gaze was constituted by a 'we' of those who finally took notice of the previously invisible essential care workers. The former looked at images of the latter from the safe distance of their homes. This pandemic gaze is spectacularly revealed in Banksy's painting *Game Changer*, which established the visual keyimage of the superhero nurse. Such compulsory heroism, celebratory applause, and the hypervisibility of care was met with resistance by healthcare workers. The fifth section looks at how nurses pushed back against clapping and being called heroes. The chapter concludes with feminist worry and feminist hope. A worried analysis is committed to understanding the ethical and epistemological implications of the power of meaning-making processes—and to not giving up hope that such understanding can contribute to feminist recovery. Reviewing the fields of critical inquiry which were opened up by my critical feminist analysis of the pandemic imperative to serve at the frontlines of care, future feminist work gains a clearer perspective on the immensity of historical violence against care as it underpins the present-day pandemic violence against care. In the name of overcoming this violence and understanding care differently, I introduce the notion of planetary care, which I see as central to the new care feminism of the twenty-first century, of which the feminist recovery plans for Covid-19 and beyond—the focus of the following and final chapter—are a central expression.

Militarized Care Essentialism

Militarized care essentialism is introduced as a tool for analyzing care in pandemic times. The concept of care essentialism has assumed different historical forms at different points in time and is therefore useful to the project of feminist analysis of cultural imaginaries, social ontologies, and material conditions of care beyond the historical moment of the pandemic, when it was transformed into the current version of militarized care essentialism. I will first lay out care essentialism and then move on to introduce militarized care essentialism. Care essentialism is underpinned by Enlightenment naturalism, which marks the beginning of modern scientific sexism and was based on what I propose to call mammalian epistemologies.

The understanding of essentialism follows Marxist cultural theorist Stuart Hall's reading of Marx's 1857 introduction to the *Grundrisse*.[18] According to Hall, "essentialism" denotes "those parts at the core of a concept" which remain "common and stable".[19] Care essentialism refers to how the modern gender system is based on a commonly accepted and historically stable concept of care viewed as women's duty on account of the specific properties and material capacities of women's biological bodies. Enlightenment naturalism provided the epistemologies for this modern gender system and its care essentialism.

The new Enlightenment taxonomy of modern naturalism redefined the human species as mammals. Enlightenment naturalist, physician, and taxonomist Carolus Linnaeus argued that the presence of "milk-producing mammae" constitutes an entire class of vertebrate animals and that human beings are part of this specific group of animals.[20] Read in political terms, Linnaeus' taxonomy connects two different strategic moves. This epistemic shift made it possible to argue that human beings are, in fact, animals and have to be included in what was at the time referred to as the animal kingdom. This meant an enormous political and social reorientation, and even a threat to the status of the emergent modern human subject of Enlightenment Man, who cast himself as supreme and dominant over nature via culture and science. At the same time, though, this new taxonomy actually asserted and even boosted Man's superior subject position, as men's bodies did not correspond with the new and highly gendered taxonomy. Only the female part of the human species had the specific biological and embodied nature that provided the justification for viewing human beings as mammals and including them in this new zoological system. This is central to the establishment of modern scientific sexism and the gender system. Modern care essentialism is firmly rooted in the taxonomy of scientific sexism. Women were regarded to be more of nature than of culture and were, consequently, obliged to fulfill the social and embodied care needs of all human beings. This modern gender system had far-reaching effects on all human genders. Based on heteronormative gender binarism, women were defined by the separatist logic of care essentialism just as much as men. Mammalian epistemologies provided the basis for the political and economic arguments and the social ontologies that have it that women were born to care. While women were viewed to be natural carers, men were excluded from the knowledge of everyday care, and to be caring was seen as unmanly.

The modern idea of the independent and autonomous subject was based on a body with clear boundaries, which a female mammal's body is clearly not. The notion of the modern subject was also based on imaginaries of control, discipline, and strength, with the mind controlling and overcoming physical and emotional needs. Care, tied as it is to both embodied and emotional needs, was therefore at odds with this understanding of modern subjectivity. Mammalian epistemology and care essentialism led to Man having to distance himself from the provision of care as well as from the embodied dependency of his own care needs, which had to be met quietly and silently. Because of the reproductive and nurturing function of mammalian glands, women were excluded from "public power", as the "maternal breast became nature's sign that women belonged only in the home".[21] This had far-reaching epistemic, political, and economic effects and drained social ontologies' access to imaginaries of care based on epistemologies of care. It led to the exclusion of women's knowledge and the knowledge of care, broadly understood, from the hegemonic knowledge tradition and from what counts as meaningful to public knowledge and politics and as valuable to the economy. Furthermore, this led to new hierarchies among women, with some women expected and forced to perform more caring labors than others. One can trace this, for example, in the history of the modern system of extracting milk from wet nurses, creating new embodied divisions among women which were based on class, caste, and race. Modern care was transformed into the labor of sexualized, racialized, and classed or enslaved human beings. Or reversely, being socially and culturally forced to perform caring labors was central to the formation of modern sexism, racism, classism, casteism, and slavery. At the same time, modern Enlightenment sexism and mammalian epistemologies impacted the historical formation of masculinity and led to men being excluded from the everyday experience of care and even viewed as having no knowledge or understanding of what it takes to care. A gender-critical investigation of the implications of the absence of care in the modern imaginaries of masculinity and what this means to hegemonic understandings of politics and the economy had, until more recently, not been embarked upon in critical feminist analysis.[22] Viewed from the perspective of the intellectual and political history of ideas, modern naturalism and its mammalian epistemologies are foundational to the formation of modern structural sexism. Looking at the development of modern medicine and healthcare, this new epistemology can be identified as the reason behind the hierarchies of modern professions, with the scientific knowledge of doctors gendered male and the caring knowledge of nurses gendered female. In broader societal and political contexts, Enlightenment mammalian epistemologies led modern state politics relying on patriarchal values to define the conditions of care, including the specific politics and economies around care under colonial, capitalist, communist, fascist, or neoliberal regimes. In cultural, spiritual, and intellectual terms, these mammalian epistemologies have led to a conspicuous lack of public imaginaries of care, from which we are still suffering today.

Militarized care essentialism, which was the response to the pandemic care needs, penetrated the essentialism of care with masculinist values of militarization. Based on the modern gender system, militarized care essentialism effectively joins together the imaginaries of care and the imaginaries of war. The modern gender system not only resulted in the profound gendering of the economy based on the idea of the *homo oeconomicus* and the realities of a highly gendered division of labor, but also led to very different expectations of what was viewed as women's national duty and what was held to be men's national duty. The Latin root of nation helps understand this. *Nascere*, to give birth, is the etymological root of nation. The national duty of women was the biological and social reproduction of the nation. This expectation to provide nurture and care as the national duty of women was aligned with mammalian epistemologies. The protection of the nation in times of war and defending the nation against attack and siege, on the other hand, was seen as the national duty of men. Joan Tronto observes that the function of the military is understood as protection.[23] Enlightenment thought not only established modern scientific sexism, which underpins the gendered expectations of national duties of women and of national duties of men, it also gave rise to new notions of modern warfare based on a new military paradigm of professionalism and its novel idea of the male citizen as soldier. Here, one can see the difference between care viewed through essentialism and war viewed through professionalism. To this day, war is closely associated with values and ideals of masculinity.

Historically war, just like care, has been organized through a gendered division of labor, which required of men to be ready to fight and to serve their people or their nations in times of war; which has, in turn, culturally shaped notions of masculinity, in particular military masculinity as the paradigmatic model for male duties and male professionalism. In her 2020 book *War. How Conflict Shaped Us*, historian Margaret MacMillan observed the following: "The assumption that it is the men who should be warriors seems to be almost universal through time and across cultures [...]."[24]. Militarized care essentialism relied on the historical gender system and forcibly joined together the deeply gendered imaginaries of masculinity and femininity as they are tied to war and to care. Following gender and militarism scholar Cynthia Enloe, "militarization is never gender-neutral" as it relies on "ideas of femininity and masculinity".[25] Militarization encompasses a range of values. Among these are most significantly, on the one hand, "dominance, [...], independence, self-sufficiency, and willingness to take risks",[26] and on the other hand, "sacrifice, compassion and cooperation".[27] While the former qualities are perceived to be gendered exclusively masculine, the latter can be considered feminine as well. The militarization of care relies on combining these values strategically and selectively. Militarization of care projects these values as expectations onto care workers as warriors, from whom it is expected that they perform self-sufficiently, take high risks, are ready for sacrifice and, at the same time, show deep compassion and a willingness to give everything in cooperation. The profound gendering of care and the profound gendering of war informed the militarization of care essentialism and were inscribed into the social ontologies of the frontline. The frontline served the purpose of overwriting care gendered as female with the masculinization of war, while keeping the structural conditions of feminization unchanged and, in fact, worsening the actualities of care through added pressures. Far beyond the context of regulatory documents or legal frameworks, the widely publicized policy term of the frontline became highly influential over cultural and visual articulations of pandemic care.

Economic Standstill and the Essentiality of Care

At the beginning of April 2020, when Kristalina Georgieva presented her diagnosis of the standstill of the world economy at the joint press briefing of the World Health Organization and the International Monetary Fund, "about half of the world's population was under some form of lockdown, with more than 3.9 billion people in more than 90 countries or territories having been asked or ordered to stay at home by their governments."[28]

I place both the standstill and the frontline in relation to modern economic imaginaries which have, crucially, been articulated in terms and metaphors of movement. Growth and progress, the two main key words of modern capitalism and perhaps even modernity at large, provide imaginaries of the economy in the service of the constant and uninterrupted movement of capital and the maximization of profit. One may also think, here, of other terms of movement, such as acceleration, upturn, flow, or expansion as well as slump or slowdown, which are widely used for describing the state of the economy. Placing these imaginaries of movement, which express hegemonic understandings of the economy, adjacent to the imaginaries of movement that typically connote care is helpful for analyzing the implications of the pandemic key words standstill and frontline. Reflecting on the way ideas of economic thought and realities of economic histories are captured through imaginaries of movement, I came to understand that there is another history of imaginaries of very different kinds of movement that shaped the ideas and realities of care. Movements centrally connected to the understanding of care are continuity and repetition. Furthermore, care is commonly seen to be a burden and to weigh heavily on the bodies and minds of those who give care. Bodies burdened or weighed down by continuous and repetitive labors of care do not correspond with the economic imaginaries of growth, progress, and acceleration. Quite the contrary: laborious, slow, and repetitive movements are a threat to the fast, unhindered, unburdened, and forever accelerating speed of the economy. These opposing imaginaries of movement that are commonly associated with the economy and with care render evident the fact that care was not only excluded from what counts as economy, but viewed as antithetical and as a hindrance that obstructs the economy's very movement. The imaginaries of movement connected to care come very close to slowing down the economy or even causing times of standstill. From this one can surmise that the kinds of movement needed for the continuity of care presented a threat to the economy. This has to be understood as one of the profound reasons why care was excluded from the hegemonic understanding of what is counted as economy. Historically, the threat of standstill to the economy was very well understood by workers. We may think, here, of the traditional German labor anthem of 1863: "All the wheels shall stand still if thy strong arm so wills."[29] The political strategy of strike in international labor movements is the organization of economic standstill. Standstill, therefore, is the economy's worst enemy. What is needed for the continuity of care has either remained disregarded by the hegemonic organization of the economy or even been seen as a threat to keeping the economy running. Conversely, the acceleration of the economy poses extreme threats to the continuity of care.

The more growth and progress accelerated, the more disruptions there are to the provision of adequate care for oneself and others. This is perhaps best understood through how capitalist economies are encroaching on sleep. In his 2014 book *24/7: Late Capitalism and the Ends of Sleep*, art historian and essayist Jonathan Crary lucidly observes that the compulsory idea of a 24/7 economy with the marketplace running uninterruptedly is not compatible with the bodily needs of sleep. Those who have to keep the economy running around the clock work longer and longer hours and do not get enough hours of sleep.[30] Sleep is being shortened. From the perspective of the economy, sleep presents the threat of standstill. Thinking of the centrality of fast and uninterrupted movement to today's globalized economic world order, standstill is the worst possible crisis, a death threat to the economy as we know it. The actualities of care under accelerated neoliberal capitalism have severely suffered from the effects of the economy's requiring more and more flexibility as it kept speeding up. The diagnosis of the standstill of the economy during lockdown conditions demonstrates not only that the hegemonic understanding of the economy completely silences the tremendous increase in care responsibilities on account of the pandemic, but that the economy has little to offer to the continuity of care. The void of silence around care and the absence of any economy providing for the continuity of care not only left the organization of care to state governance, but it also left open a vacuum. This vacuum was filled by the policy measures of the frontline, which was fully aligned with the imaginaries of war that characterized the political response to the pandemic.

The joint press briefing of the World Health Organization and the International Monetary Fund made clear that the health of the economy is viewed as separate from the health of people. My worried feminist reading of this press briefing focuses on how the imaginaries of war gripped the public response to the virus outbreak. Georgieva's speech contributed to the pandemic war rhetoric, to which she brought the metaphor of the siege. She stated the following: "WHO is there to protect the health of people; the IMF is there to protect the health of the world economy; they both are under siege."[31] The siege was her choice of war metaphor. A close and worried feminist reading of her choice of metaphor causes me to think about the siege in relation to the attack. Episodes of war produce a specific form of time, with distinct imaginaries of how bodies and environments are under threat. The most striking difference between the attack and the siege is the specific episode of war each of them stands for. Attacks are forceful, aggressive and violent. Attacks are considered to be fast, with the aim of defeating the enemy at once. Key imaginaries connected to the attack are swiftness and unexpectedness. The enemy is surprised by the attack. Those who come under attack—those who have been attacked—can suffer from the effects of the attack for years, decades, or even centuries to come. In contrast, a siege is very different from an attack. Central imaginaries of the siege were formed by medieval warfare. Besieging begins with an attack and can then go on for months. Populations of cities under siege are expected to be resilient. They are expected to not give in, to hold out, to rely on what they have prepared for their protection, to make do with the resources they have and to cope with shortages. For a deeper understanding of the war metaphor of the siege as chosen by the director of the International Monetary Fund, one has to relate the imaginaries of the siege to the imaginaries of the attack as they are connected to Covid-19 conditions. In public political oratory, the coronavirus outbreak was framed as an attack. This is aligned with popular medical imaginaries that engage the war metaphor of the attack in order to describe what viruses do to human bodies. *Medline*, an online information service by the United States National Library of Medicine, explains what viruses do as follows:

> They invade living, normal cells and use those cells to multiply and produce other viruses like themselves. This can kill, damage, or change the cells and make you sick. Different viruses attack certain cells in your body such as your liver, respiratory system, or blood.[32]

Military metaphors shape the cultural deep structure between disease and medicine and even disease and health at large. With diseases viewed as the enemy of health scientists, doctors, nurses, and patients are seen to be fighting diseases. The metaphor of the siege builds on the metaphor of the attack. After the swift and unexpected deadly attack of the virus a siege is to be expected. Georgieva's speech invokes the siege in order to describe the condition of the lockdown and what is expected from those who have come under siege. The lockdown understood as siege demands endurance, steadfastness, and resilience of the planet's population. Through the metaphor of the siege, the director of the International Monetary Fund comes close—at least—to obliquely acknowledging the essential continuity of care, which her oratory displaced from the economy. Living on an infected planet under lockdown conditions is much like living in cities under siege: life and survival are under threat from denial of access to food, water, or energy. Life under the conditions of lockdown, much like life under the conditions of siege, depends on preparedness and protection. While the use of the war metaphor of the siege comes very close to addressing the realities of the essential continuity of care during the pandemic lockdown, the notion of economic standstill effectively silenced what has to be provided for continued life and survival. The press briefing renders legible the consequences of the modern episteme of dichotomy, separation, and independency which has dislocated global public health from the health of the world economy. This shows the historical violence of capitalist economies that separated what is needed for the continuity of care from what is needed for an accelerated growth- and progress-centric economy. Not the interests of human health and wellbeing are at the center of the economy, but the interests of capital. The episteme of mammalian epistemologies, which I introduced earlier, was highly influential to the formation of the modern patriarchal organization of the economy with its separation of care—understood as women's world and of no value to the economy—from the hegemonic economy, which was understood as men's world. The lasting impact of the modern economic gender system became obvious during the pandemic, with the continuity of care widely understood as women's duty.

The patriarchal organization of modern capitalism has led to a subordination of the needs of human beings to the demands of the economy. Put differently, the health of workers was subjugated to—or even sacrificed in the name of—the health of the economy. This has resulted in the exploitation and extraction of care as well as in the dispossession of care as knowledge. In what follows I will focus on the effects of exploitation and extraction and turn to the dispossession of care as knowledge in this chapter's concluding reflections on feminist worry and hope. The analysis of the political economy of capital as developed by Karl Marx remains a critical frame of reference for understanding how maintenance of workers' bodies and health was subjugated to the needs of capitalism. Worker's bodies were defined as labor-power and seen as a source ripe for capitalist exploitation and extraction. Workers were under obligation to ensure they sustained their own labor-power. Health, therefore, was subordinated to the needs of labor-power in the interest of capital. In 1867, Marx writes the following in the first volume of *Capital*:

> If the owner of labor-power works today, tomorrow he must again be able to repeat the same process in the same conditions as regards health and strength. His means of subsistence must therefore be sufficient to maintain him in his normal state as a working individual.[33]

Labor-power, according to Marx, is provided by the living and healthy body of the worker.[34] How is the health of the worker to be maintained? How is their strength restored? How are the means of subsistence provided for? The hegemonic idea of the economy provided no effective solutions for this. Neither did the analysis of Karl Marx.

In the 1970s, feminist Marxists began to analyze the lacunae in the political economy developed in the writings of Friedrich Engels and Karl Marx. Feminist activists, economists, sociologists, or political theorists have critically analyzed the consequences of the historical organization of the daily maintenance of the living body outside of capitalist wage relations. Using the key notion of social reproduction for their analysis of how maintaining and ensuring the continuity of care has resulted in the exploitation of women's unpaid and badly paid labor under capitalism, they are the originators of today's extensive body of critical scholarship on care and on social reproduction theory. This body of work, which has been developed and advanced by feminist scholars and theorists since the 1970s, has always remained in close communication with women's labor struggles and feminist activism concerned with the systemic crisis of care caused by the patriarchal organization of capitalist economies.[35] Since care is essential and constitutive to the continuation of life, capitalist economies have most strategically, cunningly, and violently exploited the condition of essentiality and firmly linked the essentiality of care to women's bodies essentialized as caring bodies. These gendered economic realities were built on the foundational legacies of modern naturalism and its mammalian epistemologies, which were the basis for capitalist economies that transform women's bodies into a natural resource for care. Capitalism erased the essential labor of care and social reproduction from the wage-relations that define the economy. In recent years there has been a renewed interest in this line of inquiry and in making caring labors the focus of feminist analysis and struggle. This has led to a new generation of feminists revisiting and reappraising the formation of social reproduction activism in the 1970s connected to the Wages for Housework movement, founded by Maria Dalla Costa, Silvia Federici, Brigitte Galtier, and Selma Jones, or the Black Women for Wages for Housework campaign, founded by Margaret Prescod. This revitalized interest in social reproduction has also led to a number of recent publications, in particular the new series *Mapping Social Reproduction Theory*.[36] On the analysis that the classed, gendered, sexualized, and racialized conditions of caring labor result from capitalist violence across time, today's split between the health of people and the health of the economy originates from the violence of placing the living body outside of the responsibility of the economy or, put differently, of freeing the economy from responsibility for living bodies.

Feminist Marxist theorists have tirelessly pointed out that the conditions for social reproduction are in and of themselves a "product of history" and therefore open to change.[37] This finding invites more studies on how the modern conditions of reproductive labor were historically shaped by patriarchal capitalism, racist colonialism, scientific racism, and scientific sexism. At the same time, this finding encourages feminist hope and energizes feminist struggles working to change and transform the conditions of social reproduction and care. With the outbreak of the coronavirus, social reproduction and caring labors have now become a product of pandemic history. I have shown that the diagnosis of the standstill of the economy rendered invisible and silenced the essential continuity of care. Enter the state in shaping care as a product of pandemic history. States used their powers for regulatory frameworks or legal mandates that ensure the continuity and maintenance of essential care under lockdown conditions. The frontline emerged as the term most widely used for the essential critical workforce needed to maintain the essential critical infrastructure. The continuity of unpaid caring labors in private homes was incorporated into the frontline used by states to ensure the continuity of care. Traditional gender roles were reinforced by the pandemic. Expressions like "moms on the frontline" show how the gendered imaginaries of the frontline expected women to provide care as part of the pandemic war effort.[38]

Understanding the global frontline of care as a product of pandemic history and realizing the central importance of the state in constituting the frontline imaginaries and the new frontline ontologies of care raises awareness of the state's role in shaping care as a product of history at any given time. What can be learned from the pandemic situation, in which the state established frontline rules that led to public frontline imaginaries and altered expectations of care, is that more critical research is needed on how states have, in the past, shaped public articulations and imaginaries of care. While the economies of the structural feminization and devaluation of care are well understood, there is no genealogy of public articulations of care as they were historically produced in public political oratory or regulatory frameworks and therefore no easily accessible history of how the state, regulatory frameworks, policies, and public political oratory constituted public articulations and imaginaries of care. Gaining access to care as a product of state history and public political articulations will be helpful to undoing the vast silence around care.

The pandemic presents us with a present-day example of how the state shapes not only legal frameworks and conditions of care, but also care's public imaginaries. Official mandates and regulatory frameworks that ensured the continuity of pandemic care were based on the understanding of essential critical infrastructure. The following broad definition of critical infrastructure describes it as a "term used by governments to describe assets that are essential for the functioning of a society and economy."[39] The European Commission defines critical infrastructure as a "system which is essential for the maintenance of vital societal functions."[40] The U.S. Department of Homeland Security and its Cybersecurity and Infrastructure Agency defines essential critical infrastructure as "both public health and security as well as community well-being".[41] Critical infrastructure sectors include public health, emergency services, food and agriculture, electricity, drinking water, wastewater, transportation and logistics, communications and information technology, government operations, critical manufacturing, financial transactions, and chemical and hazardous materials. The official US list of essential workers included the following:

> cleaning staff; building security staff; food workers; crop pickers; miners; armored cash transporters and ATM servicers; powerline repair people; truck operators; grocery store workers; the people who cut tree branches away from overhead electrical lines; sewage processing plant workers; road repair crews; bus drivers; plumbers; waste disposers; telecommunication repair people; IT workers who maintain the internet; metal workers; chemical workers; laundromat staff; janitors.[42]

The term frontline worker is an established term to classify a specific part of the workforce and is used in the context of law, policy, and governance as well as by researchers. The European Parliament uses the term frontline to establish that "frontline workers" are needed for "maintaining basic economic, social and health facilities" and were therefore "exempted from confinement measures and movement restrictions and often had to work in face-to-face situations."[43] According to a poster presentation at the Population Association of America Conference 2022 by Lindsay M. Monte and Lynda Laughlin, working in the Social, Economic & Housing Statistics Division at the U.S. Census Bureau, "essential frontline workers" are all those "who must physically show up at their job".[44] Elected politicians as well as high-ranking public officials were soon to give public praise and recognition for the work performed by essential frontline workers, with the militaristic imaginary informing their choice of war-related vocabulary. In March 2020, the website of the New York City Comptroller stated:

> If there is any collateral benefit (sic!) to the COVID-19 tragedy, it is that the labor and contribution of those in our social service, cleaning, delivery and warehouse, grocery, healthcare, and public transit industries have finally received the attention and respect that they are due.[45]

Such attention and respect, while of course very important, neither diminish the health risks of the essential frontline workforce nor do they translate into adequate pay.

Science journalist Debora MacKenzie, whose specialization is in infectious disease, highlights the classed dimension of the essential workforce. In 2020 MacKenzie wrote "that a lot of critical infrastructure depends on low-income people."[46]

Greater vulnerability among low-income people worsens the spread and impact of a pandemic in the most critical parts of the complex system: firefighters, paramedics, police, care workers, the people who produce everyone's food, drinking water, electric power, the list goes on.[47]

MacKenzie's sharp conclusion is the following: "More inequality, and more poverty, means more risk."[48] Economic hardship has, as studies have shown, exacerbated pre-existing inequalities and presented health risks including growing cases of depression and "mental health deterioration".[49] The essential critical infrastructures were maintained and continued by the frontline workers. Working at the frontlines presented a high risk of exposure to the virus leading to pandemic trauma or even death. The imaginary of the standstill silenced these realities of the frontline workers. Income injustices, health injustices, and the exploitative and deadly vulnerabilization of frontline workers are the result of hegemonic economic imaginaries which structurally dispossess and annihilate what is essential. This shows that systems solely predicated on economic growth and progress—the so-called health of the economy—and not on the existence, health, and wellbeing of human beings, and particularly all those human beings who provide what is essential for life and survival, are in and of themselves a deadly threat to life and survival. The imaginaries of the frontline effectively posed the pandemic imperative to care. Questions of income justice or health justice for essential workers are effectively deposed by the military ethos of obligation enforced by the frontline mobilization.

Frontline Mobilization and Covid Warriors

The call to the pandemic frontline of care must be understood as part of the general mobilization of essential workers in the name of the war against the virus. "Mobilization is the act of assembling and organizing the national resources to support national objectives in time of war or other emergencies."[50] This definition of mobilization is helpful in order to understand how care was being organized. With war presented as the political response to the global virus outbreak, mobilization took command in order to forcibly transform care into an obligation so that the national objectives of fighting the virus could be met. Following the view that the virus is the invisible enemy of human beings, roles were recast in terms of mobilization for the global war against the virus. All essential workers were required to understand their work as a war effort at the pandemic frontlines. Scientists were viewed as "the new generals", and "economists" were expected to "draw up battle plans".[51] This forcible pandemic mobilization of care as a national resource in the war effort against the disease is very different from a mobilization for care that would represent a mobilization for actual social and economic recognition, more resources, better infrastructures, and improved working conditions and higher pay for care workers. While the mobilization can be seen as an un-silencing of care, the newly gained presence in public political oratory—which, in light of the viral threats to global public health and human life, foregrounded the essentiality of care as central to the war effort—translated into the social and cultural normalization of expecting from care workers sacrifice, endurance, and even heroic deeds. These public expectations made a banality of the exposure to high risks faced by frontline workers who were obliged to continue working. The health sector, in particular, left many frontline workers without sufficient protective gear and also presented them with challenges of not being able to care adequately for those in their care, as the health infrastructure was overwhelmed and dangerously overstretched. Continuing their work, maybe more than ever before, led not only to physical exhaustion, but also to previously unknown forms of pandemic grief and trauma. To provide just one example here of how traumatic and painful it was to continue working in the healthcare sector under pandemic conditions, I quote the following from a report on the situation of nurses "caring for Covid-19 patients", published by the *American Journal of Nursing* in August of 2020:

> There are refrigerator trucks filled with bodies outside our hospitals. Many of us have to pass by them when we go into work, knowing that among those bodies are the patients we cared for yesterday, and when we leave 12 hours later, some of the patients we cared for today will join them. Even harder to handle is the knowledge that among those bodies may be a colleague or friend, fellow nurses who caught COVID-19 while caring for others. It is heartbreaking and terrifying because we know that we too could end up in a body bag shelved in a refrigerator truck.[52]

Studies have shown that the frontline condition led to extreme exhaustion as "frontline nurses" faced "enormous mental health challenges" resulting in "burnout, anxiety, depression, and fear."[53] The realities of the global frontline of care were characterized by risk, danger, exhaustion, depression, loss, and death. The imaginaries of the pandemic frontline insisted on bravery and heroism.

The frontline mobilizes a very specific military imaginary: the frontline is the line of confrontation, the position closest to the conflict in war. The meaning of frontline as the foremost part of an army is very old and originated in the early modern period. Over the ensuing centuries the frontline took on the meaning of operations in direct contact with the enemy. Today, the frontline is commonly understood as the military line that is formed by the furthest advanced tactical combat units, and regarded as the physical space where two armies face each other and engage in fighting during a war. The frontline is a space made out of bodies that move. The bodies of the soldiers who fight on the ground are the frontline. They make the war move. Their bodies are the movement of the war. The term frontline captures this movement and joins together concrete physical territories with all their human and nonhuman beings, weapons, infrastructures and other technologies of fighting, conditions of weather, and fighting bodies of soldiers. The term frontline is associated with imaginaries of battles, of death and bravery, sacrifice and heroism, suffering and perseverance. Today, the term frontline is widely used beyond the military context. It has migrated into the economy and the organization of companies. Frontline staff are all "those who interact directly with customers."[54] The frontlines of businesses include, for example, desk support and customer complaints. Social services or street-level bureaucracies are understood to be in frontline interaction with the public. Direct contact with customers, clients, or members of the public is understood through the meaning of the frontline, which has historically been shaped by the realities and imaginaries of war. It is profoundly unsettling that direct contact, be it in businesses, social services or street-level bureaucracies, be it at the counter, via phone or e-mail, is viewed as a military operation. On the website of a service learning technology company this connection to the military is well understood: "frontline employees are in the trenches, handling problems, overcoming obstacles [...]."[55] An article published on a career support website stated that "frontline employees make up 70% of the globe's work population". Quoting the findings of "a team of analysts from McKinsey & Company and the Conference Board, a business research organization" who "has studied companies known to engage the emotional energy of frontline workers", they share that the U.S. Marine Corps was not only included in the study, but that the 100 interviews conducted with them revealed that the "Corps outperformed all other organizations when it came to engaging the hearts and minds of the front line".[56] Finding that "discipline" is a key ingredient to their success, the article concludes that companies and the military have the "same critical objectives: speed, responsiveness, and flexibility." It is worrying to realize this deep penetration of civilian life and the organization of businesses, organizations, and institutions by frontline imaginaries. Understanding the other as a potential enemy is central to the meaning of the frontline.

The semantic career of the term frontline presents an exemplar for the spillover of military meanings and war imaginaries into civilian realities. Through war terminology and war metaphors, the imaginaries of war and the ideology of enmity have deeply penetrated civilian life. The language of civilian life and life in so-called peace is filled with imaginaries of war. Military imaginaries govern social ontologies. Here, my focus is on the "the ideologies" that are "encoded" in how the pandemic imperative made use of the frontline.[57] In particular, I am foregrounding the gendered implications of the imaginaries and ontologies of the frontline. All metaphors, especially when they are incorporated into legal definitions or policy frameworks, have, at once, semantic and material consequences. The frontline imaginary forcibly joins together essentiality, conscription, and duty and, at the same time, gives special meaning to frontline work as it is incorporated into the war effort against the virus. Beyond the legal definition, the term frontline allows for the political exploitation of introducing a powerful public image of essential care workers as warriors or soldiers, who have historically been gendered male. Historically, those fighting wars on the frontline have been men and those nursing the wounded have been women. This is the modern gendered political economy of war and care as it emerged since the 1800s. In contemporary usage, the frontline seems to connote that a person's activity is important. I argue that the military framing of the frontline produced not only hyper-visibility for the pandemic frontline workforce, but also attributed a different cultural and social status and a higher symbolic value by mobilizing military imaginaries commonly gendered male. The global frontline of essential workers is considered key to the war effort against the virus. The essential workers exhibit and perform the political determination to defeat the enemy and are expected, as frontline soldiers of an army would be, to give everything for the shared sacrifice. In the context of the pandemic imperative, the choice of the term frontline for essential work is strategic. It renders clear that essential work is being lent special importance—just as war, in cultural and social terms, apparently bestows special importance on human activities—and, at the same time, it manages to essentialize frontline workers as the ones who are in the first line of contact with the deadly virus. Frontline imaginaries, operating on the level of ontologies, fully incorporated the bodies of those who provide vital care and maintain essential activities into the war effort by articulating a military ethos of recruitment and duty.

This militarized care essentialism dramatically changed women's work and women's lives under pandemic realities. In December 2020, South African politician Phumzile Mlambo-Ngcuka, who for two terms, between 2013 and 2021, served as the Executive Director of UN Women, published an op-ed titled "Women working on the frontline".[58] She stated the following:

> Globally, women make up 70% of the front-line workforce in the health and social sector. They are the doctors, nurses, midwives, cleaners and laundry workers, working [...] to care for the sick and keep communities safe, often in the lowest-paying jobs.[59]

A key example of this highly militarized care essentialism and women recruited to serve at the pandemic frontlines can be found in the Indian government's organization of the *Covid Warriors*. "Starting in March 2020, nearly 1 million ASHA workers across 600,000 Indian villages were tasked with containing the community transmission of coronavirus. They survey their populations to find suspected COVID cases, monitor patients' oxygen and temperature levels daily, contract-trace, ensure patients complete their quarantine period, and help them get medical care."[60] Asha, which has a Sanskrit etymological root that means hope or desire, is the acronym for Accredited Social Health Activists. They are central to India's National Rural Health Mission. Since 2005, these voluntary community health workers, whose voluntarism is expected as community service, receive only very low pay, approximately 40 dollars per month, far below the minimum wage in India, from the Ministry of Family and Health Welfare. They are "trained to work as an interface between the community and the public health system." According to the National Health Mission, an "ASHA must primarily be a woman resident of the village married/ widowed/divorced, preferably in the age group of 25 to 45 years" and she "receive[s] performance-based incentives."[61] Healthcare provision in India is characterized by differences of class, gender, and caste. "With less than one doctor for every thousand people, and a medical system stretched to its seams, women have shouldered an enormous burden of care since the pandemic started in India."[62] In structural terms, there are a number of different interconnected dimensions to be made out in the feminization of mobile health care workers. Mobile healthcare workers have the task of introducing and working toward the acceptance of new health norms, in particular norms having to do with reproductive health, contraception, pregnancy, birth, immunization, and the prevention of infections. The mobile female health workforce was expected to embrace voluntarism and their low pay. Their volunteered time was seen as an extension of women's domestic caring in the service of the betterment of the community's health.

As part of the political response to the pandemic, Indian Prime Minister Narendra Modi turned the community health workers into *Covid Warriors*. On April 27, 2020, Modi announced "COVID Warriors", which was the "new Coronavirus-related website".[63] The purpose of the website was to act as an "umbrella portal to provide information related to doctors, nurses, ASHA workers, NSS, NCC, and people related to these industries are all present on the website. People can look for information on this and even become a volunteer to serve during the Coronavirus crisis".[64] This militaristic shift had far-reaching consequences, as in "one authoritarian move, one million ASHAs, [...] were transformed into 'frontline fighters' against the disease" with many of them on Covid duty twelve to fifteen hours every day.[65] In June 2020, Modi stepped up the war rhetoric. Addressing an event at the Rajiv Gandhi Health University in Bengaluru via video conference, Modi said the following:

> The virus may be an invisible enemy. But our warriors, medical workers are invincible. In the battle of Invisible vs Invincible, our medical workers are sure to win. [...] The world is looking at them with gratitude, hope, and seeks both 'care' and 'cure'. [...] At the root of India's brave fight against Covid-19 is the hard work of the medical community and our corona warriors. In fact, doctors and medical workers are like soldiers, but without the soldiers' uniforms."[66]

His political praise of care acts had the effect of militarized pressure, articulating a politics of expectation that *Covid Warriors* have to win the war against the virus and prove that they are invincible, while, in reality, health care workers lacked proper equipment and had to cope with enormous stresses and traumas.

Findings of a study on the situation of ASHAs during the pandemic, conducted under the guidance of development researcher, and program manager in disaster mitigation at the Intermediate Technology Development Group in Sri Lanka, Madhavi Malagoda Ariyabandu, were published in the *National Institute of Disaster Management Journal*. The findings included the "mental and physical stress a woman *Covid warrior* undergoes as she multitasks the entire day like taking care of patients at the workplace, fear of contracting Covid-19, PEE's [Personal Protective Equipment] ill fitting, lack of transportation and sanitation facilities."[67] Furthermore, essential care for themselves was under pressure, "as the community health workers "face issues concerning menstruation and lack of sanitary napkins at the workplace. They fail to eat their meals on time as they need to attend to patients or other related matters immediately."[68] The political rhetoric of the *Covid Warriors* and its deeply ingrained ideology of "heroes" and "sacrifice", as diagnosed by sociologist and scholar-activist Christa Wichterich, added pressure and led to thousands of ASHAS contracting Covid-19.[69] Using an intersectional approach, Wichterich examines interlinked dimensions of inequalities connected to "gender, class, caste, and race or ethnicity" as they "structure the division between productive and reproductive labour".[70] With many of the AHSAs Dalits, who "in the Indian caste hierarchy represent the lowest groups and must perform the most polluting and impure work", the rhetoric of the warrior and the hero has to be understood as an expression of class violence.[71] Prime Minister Modi, frequently using the hashtag #ModiWithCoronaWarriors, was aware of gendered violence and even sexual abuse against the voluntary community healthcare workers, as he stated that "violence, abuse and rude behaviour against frontline workers is not acceptable".[72] Yet, instead of investing in structural and infrastructural measures for the protection of community health workers, against sexual violence and from the risks of infection with the potentially deadly virus, Modi encouraged the public to "clap, ring bells or beat plates for health care workers" to "boost their morale and salute their service".[73]

Many in the health sector were infected with Covid-19 and died from the disease. In honor of deaths in the health sector, the prime minister "encouraged ordinary citizens to light lamps, and the Indian air force showered flower petals from helicopters on hospitals in various cities."[74] Such acts of public symbolic public recognition and the officialdom of militaristic imaginaries served to enforce care voluntarism and present a rhetoric of policing: warriors do not demonstrate, heroes do not strike. In 2020, the ASHAs did precisely that. They organized, demonstrated, and went on strikes. Dressed in their pink uniforms, they demonstrated in New Delhi in August 2020. At their rallies, they demanded "the legal status of full-time workers, better and safer working conditions, and higher pay."[75] Together with millions of other so-called scheme workers they went on strike again in September 2020, and they have continued coordinating strikes with the big labor unions since. In 2022, Tedros Adhanom Ghebreyesus, deciding on the awardees of the Global Health Leader Awards, chose to give the award to the entire team of ASHA workers, which they received during the 75th World Health Assembly in Geneva. Tedros stated that "these awardees embody lifelong dedication, relentless advocacy, commitment to equity, and selfless service of humanity."[76] In connection with this award ceremony, the All India Co-ordination Committee of ASHA workers affiliated with the Centre of Indian Trade Unions critically stated that

> scores of ASHA workers sacrificed their lives succumbed to COVID-19 and the Government of India doesn't even have statistics on them. Their families are yet to receive the ₹50 lakh [approximately 60 USD] for death due to Covid-19 for frontline workers.[77]

The paradigmatic example of the *Covid Warriors* in India demonstrates the politics of structural uncaringness and the social realities of highly exploitative and deadly care extractivism.[78] The "responsibilisation of the weakest" was based on demands for selflessness. Care workers were turned into warriors and warriors were turned into heroes. The difference in gender and caste between those in danger out there and those safe at home is clearly exposed in an article by independent journalist Priyamvada Kowshik, which was published in the *Times of India*. Titling her article "Women Warriors Against Covid" and sharing with the public "stories of the faceless (sic!) wonder women fighting on the forefront of the war against the ongoing pandemic" Kowshik writes the following:

> What did it take to keep us #safeathome, while a virus unleashed a war? An army, no doubt. An army of people researching, testing, strategising, treating and creating safe spaces—battling against a microbe that had brought the world to its knees. These are stories of some of the female foot soldiers. Stories of women at the forefront, down in the trenches, out on the field who made a difference, putting their lives on the line.[79]

The example of the *Covid Warriors* in India manifests the deep class antagonism with its split between those who have to care and those who are safer at home, which, as I will show in the next section, is articulated in the pandemic gaze. The militarist ideology of an army of *Covid Warriors* fighting the virus is not a metaphor. It is not merely political rhetoric. It created material, social, and corporeal realities. The pandemic world order was based on the class antagonism between those who were forced to fight on the frontlines and those who were not. This class antagonism was visually expressed through the pandemic gaze with its focus on frontline workers and the emergent imagery of highly militarized care heroism.

The Pandemic Gaze and the Hero Nurse

On April 23, just three weeks after the managing director of the International Monetary Fund had diagnosed the standstill of the world economy, the *National Geographic*, an American monthly known for its photojournalism, published an essay "to show the world's essential workers serving on the front lines".[80] Composed as one long visual essay, the piece contains a large number of documentary photographs showing essential workers from different parts of the world. This essay was among the first visual articulations to establish the new frontline imaginaries through photography. Using as my example the lead image of this photo essay I am able to show how the visual tools of documentary photography were employed to create the new imagery of the essential worker as paradigmatic pandemic warrior serving on the frontline. The lead image is central to the articulation of the pandemic gaze. It shows a man at work in an otherwise almost empty street, with only very few people in the background. He is wearing a white full body protective suit with a hoody attached to it, which he has drawn tight around his face. A white mask covers his mouth and his nose. Large protective goggles with an orange-brown frame, ready to be pulled down over his eyes again, are pushed up on his forehead. Both of his hands are fully covered with yellow plastic gloves that reach up on his wrists. Only a tiny bit of skin is exposed between his wrists and the protective suit. His left arm reaches across his body and both of his hands are gripped tight around a black rubber hose, which from its metal tube releases a disinfecting agent that forms a big cloud of white mist in the narrow street in Istanbul's Beyoğlu district. The man's task is to disinfect the street. His protective suit makes him look as if he were wearing a special kind of uniform. The hose can quite easily be interpreted as a weapon, and the white mist appears to be a powerful chemical agent. If this were a scene from a science fiction film, one would immediately, and without any doubt, take the man to be a sole and brave warrior, who is out on a mission to protect his neighborhood or to defend his city against an alien invasion. In the pandemic situation of April 2020, the image of this man is not read to be of a science fiction warrior, but is easily identified as one of the many "workers who now find themselves at the frontlines of the Covid-19 pandemic" in the words of Rachel Hartigan, writer and editor for National Geographic.[81] This photo was taken by Turkish photojournalist Emin Özmen, who is known for documenting human rights violations and refugees. During the lockdown conditions, like other photographers who focus on war as well as on so-called natural disasters and ecological and humanitarian crises, he focused his attention on essential critical labors and helped create the visual imagery of the pandemic frontlines. The lead image captures important elements that render previously unnoticed mundane activities, such as the cleaning of streets, legible as part of the dangerous fight against the spread of the virus. This established the frontline as a distinct perspective of pandemic visuality.

The *National Geographic* essay shows how the visual means of documentary photography were put to use to stage essential workers as warriors, whose protective gear, clothes, gestures and movements made visually manifest that they were fighting at the frontlines with the high risks of exposure to the virus. The pandemic-defining images show nurses, staff at supermarkets, bus drivers, casket makers, food deliverers, pharmacists, doctors, ambulance drivers, fumigation workers, and many other essential workers. I see these images as a new visual genre, which I propose to call frontline visuality. Such images provide visual evidence of the global frontline of care, which was created by government ordinances and legal frameworks that defined essential work as frontline work. Such images also created the public visual understanding of the frontline, as part of the political response to the pandemic, as a war effort against the virus. The images that appear in this photo essay highlight specific elements of the new frontline visuality. These elements include frontline workers wearing masks, plastic shields, gloves, or protective body suits, which made the workers appear to wear uniforms ready to fight the pandemic war. This new militaristic iconography of war visually transformed all kinds of different types of work, such as the maintenance of streets, the stocking of supermarket shelves, or the care of Covid-19 patients, into essential frontline work. Evoking associations of protection, defense, and combat, such imagery is fully aligned with the political rhetoric of "'fighting' coronavirus" and of uniting populations globally in a war against the pandemic.[82] Images like this one made the previously widely ignored and unnoticed essential work hyper-visible and raised awareness of its essentiality as it changed its image from the work of ordinary workers into the work of courageous warriors. The essentiality of the continuity of care and the imaginary of the frontline were made visually and ideologically inseparable. Frontline images created the pandemic visuality of militarized care essentialism and this makes manifest how frontline imaginaries operated visually on the level of pandemic frontline ontologies.

In the opening paragraph of the *National Geographic* photo essay, Rachel Hartigan, *National Geographic* editor and writer, makes the class antagonism between the caring classes and the others, who are dependent upon their care, explicit as a visual relation between those who are seen and those who see.

Hartigan writes that "we are finally seeing the faces of the people we need to survive."[83] This sentence kept coming back to me and provoked deep feminist worry. Reading this sentence through the lens of feminist worry raises critical and painful questions: Whom does this sentence address? Who is the assumed we of readers looking at the images of essential frontline workers? Who is made to identify with this we? Are we all the people who are now, under pandemic conditions, being found out to be the ones who had previously not seen, that is, who had chosen not to look at the faces of those who perform essential work? "We only see what we look at," writes John Berger and goes on to argue that "to look at is an act of choice."[84] Had 'we' made a public and collective choice to not look at the faces of essential workers? What had made such a choice of not looking at the faces of essential workers possible? What about essential workers, the majority of the workforce globally? Are they not assumed to form part of the readership? Are they assumed to not see the faces of other essential workers, who are their colleagues? What about their way of looking at those who depend upon them for their survival? How do they see the faces of those who are inessential workers? The regime of seeing captured in the observation that 'we' are finally seeing the faces of the people 'we' need to survive exposes the violence of structural invisibility, while, at the same time, it makes manifest new forms of class antagonism expressed in the pandemic ways of seeing care as the war fought by others—whom 'we' finally notice—on 'our' behalf. My feminist diagnosis looks at the implications of 'we'. In order for there to be an assumption of the existence of a group constituting a 'we', there is, most often, the assumption of the existence of a second group, who are not we, who are they. We and they are understood to be different from each other: 'we' are not 'them', and 'they' are not 'us'. The political, ethical, social, and cultural understandings of 'we' and 'they' are as complex as they are contested. With these notions of us and them, us against them, or us for them, global politics is continually being made and remade. With these notions of us as different from them, the globalized structures of racism and sexism were produced. Of the notions of us as superior to them, the histories of genocide and ecocide were the result. The histories of us against them are filled with nationalism, enmity, and war. Yet there exists, also, another way of understanding the histories of 'we' through the politics of organizing the formation of a 'we': histories of liberation and emancipatory struggles, histories of activism, histories of anti-capitalist, anti-sexist, anti-racist, or environmental movements. In feminist activism, the political idea of a 'we', informed by the politics of essentialism, has historically been invoked to articulate the political idea "that women are a class having a common condition."[85] The idea of a 'we' in feminism has also been articulated through the idea of universal sisterhood, which invokes a political feeling of relatedness because of a commonly shared condition as women. These figurations of a feminist 'we' through the ideas of class or sisterhood have been central to feminist organizing in struggle and solidarity. At the same time, the idea of such a homogenous female subject articulated as 'we' women united in feminism has been widely and fiercely disputed as essentialist. In particular, pushing against essentialism was a political feminist reaction to Western modernity's understanding of women as mammals and as providers of unpaid caring labor in the modern gendered division of labor, which viewed nurturing and caring as a natural resource to be freely extracted.

Historically, caring work was constructed as a biological condition of the nature of women as nurturers and carers. The formation of a political feminist 'we' in relation to the condition of women's lives and existence has, of course, to be understood in relation to the conditions created under specific economic and political regimes as they resulted in oppression, subjugation, discrimination, and exploitation. The creation of these conditions has historically been centrally organized around dimensions of women's bodies, including their capacity to care and their reproductive function. Women's bodies were essentialized as caring bodies with the patriarchal gaze rendering care invisible—or visible—in a narrowly circumscribed way, as it is depicted through imagery of maternity or domestic servitude, including domestic slavery. Thinking through and debating the implications of pushing against an essentialist and naturally assumed we, and struggling for a political we, has led to disruptions, rifts, splits, and deep wounds in feminism as well as to an extremely rich and nuanced production of feminist theories and methodologies. This immediate recognition of the pandemic split between those who have to perform essential work and those who do not as a class relation is, of course, owed to critical feminist scholarship, which has diagnosed the historical "mistress–maid"[86] relationship and pointed out that "the greater liberty of these middle-class women, however, was achieved at the expense of working-class women".[87] The social stratification among women, which is part of patriarchal racial capitalism and manifested today in a globalized division of caring labor, is classed and racialized. "Race", as Marxist cultural theorist and sociologist Stuart Hall writes, "is thus, also, the modality in which class is 'lived', the medium through which class relations are experienced [...]."[88] The same holds true for gender, which continues to be a modality in which class is lived. Decolonial feminist activist and thinker Françoise Vergès has called for "politiser le care" using a framework that connects the intersecting, yet different axes of gender and race.[89] Analysis of classed and racialized divisions between women who have to care and women who can pay for care is helpful to understanding the class relation between those who have to work at the pandemic frontlines of care and those who finally notice them in the new pandemic visuality of the frontline. The *National Geographic* essay observes that these workers "have always been essential, but we're just now noticing them."[90] Therefore, the photo essay in the *National Geographic* exposed the endemic violence of class as "the caring classes" were being made visible and documented so they could be looked at by those who did not have to work at the global frontlines of care.[91]

By December of 2020, the pandemic gaze was fully established, as evidenced by "Frontline Health Workers" chosen as "Guardians of the Year" by *Time* magazine and put on its cover.[92] In 2020, the Guardians of the Year were described as follows:

> Guardians put themselves on the line [...]. In 2020, they fought on many fronts. On the front line against COVID-19, the world's health care workers displayed the best of humanity—selflessness, compassion, stamina, courage—while protecting as much of it as they could. By risking their lives every day for the strangers who arrived at their workplace, they made conspicuous a foundational principle of both medicine and democracy: equality. By their example, health care workers this year guarded more than lives.[93]

The cover, created by illustrator and painter Tim O' Brien, who specializes in lifelike portraiture and whose work first appeared on the cover of a *Time* magazine back in 1989, quite seamlessly blends photography and illustration.[94] The cover centers on the half-portrait of one health care worker, who wears a plastic face shield with a white facemask underneath, a light blue hospital gown with a rounded white neck, a black sweater, and a white T-shirt. The chin is slightly raised, the hair is framed by a colorful twisted band, and the eyes are intently focused as they seem to look not at the reader, but beyond, facing the pandemic world. This figure, whose skin color reads as brown, is at the very front of the cover, literally at the frontline, and fills up the space of the cover with the sleeves of the gown of this half-length portrait touching the fine white line next to the bold red frame by which the covers of Time magazine are easily recognized. To the left and the right there are chest portraits of two more health workers. The figure to the left wears a turquoise mask and a white coat, and has *sindoor* applied at the root of the hair and a *bindi* between the eyebrows.

The figure to the right wears a black sports cap, eyeglasses, and a white medical shirt with the top buttons open. The figure's nose, mouth, and part of his black beard are covered by light blue surgical mask. There is one more figure to the left, behind the figure with the green mask, who is shown in full color. This figure wears a light blue surgical mask, a white coat, a blue top, and has a stethoscope around the neck. Behind them one can make out the heads of more figures, shown in shades of sepia, and then more silhouettes which dissolve into the white top of the cover. Visually, this implies to the viewers that the health workers who are shown here also represent all the other health workers, whose number goes far beyond what the space of a cover can hold. They are all wearing their pandemic frontline uniforms, their protective masks, and their blue or white hospital clothing, suggestive of a global frontline of health workers who are working together and standing in solidarity with those who need them and are dependent upon them.[95] The composition and visuality of the cover subtly counteract any notions of the feminization of care. Even though, at first glance, the cover seems to represent gender, ethnicity, race, or age in a very straightforward way, there is a conscious downplaying of gender identity, particularly in the way the central figures are being shown. This can be understood as the visual articulation of the masculinist values and the military ethos attributed to the frontline health workers. Their faces—eyes intently trained on the pandemic world, mouth and nose fully covered—show the determination to "put themselves on the line" as they are ready to "fight on many fronts".[96]

The article even encouraged readers to purchase a print of the cover. This is of interest, as it expands recognition for health workers to the level of popular esteem, or celebration, that is associated with hanging up posters of popular culture idols for admiration at home.[97] Such popular forms of visual recognition had previously not existed for health workers, the care sector, or essential workers in general. The cover art also inspired new forms of popular, and commercial visual portraiture of health workers, of which I will cite one example here. Watercolor artist Steve Derrick, a video game developer based in Clifton Park, New York, who devotes his spare time to watercolor painting, found his "inspiration in the faces of health care workers who were honored in *Time Magazine's Person of the Year* issue."[98] Painting hundreds of portraits of medical workers, nurses, and doctors, Derrick shares them via Instagram. An article in the local newspaper in Clifton Park, New York, where Derrick paints in his basement, emphasized that he "has managed to honor and capture the heroics of men and women battling on the front lines – a legacy that will far outlive this pandemic."[99] What matters to my purpose, here, of examining the condition of care as defined by frontline imaginaries and of conducting a feminist analysis of the military ethos mobilized for its provision and recognition, is how easily the frontline was popularized as a new visuality of care, celebrated through posters and watercolor portraits, and how readily it was embraced as a new value system expressing the best of humanity. While, before the pandemic, the value system of care was already widely cognate with selflessness and compassion, stamina and courage are pandemic additions that align with the idea of the frontline. The latter correspond with the process of valuation through ideals of masculinization. While selflessness and compassion have, historically, been constructed as feminine virtues of care, stamina and courage have been largely gendered as masculine virtues that are proven at the frontline. While selflessness and compassion speak to the idea of a weak self, which lives in mutual interdependence with others and opens to them through feelings of empathy, stamina and courage represent an understanding of a strong subject rooted in independence, autonomy, and power.[100] The notion of the weak self, introduced here to complicate the implications of the frontline from a critical feminist perspective, resonates with recent feminist theories of resistance as well as a queer/pandemic analytical framework for contemporary social theory. Queer theorist Yener Bayramoğlu and postcolonial theorist and trauma scholar María do Mar Castro Varela introduce the "queer/pandemic" as a distinct analytic framework: they develop their "new theory of fragility" as they argue for the "search for possibilities to train the skills and reflexes that keep alive our capacity for solidarity, empathy, and care."[101] Fragility as the basis from which to understand interdependency, interrelatedness, and inter-vulnerabilities is central to the idea of a weak and porous self, open to feeling and living with others. This is very different from the concept of a strong, independent and bounded self, based on masculinist, militarized, and heroic values which were mobilized and promoted by the frontline.

The hero nurse is, perhaps, the clearest articulation of the effects of the masculinist militarization of what is expected from care workers in everyday language and of the popularization of the pandemic gaze. Heroism is associated with powers beyond the normal, super-powers that can overcome bodily limitations or infrastructural constraints. During the first wave of the pandemic, in May 2020, a new piece by globally famous anonymous artist Banksy appeared on one of the walls of London's Southampton general hospital. The mostly monochrome, one square meter-large painting shows a young boy looking up at the toy figure of a nurse, which he holds over his head in his left hand. The only color in the painting is the red cross on the nurse's uniform.

Eyes wide open, cap firmly placed on her hair, face masked, and cape billowing behind her, the nurse is ready to fly. Her left arm is stretched out high in a pose well known from superheroes such as Batman and Spiderman.[102] The flying nurse, with her war uniform and her cape, which would typically have been worn by nurses around 1900 at the time when nursing emerged as a new respectable profession for women in the wake of the Crimean War, alludes to the essentiality of nurses in the historical theatres of war, and, of course, immediately forms a visual and semantic connection to the present-day war against the virus. The boy, who is much bigger than the toy figure of the nurse, at which he looks admiringly, is kneeling next to a garbage bin. He has disposed of his former superhero figures, a *Batman* and a *Spiderman*: they are now garbage. A new, more impressive superhero has arrived in the form of the hero nurse. Now he is playing with the toy figure of the nurse. The painting inserts the visual figuration of the essential frontline health care worker into the popular visual world of superheroes. Celebrated for decades in comic books and films, superheroes come with their own troubling legacies of ideologically stereotypical and problematic representations which, for a long time, tended to reinforce gendered, sexed, and raced tropes of heroism. Superheroes, as is widely known, have powers that are never exhausted. They never give up, and they never fail. Most importantly, superheroes always win. This translates the expectations of the politics of the frontline of care into what is expected from the nurse as superhero. The expectation is that the nurse has superpowers—which she generates all by herself—and that these powers will enable her to win the war against the virus. Reproductions of the image can be bought online as a mounted print or poster, for example at wall-art.de. While the original was titled *Game Changer*, the online reproductions of this new form of medical pandemic merchandise are named *Real Hero* and marketed as "critical social art for your walls."[103] The image immediately became immensely popular on social media and received "2,8 million likes and over 30.000 comments on Instagram", as reported by the art broker and Banksy expert Joe Syer.[104] The painting "sold to an unnamed buyer for €19.4 million plus costs—the highest ever for a Banksy painting—after fierce bidding at Christie's auction house in London."[105] The proceeds from the auction were donated to National Health Service charities. Christie's auction house stated that "as an artwork, however, it will remain forever a symbol of its time: a reminder of the world's real game changers, and of the vital work they perform."[106]

While one may think that the superhero nurse presents a welcome intervention into the highly gendered landscape of toy super heroes available for young children, I want to argue here that the painting deepens the militarized gendering of care through its celebration of the nurse as superhero associated with war and masculinity. Even though "masculinity is a malleable category" it is "always connected to war—when war is present."[107] Conversely, one can observe, when masculinity is present—it has historically been connected to war. At the same time, one can suggest that, even though femininity is a malleable category, it has always been connected to care. The hero nurse mobilizes deep connections to both femininity and masculinity. Converging child's play and heroics, the image does not in fact center on the nurse, but on the young boy, who has abandoned his former heroes in favor of the hero nurse, who has taken their place. Discarding one's old, previously much-loved toys is a gesture of power and neglect, as is the transformation of a health care worker into a super-hero toy figure and visual merchandise, neglecting the realities of care in pandemic times. Super heroes, as is widely known, never work for pay. They can always give their super powers for free and they are always ready to save the world. The celebration of an image of heroism makes invisible and silences the exhaustion, trauma, stress, fears, pains, and anxieties real nurses suffer from. Furthermore, the hand that wields the power to make the nurse fly is the hand of a child clearly gendered male. He has the power to lift the nurse and raise her up. He also has the power to drop her and toss her into the bin, where he previously dropped his other unwanted superheroes. The painting, perhaps unwittingly, exposes the vulnerabilities and risks of what it means to be raised to the status of superhero. Rather than an image of the valuation and celebration of care, the *Game Changer* portrays the violent logics of masculinist powers and dependencies, with the hero nurse, reduced to the status of a toy, dependent upon the hand that lifts her up. The hand is not stretched out give help, support, consolation. The hand symbolizes the power to bestow symbolic value and recognition. The hand does not represent a politics of solidarity, mutuality, or reciprocity.

The *Game Changer* does not provide transformative social and cultural inspiration concerning how to better care for care but, rather, exposes masculinist imaginaries of power and their violent effects of super-heroism. Unlike real nurses, who need to look after themselves, who need to sleep, to take care of their own kin and friends, who have to pay the rent, cannot continuously work double shifts and are dependent upon reliable infrastructure, superheroes are not burdened by any of these social, economic, and infrastructural realities of care. Failure, stress, sadness, depression, or low pay are absent from the world of superheroes. Marketing and selling reproductions of the image under the name *Real Hero* suggests that the powers of super heroes, understood to be fiction, have now become expected from the real heroes, the nurse heroes. In many places around the world, public consciousness was informed visually and rhetorically by the image of heroism. StreetARToronto started the *Front Lines Heroes Art Project* with a series of murals honoring essential service providers, including portraits of nurses. The hero imaginary was even taken up by the profession in the television special American Nurse Heroes, produced by the American Nurses Association, Al Roker Entertainment, and HealthCom Media, which premiered on Thursday, June 24, 2020 on *Discovery Life*. The documentary was announced on *GlobeNewswire* to "feature inspiring true stories of nurses who selflessly provide expert, compassionate care on the frontlines of the COVID-19 pandemic."[108] With the imaginary of the hero as nurse firmly entrenched in public consciousness, heroism came to be viewed as normal and to be expected from those in caring professions. This not only continues to place essential care outside of the economy and thus disconnects, and depoliticizes, all forms of public recognition of labor struggles or wide public political support for fair pay, but it also comes to consider normal the heightened exposure to risk and death which is historically connected to the ideology of war heroism.

The pre-pandemic silence around essential work and the cultural and social devaluation of caring labors was replaced by militarized hyper-visibility. These articulations made traditional assumptions of caring femininity and military masculinity hyper-visible and informed, as I have shown, a new pandemic visuality of the global frontline of care. The frontline was established as visual pandemic motif, which was primarily articulated through imagery, in particular portraiture, of frontline workers. The imagery of the frontline rendered public the pandemic class division between those in standstill, instructed to shelter in place, and those at the frontlines, who were obliged to leave their homes in order to fulfill their national duty of ensuring the continuity of essential critical infrastructures. In response to and in visual support of the political imperative to fight a war of care against the virus, there was the emergence of popular pandemic imagery that translates the masculinist ethos of militarized heroism circulating in public political oratory and media commentary into a new public visual language of the pandemic. I argue that the violence of militarized care essentialism so easily conquered public imaginaries of care because of the acute historical lack of public articulations and imaginaries of care and the poverty of understanding care as valuable work and a form of useful public knowledge. The legacies of modern Enlightenment epistemologies of separation, which split bodies from minds and humans from all other living and non-living planetary beings, have to be understood as politics of violence, which ultimately gave rise to defining the provision of care through imaginaries of war and enmity and to militarized care essentialism. The expectations of heroism from essential workers not only led to headlines calling frontline workers heroes or to the visual imagery of nurses as heroes, but also to other forms of symbolic recognition, such as public applause and collective clapping for healthcare workers during lockdown: people in cities around the world gathering on their balconies or at their open windows at an agreed hour in the evening to show their thankfulness and their respect. This shift from invisibility to visibility, from silencing to applause, did nothing to change the structural and systemic conditions of care. Quite the contrary: militarized care essentialism enforced a public view that essential work and care, while finally noticed, was to be expected as a duty which frontline workers were obliged to fulfil for the pandemic war effort. Statements by nurses highlight that care workers were very well aware of these new and violent pressures that resulted from the militarized imperative to care and its imposition of heroism, which was culturally affirmed, and even celebrated, in visual hyper-visibility and public applause.

Stop the Clap, Stop Calling Us Heroes

On April 3, 2020, the very same day the joint press conference of the World Health Organization and the International Monetary Fund took place and the diagnosis of the standstill of the world economy took effect, an American online publisher of medical news and information on human health reported the following: "Worldwide, People Clapping for Hospital Workers."[109] In cities around the world, people organized and coordinated public applause for health workers and medical staff to show their respect and their thankfulness. "New Yorkers have leaned out of windows, stepped onto balconies or fire escapes, and even climbed onto roofs to applaud hospital workers during the evening shift change."[110] Hashtags like "#ClapForOurCarers" were trending. In Italy, people "shared videos of their neighbors chanting and singing from windows, in an effort to cheer on hospital workers and lift their neighbors' spirits."[111] During the first lockdown, the clapping for the NHS—the National Health Service in the UK—had been named *Clap for Carers*; for the second lockdown, the organizers wanted to bring the applause back, calling it *Clap for Heroes*. *Nursing Times*, a monthly magazine for nurses published in the UK, titled "Nurses say they do not want return of applause" and reported strong pushback on social media.[112] Clapping, and calling nurses heroes, had become political. Commentary diagnosed the clapping as a "hollow gesture" and called "on the public to campaign for fair pay for nurses." Nurses emphasized that they had "seen too much Covid denial, general abuse and harshness towards the medical profession [...] to fully believe the sentiment is real" and that they wanted "people to stick to the guidelines and for the government to raise wages for nurses." In particular, the term hero was viewed as dangerous. "We aren't heroes or brave. We are educated professionals with careers in nursing", stated Vickey Bintley, one of the persons quoted.[113] Kirstie Hill, another of the persons quoted in the article, observed that "they believed hero was a "dangerous" term, because it "implied invincibility". "We are not invincible and when we do say we're struggling, we're not believed."[114]

Already in July 2020, David Berger, an Australian remote general practitioner advocating outspokenly for public health education and Zero-Covid, had published an opinion piece in the *Sydney Morning Herald*: "Please stop calling healthcare workers 'heroes'. It's killing us." Berger lucidly diagnosed a necropolitical normalization of death that is characteristic of militaristic and emotionalized reporting on the deaths of health care workers. He writes:

> The military rhetoric in emotional news reports of healthcare worker deaths has normalised the notion that healthcare workers caring for sick patients will inevitably die of COVID-19 contracted while doing their duty, when the truth is that this doesn't have to be normal at all.[115]

Insisting on not being "soldiers in some kind of war" he states: "I don't recall pledging to unhesitatingly sacrifice my health or my life to protect my patients, when that risk was entirely due to organisational incompetence and negligence."[116] In 2021, the WHO published a working paper on the impact of Covid-19 on health and care workers coming into close confrontation with death. The WHO estimates that "between 80 000 and 180 000 health and care workers could have died from COVID-19 in the period between January 2020 to May 2021, converging to a medium scenario of 115 500 deaths". Yet the actual number of deaths may be much higher, as the "figures largely derive from the 3.45 million COVID-19-related deaths reported to WHO, a number that by itself is proving to be much lower than the actual death toll (60% or more than reported to WHO)." The report states that there is "mounting evidence that the number of deaths due to COVID-19 among HCWs is much greater than officially reported."[117] In India, where *Covid Warriors* was the political term of choice for healthcare workers, the public viewed them as heroes who were under the obligation to be the "foot soldiers of India's battle to improve public health".[118] The "Indian state government" had initially "knowingly put ASHAS at a high risk of contracting COVID-19 by failing to provide proper protective equipment like masks or gloves" and "ASHAS were injured, infected, or died as a result of their work."[119]

Political metaphors can be very dangerous, even deadly. The imaginaries produced by the frontline as a designation for essential workers, along with the expressions of the pandemic gaze—which made hyper-visible the masked faces of those who had to perform care across many different sites of care, in hospitals, in intensive care units, in nursing homes, and in private homes—articulated the expectation that caring classes had to be heroic and selfless. The re-gendering of care through its association with masculinist values of warriors and heroes articulated a militarized care essentialism based on an ethos of war, which moved all frontline care workers closer to associating the profession with exposure to high risks and death. Overstretched and failing provisions by states and the existence of a profound class antagonism between the caring classes and the others led to new forms of structural carelessness and "necro-care, a unique mode of care in which the death of certain individuals is an integral part of care for others".[120] This philosophical and theoretical understanding of necro-care builds on analytical lineages of "necropolitics", as introduced by Achille Mbembe, and of "necroeconomics", as written about by feminist sociologist Beverley Skeggs in the context of the pandemic.[121] This approach to care assumes the power to decide over life and death. This is the ultimate expression of the deadliness of power produced and delivered in the name of care.

Hands that clap can easily stop clapping. A hand that firmly holds a toy celebrating the nurse as superhero can easily drop its new hero and bin it alongside other toys no longer needed. Recognizing and celebrating what is essential through symbolic gestures aligned with metaphors of war-heroism is harmful. With the pandemic fully exposing the crisis conditions of public health, social care, and care in general, the frontline allowed talk of an acute crisis, while camouflaging the pre-existing conditions. Reasons for the crisis in care include austerity measures, shortages of equipment, and lack of infrastructural investment, combined with the rampant bureaucratization of care as well as shortages of personnel. The low pay in the care sector also presents a form of crisis made permanent, as many working in low-pay sectors—many of them women, who continue to have more care obligations—have to work longer and longer hours to prevent impoverishment and are thus faced with increasing levels of exhaustion and less time for care for themselves and others.

The pandemic imperative to care at the frontlines shows that the borders between essentiality, essentialism, and conscription were being redrawn. The military imaginaries embedded in policy frameworks, political rhetoric, and public commentary reordered the social and material actualities of caring work. The term frontline has strong connotations of crisis, risk, and death. The frontline is the mobile frontier of crisis, its avantgarde, meeting the crisis first, wherever and whenever it hits. Frontline imaginaries and war heroism came to define the realities of essential frontline workers. They were obliged to fight a war against the virus. The notion of essential frontline work invoked heroism with associations of masculinist honor and bravery. With heroism normalized as social expectation, care workers were viewed as foot soldiers serving at the pandemic frontlines, as a vaccination army and as hero nurses. After wars, soldiers returning from the frontlines went on to live with bodies that had lost limbs, and struggled with shellshock, with emotional, psychological, and mental illnesses and post-traumatic stress. Because of the pandemic war, care workers live with grief due to pandemic death and loss, traumatic stresses, exhaustion and chronic fatigue, and the impact of long Covid. There is also awareness of the effects of militarized hyper-visibility and new pressures on care due to social expectations of compulsory heroism. Moving care as virus-fighting into the masculinist tradition of war will leave behind physical, mental, emotional, and spiritual scars and wounds that will be difficult to diagnose and heal.

The public visibility and celebration of care must not be confused with structural change. In fact, celebratory gestures expressing honor and gratitude are not at all helpful to labor struggles organizing for adequate economic recognition of essential work and for acknowledgement of demands to transform the world economy in such a way that essential work is actually placed at its center. Such gestures, even though perhaps unintentionally, contribute to confusing symbolic recognition. The realities of work in the care sector have actually worsened. Because of the pandemic working conditions, many in the sector are now physically and mentally ill, and even unable to continue working. In July 2022, Kelly Fearnley, who is a foundation doctor at Bradford Royal Infirmary, and Shaun Peter Qureshi, who is a specialist registrar in palliative medicine in Glasgow, published a joint article titled "Who's clapping now? UK healthcare workers with long Covid have been abandoned" in the *Guardian*.[122] The two authors report that thousands of healthcare workers are suffering from the chronic illness and disability of long Covid. These healthcare workers acquired the infection in the workplace. Now these very same workers, who risked their lives for others to whom they provided essential care, are faced with disciplinary procedures, the risk of losing their jobs, and financial destitution.

> Meanwhile, as tens of thousands of us NHS workers face this precarious and frightening situation, we cannot help but feel we have been treated as though we are expendable, and are now being abandoned. Somehow the faint memory of people clapping and banging pots and pans on Thursday evenings doesn't quite make up for it.[123]

Living the afterlife of infection and with chronical illness, essential frontline workers are faced with failing support and an absence of actual social and economic recognition for having delivered essential frontline care. The crisis of care is deepening, as the virus continues to mutate.

Feminist Worry and Feminist Hope

The imaginaries of the frontline, operating on the level of military ideology, led to the formation of frontline ontologies of care, which was supported by the conspicuous silence around care in the hegemonic view of the standstill of the economy. My examination of how public political oratory, policy, and publicly circulating pictures redefined and re-gendered care through frontline imaginaries, militarized care essentialism, and hyper-visible heroism has introduced feminist worry as an analytic. Feminist worry, at once an ethical stance and a methodological orientation, directed at public imaginaries of care, also opens up new fields of future inquiry dedicated to examining how political oratory, policy, reporting, and public imagery have, in the past, re-defined care in times of crisis and beyond. Political speech in times of crisis relies on metaphors. Terms like standstill or the frontline raise awareness of the need for more feminist cultural analysis in order to understand better the interconnectedness of political, economic, and military imaginaries, and in particular crisis imaginaries, as they impact on the ontologies of care. A critical feminist analysis of terms of the military and of war is needed in order to understand better what it means that so many of these terms have migrated to contexts beyond the military and actually unfold their deep meaning in many different contexts beyond times of war and the military. Militarized and warring cultural and social imaginaries have profoundly shaped how human beings relate to one another and all other living and non-living beings on the planet in times of so-called peace.

The way in which states and economies have worked together to produce pandemic care also requires us to think of future analysis on how historical care regimes were organized and what the specific roles of the state and of economies were in this. Care, understood through the historical conditions of political and economic regimes and their specific violence, will need to be more extensively studied. This requires future inquiries on imperial care, "colonial care", fascist care, socialist care, communist care, or welfare care. Such critical analytical work will lead to a more complex understanding of the impacts of ideologies and imaginaries on care practices and allow for a widening understanding of the functions and doings of all those responsible for creating the conditions of care, who include, among others, politicians, policy makers, scientists, educators, and the whole range of different care workers as they are historically specific.[124] This will have to centrally include intersectional approaches to sexism, racism, classism, and casteism in the organization of all essential work, along with a deeper understanding of how caring labor, understood as feminized, relates to other forms of essential work, which were historically masculinized.

My observations on the visuality of care under pandemic conditions and my reading of the frontline imagery led to my diagnosis of the pandemic gaze. This analytical framework of the pandemic gaze suggests a wider historical investigation in order to understand, in visual and epistemic terms, the formation of the modern gaze on care with its public articulations of care imaginaries across social, political, cultural, aesthetic, spiritual, and religious contexts. This will necessarily have to include the study of how imagery and imaginaries of care were visually articulated in previous times of public health emergencies and pandemics.

There is an urgent need to understand better the poverty of public articulations and imaginaries of care which, as I argue, have been caused by the centuries-old dispossession of care as knowledge. This lack of knowledge and its concomitant lack of language and articulations is hugely damaging. If the knowledge of care had informed modern epistemologies, politics, and economies, we might today have a rich and complex knowledge of care and established epistemologies of worry and of hope. Worry and hope are learned, experienced, and practiced with care. The interlocking devaluation of class, caste, race, gender, sexualities, and the environment, which is foundational to patriarchal epistemologies and their ways of knowing, has excluded the knowledge of care from what is considered valuable knowledge. This has violently harmed the understanding of knowledge and deprived ways of knowing of the resources to know how we relate to one another and the planet with worry and with hope.

My critical feminist analysis of the response to the pandemic catastrophe in terms of war and militarization started from worry. Worry, therefore, has to be understood as central to feminist epistemologies. Worry is a method that comes from the knowledge of care. Marxist feminists have pointed out that care is a product of history. This allows the following thoughts. If care is a product of history, then there is hope that the conditions for care can be changed. If the knowledge of care is a product of history, then the knowledge of care can, in fact, be made central to the organization of politics and economies, which would not displace care but put its essentiality and continuity at the center of how they organize the conditions for care. In Covid times and beyond, care has to be understood as a product of pandemic history. Feminist worry, as a method, has allowed critical analysis of how the political response to the pandemic resulted in militarized care essentialism. Feminist worry raises awareness of the harmful, exploitative, extractivist, and deadly consequences of these frontline ontologies of care. Such analysis is needed in order to understand what present-day and future feminist work is up against and what feminist hope needs to counteract and overcome. Worry and hope in critical feminist cultural analysis are helpful to understanding how care is shaped as a product of history and what needs to be changed so relations to interdependencies, inter-vulnerabilities, and complexity are placed at the center of organizing care differently. Working against the necroeconomics and necropolitics of care extractivism and the dispossession of care as knowledge is central to new forms of feminist activism, thought, and organizing in the twenty-first century.

Through the novel care feminism of the twenty-first century, one can learn that care is planetary. While not all feminist organizing and activisms are connected with all the different interdependent and interconnected dimensions of care, there is rising awareness of how the historical epistemologies of separation that split the public from the private and human bodies from their environments, also known as nature, have been most harmful to the essential continuity of care, in which all human bodies and minds, living and non-living beings, environments, technologies, and infrastructures are interconnected and interdependent. Such is the complexity of care that epistemologies of splitting—separating minds, bodies, environments, technologies, and infrastructures from one another in order to enact power relations of subjugation—always result in violence. Therefore, care has to be understood through planetary interconnectedness, interdependencies, and inter-vulnerabilities. Today, this means finding new caring ways of relating to and living with our infected planet, with the Covid-19 pandemic and future pandemics resulting from the Man-made careless ruination of the planet. Understanding how this pandemic introduced the imperative to serve at the global frontlines of care provides insights into the immensity of violence and the warification of the mind, the consequences of which current and future feminist work will have to repair and overcome. Analysis of the forcible outsourcing of care to global frontlines of essential workers leads to understanding how care workers have been subjugated to new forms of care extractivism presented as the national political duty to care. At the same time, the harms of pre-existing care injustices have not even begun to be taken care of so they can start to heal. All this will result in new care divides and heightened planetary care injustices.

Feminist work for planetary care not only responds to care as a product of contemporary pandemic history, but also to care as a product of previous histories of care violence and structural carelessness.[125] Planetary care views the whole planet as a territory of care consisting of interdependent sites of care with locally distinct care needs that arise from uneven and unequal histories of carelessness, uncaring, and neglect. While care needs are always locally distinct, the ways in which they are taken care of—or not taken care of—have planetary consequences. Understanding care as planetary, in political, economic, and ethical terms, needs new imaginaries and ontologies. Feminist recovery plans, which emerged as a feminist response to pandemic conditions, and the collaborative local and transnational efforts of feminist policy, care workers, activists, grassroots organizations, researchers, and scholars behind these recovery plans, introduce such new care imaginaries. These feminist recovery plans for Covid-19 and beyond are the focus of the following and final chapter of this book.

Chapter 3: Feminist Recovery

Immediately after the outbreak of the novel coronavirus and the introduction of measures to prevent the virus from spreading, many new hashtags began to appear online: #stopspreadingthecoronavirus #washyourhands #covercoughs andsneezes #stayathome #wearamask #becalmbesafe #besafe #keepingpeoplesafe #stayhealthy #keepadistance #socialdistancing #quarantinecare #protectothers #wereallinthistogether #takecareofyourself #takecareofothers #takecareoftheworld. Such hashtags show how policy measures and public health rules like self-isolating, physical distancing, wearing a mask or washing one's hands, as advised by the World Health Organization and implemented by governments around the world, created new social realities, which were immediately reflected online. Rules translated into new behaviors and routines, as people had to change habits and adopt new ones. A number of hashtags speak of responsibility, mutuality, and of protecting others. There was also the claim to pandemic solidarity based on the understanding of all of us being in this together. It was well understood that a pandemic, with the Greek word *pan* meaning all and *demos* meaning people, involves all people on their shared planet and requires societies around the world to develop new collective social practices globally. States and their societies, which make up the planetary society, of course responded in highly differing ways to these measures in terms of politics, policy, economy, and stratifications within the societies living within the borders of nation states.

While the World Health Organization communicated the physical distancing rules by means of appealing to a military ethos as they encouraged people to "be a hero and break the chain of Covid-19 transmission by practicing social distancing", such militarization was conspicuously absent from the translation of the new rules into the digital language of hashtags which emerged in March and April of 2020.[1] Metaphors of war, as they were mobilized in public political oratory, were not much used in these new pandemic hashtags. Quite the contrary: in the online language, care was omnipresent. Care was being understood at the different and interrelated scales of the individual, the social, and the entire world: takecareofyourself, takecareofothers, and takecareoftheworld. Even in many of the personal e-mails along with other digital messages which I received from colleagues as well as from family members and friends who live in different parts of the world, such expressions of care and concern for each other's safety and protection formed a new and central part of the communication during the first months of the pandemic. Practically overnight, this new practice had formed, and e-mails I received right after the global virus outbreak began with sentences like the following: 'Hoping that you and your loved ones are safe', or ended with 'Stay safe and take best of care.' There seemed to have been a mutually understood reciprocity of the need for care and a real desire to know how others were living and surviving in the pandemic catastrophe. New practices for giving answers to such questions had to be found in order to share, but not to overshare; in order to appreciate the other's concern, but not overburden them with one's own worries, fears, and sadness. It was also necessary to practice new ways of expressing empathy and sorrow when learning that someone had caught the virus, had fallen seriously ill, was having a hard time recovering, had family members whom they could not visit in hospitals or nursing homes, or was grieving loved ones they had lost to the pandemic or during the pandemic. I began to understand how extensively expressions of emotional caring are still connected to physical presence and closeness to others, with facial expressions, gestures, and moments shared in silence often taking the place of words. In e-mails and other digital exchanges with my friends, colleagues, and collaborators, there was also, maybe even paradoxically, an expression of hope for more care, precisely because of the rising awareness that the catastrophe of the global pandemic was Man-made. Massive urbanization and deforestation led to increased human exposure to new and deadly viruses. This specific responsibility for the pandemic catastrophe—and that catastrophe arises from the historical situation in which the capitalist economy has taken command of the planet as a resource—, for what political scientists Ulrich Brand and Markus Wissen call the "imperial mode of living", gave rise, perhaps counter-intuitively and paradoxically, to the hope that care, for the planet and all its living and non-living beings, would finally be placed where it belongs: at the center of politics and economies.[2] There was hope that the "new awareness that each of us belongs to the whole and depends on it" in Rebecca Solnit's words would finally lead to the recognition of interconnectedness and interdependence as the ground for organizing responsibility and mutuality.[3]

There was hope for change in real time, not abstractly, in and for the future, but in the here and now. There was feminist hope for recovery and what I have suggested seeing as a call for building a new "international global care order".[4]

This chapter focuses on recovery, identified as a pandemic keyword and, in my interpretation, also a keymetaphor. Approaching the public imaginaries of care in pandemic times as they were articulated through keywords, my feminist cultural analysis places recovery adjacent to war and the frontline. War, frontline, and feminist recovery as new political terminology emerged in response to the pandemic lockdown conditions in March and April of 2020. While war and the frontline articulate the militarization and forcible conscription of care, the meaning of recovery is closely associated with processes of healing, mending, and getting better. Feminist recovery is a novel concept that was introduced in response to the pandemic catastrophe or, more precisely, in response to how hegemonic politics and economies led to a new regime of care dictated by militarized essentialism and care heroism. Feminist recovery was elevated to policy level in feminist recovery plans, which this chapter presents and analyzes. Refusing the hegemonic imperative of returning to normal, feminist recovery plans centered on the essentiality of care and on care justice. Normal would mean the continuation of massive urbanization and environmental destruction as well as deadly extraction, and exploitation. Normal would mean a continuation of inequalities defined by health, by housing and food insecurities, failing infrastructures, impoverishment and no access to basic provisions. Normal would mean continued care extractivism and exhaustion for large swaths of the global population. Therefore, feminist recovery plans defied the warring logic of back to normal. The policies for the feminist recovery plans were developed horizontally and transversally by policy makers, public administrators, and scholars and researchers together with feminist grassroots organizations, activists, and civil society groups. Feminist worry was a central method to my approach of war and frontline as political imaginaries in pandemic times. Feminist hope is key to my reading of feminist recovery plans, yet feminist hope is not separated from feminist worry. On the contrary, feminist hope makes space and time for shared worry in recovery, seeking to re-imagine the rights to care through a new international global care order.

How, then, to collectively imagine rights to care in light of the interlinked pandemic and climate catastrophes? How, then, to begin to work for the imagination of care's recovery from the necro-epistemic patriarchal violence that is based on epistemologies of separation, of policing, and regulating the boundaries of life and death. How to imagine healing so that planetary being can recover from the ideological onslaught on ways of thinking and imagining that led to separating humans from one another by means of hierarchies that result from ableism, classism, casteism, sexism, or racism as well as speciesism, which separates humans from all other living and non-living beings by placing the former above the latter? The violence of the epistemology of separation has been diagnosed in many different traditions of feminist thought, in particular Afrodiasporic, indigenous, environmental, or materialist perspectives, as a regime of domination through the logic of binary oppositions. Binaries—even though always reductive, as they describe states of being to be fully understood in pairs of two—do not, per se, have to be oppositional, hierarchical, or necro-epistemic, as in you can live and I cannot, or I can live and you cannot. Feminist theory, particularly from the 1970s onward, has analyzed the impact of binaries such as Man/Nature, Black/White, culture/nature, mind/body, productive/unproductive, active/passive, man/woman. These binaries have captured the imagination. They have informed Western and globalized ways of thinking that underlie economic, legal, or policy imaginaries. Binaries, separations, and boundaries are ideas, imaginaries, and realities. Imagination is needed to imagine otherwise, to re-learn how to think, feel and care beyond and outside of them. In this context, recovery, and in particular the novel notion of feminist recovery, provides inspiration and, at the same time, requires reflection on what it can, our could, mean when approached through a feminist cultural analytical perspective.

Recovery is an interesting term. Recovery takes time. One can plan for recovery, but recovery cannot be planned. There is an element of unpredictability in recovery. Recovery requires patience, endurance, and care. Recovery is always tied to what one needs to recover from. At the level of language, the semantics of recovery are closely connected to disease, war, and economy. Recovery is the process after a disease, recovery is the process after economic collapse, and recovery is the process after war, genocide, and ecocide. Recovery, most broadly understood, is the process of getting better after a crisis. The medical view on crisis is useful to understanding this, with crisis meaning the turning point for better or for worse in an acute disease. The pandemic is a moment of global crisis, in which it is socially and politically decided whether this crisis presents a turning point for the worse or a turning point for the better in relation to the Man-made conditions, which have not only caused the pandemic to break out but also include insufficient preparedness for pandemics despite abundant warnings by scientists, epidemiologists, and public health policy makers.[5] In the pandemic situation, recovery has to be understood at the scales of the individual, the social, and the planetary, which are most intimately physically and materially interconnected. No-one can recover on their own. Recovery, when one is still weaker, when one is still more vulnerable and more fragile than usual, makes one even more dependent on structures of care and support and their dependable availability. All living and non-living beings depend upon others for their recovery.

The infected planet needs the support and care of human beings for its recovery. Thinking of individuals as planetary beings constituted by the conditions of the planet is helpful to understanding what living with an infected planet means. The different scales of the individual or personal, the social, and the planetary are interconnected, as they foreground needs for different infrastructures and supports, as they actually enable caring for one another's interdependent recovery. Recovery is mediated across the personal, the social, and planetary through environmental, material, infrastructural, and technological conditions. Processes of physical, mental, and spiritual recovery are tied to the specific local environmental, material, infrastructural, and technological conditions, which makes clear that recovery is very much about these conditions as well. One cannot recover independently from these conditions. Therefore, people need to work together so these conditions, which are themselves not well, can recover from the centuries-old onslaught of patriarchal colonial violence, extraction, and exploitation. The conditions for recovery need to be restored in order for recovery to actually become possible. Bodies, minds, spirits, environments, materials, technologies, and infrastructures have to be understood not as separate from one another in their processes of recovery, but as deeply interdependent. Feminist activism and theory have long proclaimed that the personal is political. One has to add many more dimensions to such a conception of the personal: the personal is social, the personal is environmental, the personal is material, the personal is infrastructural, the personal is technological, the personal is planetary. In short, the personal is never alone, the personal is never on its own. There is, therefore, the need to recover from the modern ideology that the personal can be thought of as standing alone, separate from all these other dimensions that constitute it and support it, and, in turn, make persons able to have what is called personal relations, that is relations with other living and non-living beings. Modernization and large-scale urbanization define these relations through infrastructures. Therefore, modern life has to be understood as infrastructuralized life. The modern infrastructural condition reshaped not only the relations among humans, but also the relations between humans and their planet with all its living and non-living things. Modern human inhabitation of the planet is founded on systems of infrastructures that intimately connect bodies and environments. One may think, here, of modern sewage or ventilation systems as salient examples that bound infrastructure and bodies as they began to reshape nature into a Manmade environment. Expanding inhabitation means encroachment onto territories that were previously nowhere near humans. The Covid-19 pandemic was caused by zoonotic spillover, which occurs when pathogens are transmitted from wild animals to humans. Such virus spillover results from infrastructure stitching bodies and environments closer together. The modern infrastructural condition, which I understand through dimensions of social equity and notions of support in tension with harmful and violent effects on bodies and environments, is a crucial starting point for understanding what feminist recovery entails and for reimagining care. In historical terms, periods of recovery after wars are linked to investment in reconstruction and rebuilding. Twentieth-century realities and imaginaries of post-crisis, after the 1929 Depression or of the post-war period after World War II, are firmly linked to investments in large-scale infrastructures. Understanding how deeply linked wars are to the research and development that result in new technologies, which in post-war life are immediately translated into everyday infrastructures that define bodies and environments, is important to understanding how war has materially, infrastructurally, and technologically extended into life in so-called peace.

Technologies and infrastructures invented for preparedness for wars—or even during times of war—have fully penetrated the everyday life of all living and non-living beings on their shared planet in times of so-called peace. One may be put in mind, here, of DDT—called "the atomic bomb of the insect world"—or of the military origins of the internet: those go back to the work of the Advanced Research Projects Agency of the US Defense Department in the 1940s, which was motivated by bringing "computing to the frontlines".[6] Military infrastructures and war weaponry migrated into so-called civilian use and have profoundly defined everyday life, as such infrastructures not only surround living and non-living beings, but pass through them and unfold their effects inside of them. In this sense, a feminist recovery from infrastructural effects and within infrastructures that bring technologies of war into everyday life would need to expand the understanding of care to go far beyond the establishment of care infrastructure, which is understood primarily as healthcare or social care infrastructure. Imagining such recovery as necessary is made possible by the term feminist recovery. (Re)building and (re)constructing infrastructures that care, as well as infrastructures of care more narrowly understood, are both central to feminist recovery. Such rebuilding and reconstructing needs to include infrastructural awareness-raising and work on cultural imaginaries that enable people to actually envision care-full and peace-full infrastructures that would come into being through a coming together of bottom-up social movements and grassroots knowledge in collaboration with top-down state politics that enacts infrastructural responsibilities. Making infrastructural politics matter to the continuous labors of feminist recovery, and to public policy and public imaginaries at once, will necessarily have to include the development of robust collective forms of "feminist infrastructural critique" in order to understand better how infrastructuralization, with its origins in war, is the main cause behind today's conditions of living with infected planet.[7] At the same time, critique as awareness of these conditions is crucial to a politics of hope for imagining and building new care-full infrastructures for planetary recovery.

The notion of feminist recovery was introduced in feminist policy which was written during the first months of pandemic lockdown. I understand feminist recovery to be a response to the language of war present in public pandemic oratory and the organization of the global frontline of care. *Feminist recovery plans for Covid-19 and beyond* articulate a dual aim: equitable preparedness, and accountability to the harms caused by centuries of (infrastructural) patriarchal violence. I see the work of feminist recovery as preparedness, understood as accountability to the future, and as reparation, understood as accountability to the ongoingness of the past: a different present is imagined as possible through the coming together of preparedness and reparation. The violence and deadliness of inequality is caused by the lack of infrastructural supports. This led to broad swaths of the planetary society not being enabled to follow pandemic measures. The feminist response to the pandemic centered on this inequality. I find inspiration for critical hope in the term feminist recovery, the meaning of which this chapter explores through my close reading of the feminist recovery plans as, at the same time, the chapter seeks to expand the meaning of feminist recovery in relation to patriarchal history as a whole and to imaginaries of healing the infected planet. The concept of a specifically feminist recovery is useful for questioning the "epistemology of mastery" inherent in modern ideologies of policy and planning.[8] Processes of recovery are, per se, unpredictable. What bodies and environments that have been critically infected need to really heal today is still largely unknown, and might even change in surprising and unforeseen ways along the process of recovery. Therefore, planning for feminist recovery needs to stay attuned to such long-term processes of recovery, which, above all, require the responsiveness of care to changing needs of care.

In order to imagine feminist recovery from within, and beyond, the pandemic catastrophe, I apply the following questions: What does the infected planet, beyond the acute disease of the current pandemic, need to recover from? What does the infected planet need in order to recover and heal? When will the planet have been enabled to recover? While there is, as we have seen in the previous chapters, an official politics of beginnings and endings when it comes to declaring wars or pandemics, one can never declare the end of recovery. One can never be really certain that recovery, or healing, are over or complete. One cannot declare the end of recovery. One cannot declare the end of healing. Quite the contrary: recovery is always durational, marked by ongoingness and unfinishedness. The temporality of recovery, like all processes concerned with healing and restoring, is complex, never linear, unpredictable, and, in a certain way, never ending. When recovering from a disease, one may feel better one day and worse again the next. Recovery can be slow and unpredictable. Recovery is, first and foremost, a process and, therefore, has to be understood in temporal terms. While not only plans for disaster preparedness, but for recovery preparedness and all the necessary support structures and infrastructures are most certainly needed, there needs to be, at the same time, a better understanding of the uncertainty and the unpredictability of recovery. Planning that remains open to such uncertainties can be most responsive to recovery needs as they emerge, and to adapting supports and infrastructures accordingly. Planning based on mastery would assume knowing for certain what recovery needs. Planning that followed the needs of recovery would remain responsive to the kinds of changes needed during processes of recovery. The impact and traces of previous trauma and diseases live on in bodies, societies, environments, and the planet as a whole. The historical inequality and the harms enacted on bodies and their environments by sexism, racism, and speciesism on a planetary scale is an expression of war: war against Black and Brown people, war against indigenous populations, war against nature, war against poor people, war against vulnerable populations, war against women. This logic of war extended, in pandemic times, to forcibly enlisting care.

Feminist recovery does not only address the current pandemic situation, but the historical ongoingness of multiple and interlinked wars against women rooted in the violence of colonial-patriarchal ideology as warfare. The effects of this ideology continue to penetrate conditions of life and death. Silvia Federici diagnoses that "capitalist development begins with a war on women".[9] Feminist anthropologist Rita Segato argues that femicidal violence has to be understood as "femigenocide".[10] Colonial-patriarchal warfare takes many forms that interpenetrate and support each other, economic and intimate, militarized and legal. Domestic violence has been described as "invisible war" or as "shadow war".[11] In pandemic times, as yet another example of the close traffic between imaginaries of war and epidemiological imaginaries, the so-called shadow war of domestic violence was referred to as "shadow pandemic".[12] Taking the notion of feminist recovery to refer to recovery from pandemic conditions and the lasting aftermath of ideological and material patriarchal warfare on bodies, minds, and environments as well as to recovery from the historical violence of patriarchy, which has led to the production of gendered, sexualized, racialized, and classed vulnerable populations and the large-scale ruination of their habitats and environments, requires an understanding of recovery as a slow and lasting process, the end of which can neither be planned for nor easily predicted. Feminist recovery is about never giving in to the afterlife of patriarchal violence and never giving up on the possibility of recovering. Perhaps, a politics of hope for continued living with an infected planet begins with understanding that feminist recovery will necessarily have to be never-ending, that it is ongoing for, and in futures to come.

Providing in this chapter an attentive reading of feminist recovery plans as they were developed in different parts of the world, along with the policy advice for caring economies as well as the imaginaries for broader social and cultural transformation, I want to bring into play one additional dimension of recovery. Recovery can also mean the possibility of regaining something that has been lost or taken away. I argue that placing this meaning of recovery in relation to patriarchy's centuries-old ruination of care, which includes the loss of care's centrality and the taking away of its fundamental importance, value, knowledge, and visibility, makes for both a much more complex and, at the same time, more insistent and hope-full reading of what feminist recovery would need to entail. Regaining care from patriarchal capitalism and making the essentiality of care a source of value and recognition will require hard work, a new and much richer and more nuanced language for care as knowledge, and new social and cultural imaginaries.

The idea of modern Man as an autonomous and independent individual which underpins care under patriarchy led to the silencing of the interconnectedness and interdependencies of bodies, minds, and natures. Feminist recovery, therefore, will need to regain, relearn, and retrain a deep sense of interdependency, which was violently taken away by toxic patriarchal "epistemologies of separation".¹³ The political and economic silencing, and persistent structural devaluation of care included the erasure of care as knowledge in hegemonic understandings of what counts as knowledge, of what matters to knowledge and what does not.¹⁴ Such silencing and "epistemic ignorance" is not a-historical, but continually reproduced, as care theorist Riikka Prattes has recently diagnosed.¹⁵ Central to the feminist recovery of care will be continuous work on epistemic and economic imaginaries that overcome the lasting epistemic violence of separation and ignorance, which have led to political, intellectual, spiritual, and cultural silencing and economic devaluation and deprivation of those who perform caring labors.

Common to recovery and care is that they are characterized by temporalities of ongoing-ness and the complexities of unpredictability. Processes of care and recovery are also, perhaps in differently felt ways, shaped by the continuous experiences of learning, which may be filled with disappointment, disenchantment, and hope-making surprise, as one understands better oneself and others as not only maintained or restored, but also as transforming as a result of caring activities, and as one understands bodies, minds, spirits, or environments as changing in the process of recovering. This has epistemic and economic implications. The knowledge of care and the economies of care are concerned with maintaining consistency and duration, while they need to respond to complexly unpredictable change and the process of ongoing re-learning. This, as one can readily see, does not conform with the patriarchal economization of time as efficiency and Fordist and post-Fordist rationales of productivity. The need for new and differently care-full economic imaginaries based on different ways of knowing resonate with what Carol Anne Hilton, founder of the Indigenomics Institute and the Global Centre of Indigenomics, has described, in a special issue of *Site Magazine* dedicated to *Provisions, Observing & Archiving Covid-19*, as "a collective response to the systemic de-valuing of Indigenous ways of being and knowing" and as "economics from an indigenous worldview", which is premised on "care for all".¹⁶ Seeing the premise of care for all and the idea of feminist recovery as part of a larger twenty-first century feminist movement, I propose understanding this newly emergent feminist organizing and theorizing as care feminism. This means working through the aftermath of violent epistemologies of separation that result in extreme social, economic, political, infrastructural, technological, and environmental inequality. Furthermore, this includes a more profound acknowledgment of the nascent imaginaries of what I suggest calling the rights of care which go beyond human rights and include the rights of nature. Care feminism provides the potential to move beyond the separated feminist traditions of care ethics and social reproduction theory, placing at the center the essentiality of care and the inseparability of bodies, minds, and natures as mutually constituted and ontologically co-vulnerable and interdependent. This is foundational to a new international global care order, which will have to overcome human-centricity. While equitable access to care, and new cultural and economic value systems that counteract the systemic silencing and extraction of caring labors are paramount, the interconnectedness and interdependence of all living and non-living beings with their planet demands that care overcome regimes of separation that regard the care needs of human minds and bodies as being separate from the care needs of all other living and non-living things.

Inequality Is Death-Making

How can one respect physical distancing rules in overcrowded spaces? How can one wear masks when there are no masks being made available or when they are unaffordable? While policy measures sought to counteract the spread of infection and to ensure public health for all, there was evidence that, for the most vulnerable populations around the world, it was not possible to follow pandemic rules. This put their own care and safety at risk, but also the care and safety of others. Interconnectedness in care, safety, and risk came to the fore because of the pandemic. Lack of infrastructures and resources, combined with shortages of supplies, prevented people from being enabled to follow pandemic rules. Informal settlements, which make up about thirty percent of the world's urban population with an estimated total of 1033 million dwellers, and the living conditions of displaced people and refugee populations, with the United Nations High Commissioner for Refugees estimating that there are 89.3 million forcibly displaced people worldwide, make physical distancing or handwashing for disease control a huge challenge.[17] Handwashing, as communicated by the World Health Organization and governments around the world, is one of the best ways to protect oneself and those with whom one lives in a household against transmission of and infection with Covid-19. With pathogens spreading from person to person, or from surfaces to persons, preparing food or drink with unwashed hands or touching surfaces presents a heightened risk of infection. In order to curtail these risks of infection, people were instructed to always wash their hands before touching their face, after touching their mask, after touching surfaces touched by others, and after having been outside of one's home in the street or anywhere else. How can one wash one's hands frequently with soap for a minimum of twenty seconds when there are severe water shortages, when there is no hygiene infrastructure, when no good and cheap soap is available? The compound effects of poor housing, overcrowded living conditions, lack of adequate infrastructure as well as the impact of extreme weather events—the results of the ongoing climate catastrophe—made it impossible to follow the pandemic rules. The infrastructural dimensions of inter-vulnerabilities and the interdependencies in infrastructural shortages were thrown into stark relief by the pandemic, with exacerbated risks of disease and heightened vulnerability of individual lives and equally of global public health. Such shortages are a form of infrastructural violence. Such violence is produced by political and economic systems and largely defines how lives can or cannot be lived, how health can or cannot be maintained. Judith Butler has written that

> our enduring dependency on social and economic forms of support for life itself is not something we grow out of [...]. When there is nothing to depend upon, when social structures fail or are withdrawn, then life itself falters or fails: life becomes precarious.[18]

Just as violence to body, mind, spirit, and health is infrastructurally produced, acting responsibly also has to be understood as being produced, and enabled, by infrastructure. What, then, does one make of international organizations and governments which implement responsible preventive measures to reduce transmission of Covid-19 in order to keep oneself and others safe, when one knows that the people in these organizations and governments are very well aware of the catastrophic situation of infrastructural shortages and what they mean to populations who are at heightened pandemic risk precisely because of missing infrastructures?

When responsibilities and risks are offloaded onto those who have been instructed to keep as safe as possible, without, at the same time, having been provided with the necessary infrastructural support systems that would make it possible for them to actually follow these instructions, we see a form of politically produced care violence take shape. Pandemic measures then become an expression of pre-existing inequality with its structural carelessness. Such inequality defined the lives of many long before the outbreak of the virus and led to increased pandemic risks and higher mortality rates for vulnerable populations whose lives are defined by everyday infrastructural neglect and the political failure to organize economies in such a way that there is access to adequate and good public health infrastructures for all. Covid-19 disease and mortality statistics provide evidence of this infrastructural neglect and political failure. There were significantly higher Covid-19 death rates among ethnic minority groups. In the United States, as observed in mid-2021, "people of colour are two to three times more likely to die from COVID-19 than white Americans".[19] The office for National Statistics in the United Kingdom reported that during the first wave of the pandemic between January 24, 2020 and September 11, 2020

> [t]he rate of death involving COVID-19 was highest for the Black African group (3.7 times greater than for the White British group for males, and 2.6 greater for females), followed by the Bangladeshi (3.0 for males, 1.9 for females), Black Caribbean (2.7 for males, 1.8 for females) and Pakistani (2.2 for males, 2.0 for females) ethnic groups.[20]

The pandemic has not only made highly visible such inequalities, but, in fact, worsened existing inequalities, producing heightened vulnerability and higher mortality rates among people living in poor conditions and low-income neighborhoods. An intersectional economic, legal, statistical, and empirical social and environmental studies approach reveals class, caste, race, gender, and sexuality as determining factors of the compounded impacts of environmental degradation and structural injustices that arise from deep-rooted classism, casteism, racism, sexism, ableism, and speciesism.

Furthermore, many of the essential frontline workers were confronted not only with the new militarized public imaginaries of care as heroism, but faced with everyday realities defined by feminization, racialization, classism and casteism as well as infrastructural vulnerabilities. If anything, the myth of the hero—able to overcome and surmount all obstacles, hindrances, or lack by relying on their own superpowers, and thus seen as not dependent upon essential infrastructural support systems—worsened the condition of carers, who were expected to heroically make do without proper infrastructures of support. The convergence of masculinized values and feminized realities worsened the conditions for care on the ground. Those whose bodies, minds, energy, capacities, knowledge, and skills performed the caring labors required by the frontline policy of critical essential infrastructure, indispensable to the basic functions of society and the economy, were failed by the infrastructure in their sectors. Underpaid and mentally as well as physically stressed, drained and exhausted, these essential care workers faced grave dangers and heightened risks of infection as they had to cope with infrastructural neglect, which resulted in unsafe working conditions and shortages of personal protective equipment. The frontline ontologies were marked by masculinist and militarized values of duty and heroic selflessness, but the essential critical infrastructure workforce is not only confronted with feminized labor conditions, but is also majority female. This did not go unnoticed. Early on, in March 2020, Phumzile Mlambo-Ngcuka, who has been serving as United Nations Under-Secretary-General and Executive Director of UN Women since 2013, observed that women were "front and centre" as the world changed dramatically because of the virus.[21] At the very beginning of the pandemic, data collected showed that the mortality rates of men were higher than those of women. Yet the reason for this reported higher mortality of men may actually be a result of the lack of accurate data brought about by profound gender bias, as economist Yeva Aleksanyan and radiologist Jason Weinman observe. They write that in social contexts where women are devalued, as they rely on family resources to have access to healthcare, households are likely to prioritize men's health, with more men being tested and going to the hospital. Thus, their hypothesis is "that countries are reporting higher male COVID-19 cases and deaths due to underreporting of women's cases and deaths."[22] What was evident, though, was that women were the frontline of the frontline, with many of their working hours performed in the context of private homes as women had to meet the increasing care needs of those dependent upon them, who included children, the sick, the frail, or the elderly. The increase in care needs was caused by lockdowns, but also by pandemic conditions in general, with people not only acutely sick with Covid-19 but also developing long-term symptoms, which include physical, neurological, and mental health symptoms. Gender-responsive policy needs to examine "differing rates of infection, differential economic impacts, differential care burden, and incidence of domestic violence and sexual abuse."[23]

In the *Responses to the Coronavirus* published by the Organization for Economic Development, OECD, in April 2020, one reads that

> around the world, women carry out far more care work than men – up to ten times as much according to the OECD Development Centre's Social Institutions and Gender Index (SIGI). The travel restrictions, at-home quarantines, school and day-care centre closures, and the increased risks faced by elderly relatives can be expected to impose additional burdens on women, even when both women and their partners are confined and may be expected to continue working from home.[24]

This brings back the historical memory of feminist conflict in domestic settings, for which socialist feminist, journalist and columnist Barbara Ehrenreich used the expression "chore wars", which were typical of feminists disagreeing and fighting with their male partners or husbands over who does the care work at home in the 1970s and 1980s.[25] Under lockdown conditions, women globally worked much longer hours at home to take care of all the chores. At the same time, women suffered increased domestic abuse and violence. This leads to the diagnosis that imaginaries and ideologies of war and realities of physical, sexual, intellectual, spiritual, and emotional violence have long infiltrated the domestic territories of the home, as they shaped cis-gendered heteronormative relations between men and women. In the context of lockdown and quarantine, theorist of architecture Henriette Steiner and theorist of culture Kristin Veel diagnosed this situation as "pandemic stuckness", highlighting the home as a site of "tension" and "contestation".[26] The home is where reproduction takes place, at once "a sanctuary and a site of caring duties, labor, abuse and violence".[27] Following the metaphor of chore wars, social, emotional, and sexual reproduction are shot through with fighting and struggles. The use of the metaphor of war in the context of the gendered social and emotional responsibilities and bodily availabilities for reproduction at home renders clear that feminist analysis saw power struggles and violence as constitutive of an understanding of the home as a site of work. Viewing feminist struggle over housework the 1970s and 1980s through the lens of chore wars allows us, today, to put into historical perspective the lastingness of imaginaries of war, which captured feminist politics and desires and—this is of particular relevance to the notion of care feminism—informed ways of seeing care as a central cause of a gender war. Ehrenreich has also observed that these chore wars of the 1970s and 1980s—which coincide with a time when much caring labor and caring services were transformed into a paid-for commodity with large numbers of women joining the workforce, particularly in jobs in the care sector—were solved by hiring badly paid domestic workers to perform these chores and the caring labors needed for maintaining households. This gave rise to new classed and racialized uneven economic relations among women during, and since, the heyday of feminist struggles in the 1970s and 1980s, which were described by Ehrenreich as the "mistress-maid relationship"[28]. This not only led to new forms of economic, infrastructural, health, and legal inequality and violence during the pandemic, with many domestic workers—who work in the informal economy—losing their income due to lockdown and pandemic conditions more broadly speaking, but it also exposed these workers to vaccine injustice, as they often have immigrant status and are not part of a country's public health system (if there is such a system in place), or are unable afford to access paid-for health services; or, with mobility restricted in pandemic times, they are confined within the boundaries of their country of work and thus hindered from reconnecting with their own families.[29]

Gendered Conditions of Care and Health: Feminist Activism and Policy

Early on in the pandemic, the human rights dimensions of the gendered conditions of care and health were internationally recognized and became a focus of feminist activism and global feminist debate and policy writing. In July 2020, the forty-fourth session of the Human Rights Council of the UN included a full-day discussion on the human rights of women, specifically dedicating one of its panels to Covid-19 and women's rights. As background information to their panel discussion on the gendered impact of the pandemic on the economic and labor condition of women, they provided the following information:

> Globally, women comprise 70 per cent of health workers, including midwives, nurses, pharmacists and community health workers. Women are also playing key role in essential services, such as in the food production and supply chain, cleaning and laundry, and care work. And yet, many of them are working in low-wage and precarious conditions. In many countries women are concentrated in irregular employments and in the informal sector that are highly prone to disruption and with no or limited access to social protection. In formal economy, women are also over-represented in hospitality (hotels, restaurants), manufacturing, retail and leisure and recreation industries that have been among the hardest hit by the response to COVID-19. Pre-existing gender inequality, such as gender pay gap and gross imbalances in the gender distribution of unpaid care and domestic work, is likely to lead to women giving up participating in labor market during the pandemic and beyond.[30]

One may also be put in mind, here, of the *Equal Care Day*, which was initiated in 2016 by journalists Almut Schnerring and Sascha Verlan in Germany. It is conceived as a day of public action on February 29—an extra day added to the year every four years to keep the human calendar synchronized with the astronomical seasons—and draws attention to the fact that it takes men four years to perform the same amount of caring labors in private, volunteer, and professional contexts that women perform in one year. In 2020, in response to the pandemic's effects on care, they added to this day of action the German-language *Equal Care Manifesto*, which focuses on fair labor conditions, fair distribution, and fair remuneration of caring labors.[31]

Early on, there was a decidedly feminist response to the coronavirus outbreak situation. This included the critical analysis of, and a push-back against, the hegemonic political and economic response. Many international organizations and local state level organizations—including UN Women; global networks of women politicians, like Women Political Leaders; transnational NGOs, like the Feminist Alliance for Rights; feminist research advocacies, like the Centre for Feminist Foreign Policy; health care worker unions, such as Global Nurses United—organized transnational exchanges, provided information, and went public with their response to the situation. In mid-April 2020, the anti-sexist and anti-colonial *Hawai'i Feminist Recovery Plan*, the first of its kind, which was soon followed by other such plans, articulated this new policy activism in response to the pandemic catastrophe. This global transnational and national policy activism not only highlighted and responded to the highly gendered and racialized dimensions of the pandemic, but also started to immediately work horizontally with many different local and transnational women's organizations, groups, networks, and individuals on such feminist plans to do everything possible to prevent a return to normal. Feminist advocacy, policy activism, and relentless work, on local levels as well as on the levels of transnational knowledge exchange, led to writing, and implementing, other such multi-sector feminist recovery plans, which included the *African Feminist Post-Covid 19 Economic Recovery Statement*—presented in the form of a policy recommendation to the African Union by the NAWI Collective, a pan-African feminist initiative—the *Feminist Economic Plan for Recovery in Canada*, the *Feminist National Recovery Plan in Northern Ireland* as well as the *Covid-19 Feminist Recovery Plan to Achieve Substantive Gender Equality* by the Center for Women's Global Leadership at Rutgers and the *Feminist Recovery Plan Project at the University of Warwick*. It is of particular interest that writing feminist policy happened in very close connection with grassroots feminisms, with, for example, the *International Women's Rights Activism Watch Asia Pacific* organizing online workshops in order to learn from transnational grassroots activism and its visions for policy when writing feminist recovery plans. Understanding that a plea for a return to normal is a plea in favor of politics and an economy that, in fact, caused the anthropogenic Covid-19 pandemic catastrophe as well as the climate catastrophe, the UN Women *feminist recovery plan*, in resonance with many other feminist plans for recovery, advocates for nothing less than a "a new social contract".[32]

Feminist Pandemic Studies and Feminist Organizing

Feminist collection of data, critical analyses, research, and theory across many different fields and disciplines gave rise to what I view as the formation of a new field of feminist pandemic studies, which, even though still nascent, is very active and has, in many instances, moved research, activism, and policy closer together. A large number of feminist researchers, scholars, theorists, and educators in the disciplines of law, public health, political theory, international relations, economy—in particular, feminist political economy—, heterodox economy, and development economics—but also feminist political ecology, health and environmental humanities, cultural studies, sociology, anthropology along with feminist, gender, queer, decolonial and critical race studies, broadly understood—focused their intellectual energy and their different methodological perspectives on dimensions of discrimination, injustice, violence, and the rights of humans and nature under pandemic conditions. Feminist academic journals, such as *Signs*, *Feminist Studies* or *Feminist Economics*, devoted special issues to the pandemic, or made calls for special issues, as did the *Journal of Social Politics*, which in 2021 called for papers for a special issue on Covid-19 and the Social Politics of Crises.[33] Michael Fine and Joan Tronto guest-edited a special issue of the *International Journal of Care and Caring*. Published in 2022, it is titled *Care, caring, and the global Covid-19 pandemic*.[34]

Feminist pandemic scholarship and theory examine Covid-19 realities and the societal and cultural consequences of the disease's effects. In this scholarship, there is a clear focus on making categories such as gender, sexuality, race, ethnicity, indigeneity, and class and caste matter to the analysis. Feminist academics and scholars, who carried out their research in the context of universities as well as through special funding obtained from governments, NGOs, or philanthropic institutions, actively sought to transcend the academic community in order not only to produce analysis, but to effectuate change together with care practitioners and policy makers. One such example of self-organized transnational feminist scholarship is the *Gender & Covid 19 blog*. Starting with the outbreak of the virus, the group of researchers began to organize regular meetings every third Wednesday each month, actively encouraging and inviting people's contributions and sharing publicly a growing list of resources.[35] The new Gender Working Group behind the Gender & Covid 19 blog grew out of a small number of academic researchers, who immediately took action as they recognized that the gendered effects of the pandemic were not taken into consideration in government response. They were able to obtain funding from the Canadian Institute of Health Research in order to study the gendered effects of Covid-19 in Canada, the UK, and China and Hong Kong in real time, and have expanded the original scope of their study to include the following additional countries: Bangladesh, Nigeria, Kenya, the Democratic Republic of Congo, and Brazil. The publication of their findings in the *Lancet* in early March 2020 marked a turning point in the way in which the pandemic was studied. Pointing out that, in past pandemics as well as in the current Covid-19 pandemic, "policies and public health efforts have not addressed the gendered impacts of disease outbreaks", they were able to raise awareness for this data gap and contributed to making it understood that the impact of the pandemic on the lives of men* and women* were very different.[36] This rendered evident that dimensions of gender had, in the past, remained unrecognized in the political and policy responses to disease—and catastrophes more broadly—and therefore dimensions of gender have also been absent from the policies for pandemic preparedness. This also showed that a collaborative effort by a transnational group of feminist researchers who set out to organize and collect important data so that "primary and secondary effects of a health emergency on different individuals and communities" can actually effect immediate change and provide the basis for "effective, equitable policies and interventions."[37] Their initiative to introduce gender as an analytical and simultaneously a policy category contributed to public awareness not only of the highly gendered impact of the pandemic, but also of the importance of working out gender-responsive plans for pandemic preparedness, response, and life in the aftermath of pandemics. The virus outbreak was immediately followed by new forms of remote feminist organizing, transnationally and on a local scale, where use was made of online tools for gathering and meetings, for disseminating findings and reports via webinars, digital townhall meetings, and other forms of digital sharing and publishing. It also led to developing and testing new research methods to gather data, counteract the impossibility of travel, and understand pandemic impacts in global comparisons.

Counteracting Gendered Pandemic Violence

With feminist organizations highlighting the gendered differences of pandemic impacts, other international organizations began to pay more attention to studying these differences as well. Women and girls suffered disproportionately because of the pandemic, not only because of many societies considering women to be of less value than men, but because of a globally observed (re)turn to stereotypical gender norms and expectations, particularly with regard to the heteronormative gendered division of domestic labor, with men considered breadwinners, and women losing their jobs. There was a globally observed increase in domestic violence against women, and rising rates of teenage pregnancy and early marriage. In May 2020, UN Women launched the *Shadow Pandemic*, a campaign to raise awareness for "the global increase in domestic violence amid the Covid-19 health crisis."[38]

On the occasion of the *16 Days of Activism Against Gender-Violence Campaign* in 2021, Rowan Harvey, an activist and consultant who specializes in gender and development, writes in an OXFAM brief that even though

> it is evident that the Covid-19 pandemic has intensified gender based violence, including domestic violence and intimate partner violence [...] the investments in GBV prevention and response are dramatically inadequate with just 0.0002% of the overall COVID-19 response funding opportunities going into it.[39]

The pandemic also increased gendered education inequality and reinforced gendered stereotypes when it comes to families supporting girls' access to education. Girls dropped out of secondary education during the pandemic and the risk that they will not return is high. A brief on *Covid-19 and Girls' Education in East Asia and Pacific* released by UNICEF, the United Nations Children's Fund, in October 2020 reported that the disruption to education systems had a devastating impact on girls' access to education and learning, with many having no internet or very limited access to distance learning. This report also observed increases in gender-based violence against girls as well as rising numbers of early marriage and teenage pregnancy.[40] Furthermore, as a report by the World Bank highlighted, girls are less likely to return to school after the pandemic, as many "caregivers are missing from the household" and they "typically have to (partly) replace the work done by the missing caregiver, who might be away due to Covid-19 related work, illness, or death."[41] With 129 million girls out of school there is an estimate that "globally 20 million additional secondary-aged girls could drop out of school due to COVID-19."[42] The international healthcare crisis, which predates the pandemic, deepened. In 2020, the *World Health Organization* estimated that "there was a global shortage of 5.9 mn nurses – almost one-quarter of the current global workforce of almost 28mn."[43] Faced with infrastructural shortages, physical, mental, and emotional pressures, and mass death, nurses globally are suffering. Jama, a US research network, "found female nurses were twice as likely as women in the general population to commit suicide" during the pandemic, and a survey by the American Nursing Association found that "one-third of nurses were not emotionally healthy."[44] Nurses are suffering from Covid-19 exhaustion, burnout, anxieties, trauma. They are also feeling a growing sense of betrayal with so many lives lost despite their efforts, with the declaration of heroism a shallow and uncaring form of recognition, and with no structural and systemic changes to labor and infrastructure conditions of the health sector in place yet. The *Understanding Coronavirus in America Tracking Survey* found out that women were "disproportionately affected by job loss, childcare duties and mental distress."[45] Despite the hyper-visibility of critical essential infrastructure and the frontline of care, there was a pronounced lack of policy provisions and political aims with regard to caring better for care infrastructures and for those who perform caring labor, be it for pay or unpaid. Politics, and hegemonic economics, failed the complex realities of care and those who worked tirelessly to produce it.

Worried about the grave pandemic realities marked by injustice and discrimination, and despite personal experiences of pandemic stresses, anxieties, and work overload, feminists relentlessly organized in real time in order to respond to these multiple crises within the pandemic, counteracting gendered injustices. The feminist response to the pandemic shows that feminists were discontent with the way in which the political response was organized and articulated, in particular under the notable absence of gendered differences in a global health emergency. Infrastructural violence and care inequality and injustice result from the specific ways in which the world is organized and structured through dimensions of class, caste, race, indigeneity, gender, sexuality, and species. Organizing around produced vulnerabilities and against structures and infrastructures of violence is key to the feminist response to the pandemic: a response to emergency policies and measures that failed to account for the gendered dimensions of a disease outbreak and the lived realities of women and girls, while the political imaginaries and the use of war vocabulary led to a dramatic re-gendering of the global frontline, with essential workers viewed as the foot soldiers of pandemic care services. Across many different scales, times zones, and locales and, perhaps, more than before, there were swift exchanges and effective collaborations among feminist activism, advocacy, consultancy, campaigning, researching, policy-making as well as women and feminists working in academia, international organizations, and politics. Very many different women's and feminist organizations, working groups, and networks and informal gatherings around the world are enacting feminist responses to the pandemic, questioning the hegemonic responses and proposing feminist visions for societal change, transformation of the economy, and new understandings of care beyond the pandemic. Researching and analyzing the compounded effects of the pandemic on women's and girls' lives, minds, bodies, labors, education, economic realities, social relations, and sexualities, feminist scholarship and militant research highlights how addressing the interdependencies in bio-material and eco-social realities are dependent upon how the response to the pandemic is organized. Living in the aftermath of infection places new demands and pressures on care. There are the still little-understood conditions of long Covid that continue for weeks, months, and even years after the original illness. There is an observed lack of cultural practices of mourning mass death and expressing collective grief. Extra care for those who cared for the infected and are directly confronted with the consequences of infrastructural violence, complete exhaustion, and pandemic loss is not being provided. Understanding that the pandemic catastrophe and the climate catastrophe are interlinked and Man-made and result from the death-making exploitative and extractivist imaginaries of hegemonic politics and economies is heavily incumbent upon feminist political imaginaries of hope for futurity.

Care Feminism and Recovery

Situating the feminist response to pandemic realities in the larger context of what I consider to be the formation of new expressions of present-day feminisms concerned with working against and transforming economic and political regimes, institutions, and infrastructures that violently and unjustly regulate conditions of life-making and death-making across bodies, minds, and natures, this chapter is particularly interested in the notion of feminist recovery and in understanding how this notion of recovery can be seen in relation to the larger contemporary developments in feminism, which I propose to call care feminism. Recovery makes for a very interesting keyword in the pandemic vocabulary, as it so closely conjoins the contexts of disease, war, and economy, which are central to pandemic realities and imaginaries. In everyday communication people wish their loved ones, friends, acquaintances, neighbors or colleagues who have been ill a speedy or quick recovery. They inquire what they can do to make the recovery easier. Recovery is thus understood as a process of healing and transition, which is still defined by special needs and requirements because of the effects, the pains or weaknesses, the disease still has on body and mind. While recovery is very closely associated with medical conditions and with the period after a disease or a medical intervention, the term is also central to wars and economic crises. We may think, here, of the *European Recovery Program*, maybe better known as the *Marshall Plan*, as one such historical example of a post-war situation framed through the lens of recovery. After World War II, material and economic reconstruction was considered primary to recovery—perhaps in pursuance of the belief that from material recovery and economic well-being social and political recovery and democracy will result. This understanding of post-war, post-conflict and post-trauma recovery also extends to notions such as "recovery after genocide".[46] In the context of economic or financial crises, the term recovery pertains to how what the economy does after a crisis is understood: for example, after the 2007/08 global financial and economic meltdown, the economy was framed by the OECD as moving "from crisis to recovery."[47] These examples served to underline that imaginaries of recovery are constitutive of how conditions of crisis and catastrophe owed to disease, war, or the economy are seen as a situation that will pass. Recovery means that the effects and impact of crisis can, and will be, overcome.

My reading of feminist recovery aligns this new concept with existing anti-capitalist, anti-racist, decolonial, and ecological struggles and insists that recovery can be slow, unpredictable, fitful, and forever incomplete. Placing the notion of feminist recovery from colonial and racist patriarchy adjacent to decolonial and indigenous notions, as well as critiques of hegemonic understandings of restitution and reconciliation, and understanding recovery as the articulation of the need for not only long-term, but permanent planetary care, I see the emergence of a new twenty-first century care feminism. Care feminism organizes around interdependencies and vulnerabilities in and of care. This is evident in movements such as Black Lives Matter, Ni Una Menos, Idle No More, and many emerging forms of climate activism for climate justice, especially in the Global South, but also in the Global North.[48] Foregrounding intersectionality, interrelatedness, and interdependencies in economic, environmental, social, and sexual vulnerabilities and violence, care feminism can be observed across many different strands of feminist approaches including among others, but not limited to, African feminism, Asian feminism, Afrodiasporic, indigenous, immigrant, decolonial, and transnational feminisms. There is also newly invigorated social reproduction theory and care ethics in many different fields. And there are many new forms of ecofeminism, many new forms of climate feminism as well as anti-sexual violence and anti-femicide movements.

Scholarly, theoretical, and activist articulations of the formation of this new twenty-first century care feminism can be traced through a large number of publications, of which I can name only a few here: the call for "a care movement" by researcher on the politics of public policy researcher Deborah Stone, who focuses on the politics of policy making; political theorist and care ethicist Joan Tronto's *Who Cares? How to Reshape a Democratic Politics*, the Network Care Revolution and social scientist Gabriele Winker's book on the *Care Revolution*; feminist theorist, science and technology studies and environmental humanities scholar Maria Puig de la Bellacasa's *Matters of Care*; the transnational research project and network of activists, scholars and practitioners *Pirate Care Project* convened by Valeria Graziano, Marcell Mars and Tomislav Medak; the manifesto *Feminism for the 99%*, written jointly by philosopher and one of the main organizers of the International Women's Strike, Cinzia Arruzza, Marxist historian, expert on social reproduction theory and also one of the main organizers of the International Women's Strike, Tithi Bhattacharya, and philosopher and critical theorist Nancy Fraser, who actually coined "feminism for the 99 percent"; curator and architectural theorist Angelika Fitz's and my own work on *Critical Care. Architecture and Urbanism for a Broken Planet*; *Decolonial Feminism* by Françoise Vergès, who has written widely on the racialized dimensions of women cleaning the world; the *Care Crisis: What Caused It and How Can We End It* by sociologist and feminist political economist Emma Dowling. Further, there is *Rebelling with Care. Exploring open technologies for commoning healthcare* edited by Valeria Graziano, Zoe Romano, Serena Cangiano, and Maddalena Fragnito; the *Care Manifesto. The Politics of Interdependence*, written jointly by The Care Collective which includes Andreas Chatzidakis, Jamie Hakim, Jo Littler, Catherine Rottenberg, and Lynne Segal; climate activist Vanessa Nakate's *A Bigger Picture: My Fight to Bring a New African Voice to the Climate Crisis*; and sociologist and journalist Anne Karpf's *How Women Can Save the Planet*.[49]

Care feminism recognizes the ontological vulnerability of life and the interdependencies of all life and non-life on planet Earth as well as the political, economic, and social responsibilities that result from the centrality of care to living interdependently in vulnerability. Care feminism fully investigates and seeks to dismantle the colonial-patriarchal ideology of warfare based on turning care into a means of deadly bodily, environmental, emotional, and epistemic violence, relentless extraction, and ruthless discrimination. Yet care feminism is also impacted by legacies of epistemologies of separation that split the social from the ecological, that split care for humans from care for all other living and non-living beings; this is something which, as I explain in more detail later, needs to be addressed and overcome. Taken together, vulnerability and interdependency make it explicit that the ways in which interdependencies are socially, economically, and politically organized and culturally understood define how lives can be lived. The ways in which interdependencies are organized through imaginaries of reciprocity, mutuality, and peace or imaginaries of exploitation, exhaustivism and war make lives less or more vulnerable, that is less or more livable. Vulnerabilities, therefore, are politically, economically, and socially produced, as life and nonlife are always open, that is vulnerable, to systemic and structural infra-political, economic, and epistemological violence. Returning to and insisting on the inseparability of bodies, minds, and natures, care feminism—in particular when conceived of as recovery from patriarchy—works to overcome the aftermath of violent epistemologies, politics and economies. Judith Butler has written most lucidly on vulnerability, equality, and interdependency. Butler has explained that "equal treatment is not possible outside of a social organization of life in which material resources, food distribution, housing, work, and infrastructure seek to achieve equal conditions of livability."[50] The situation of pandemic catastrophe and climate catastrophe has exposed the extreme inequality of access to resources and infrastructure as well as the extreme labor inequality impacting those who are required to perform the essential work of keeping resources available and infrastructures running. The patriarchal violence of the social organization of life results in the rampant destruction of livability and in the denial of interdependency as primary. Judith Butler observed that "the facts of global interdependency are denied."[51] Such denial of interdependency is the epitome of structural carelessness connected to the warification of hyper-individualism, where all compete against all for livability, and also, as I have shown in the second chapter, the epitome of the forceful militarization of obligations to provide care, with individuals heroized as Covid warriors and corona heroes who are expected to have the superpowers necessary to overcoming dependencies—especially those of infrastructural shortages, failures, and lack—with their individual physical powers. During the pandemic, Butler has explained in public essays and online lectures why "rigid individuality" stands in the way of organizing social obligations, of raising awareness of what it means that a body is always "bound up with other living creatures, with surfaces, and the elements, including the air that belongs to no one and to everyone."[52]

Aware of the interdependency in pandemic care needs, and in particular critical of the violent impact on the present economic organization of social life, which renders lives and labors of care vulnerable, the new Global Alliance for Care, which was publicly launched by the National Institute of Women in Mexico in alliance with UN Women at a so-called high-level event on International Human Rights Day on December 10, 2021, argues for "care as human right".[53] This leads to a reflection on how this notion of recognizing care as a human right relates to the international care order as it was established in the twentieth-century as part of the recovery process after the Great Depression as well as after World War II, along with a reflection on how the right to care can be understood in relation to today's struggles for the rights of nature which, in fact, need a much more expansive and inclusive understanding of care than does any right of humans. Finally, this chapter ends with placing in conversation the newly emerging legal imaginaries of the right to care and the rights of nature, which I approach with critical feminist hope.

Hawai'i's Feminist Economic Recovery Plan

By mid-April 2020, in the short space of five weeks, a group of close to forty feminists, gathered together by Khara Jabola-Karolus, a specialist in native Hawaiian law and the Executive Director of the Hawai'i State Commission on the Status of Women, which is a feminist government agency located in Honolulu, had written a feminist recovery plan. By June 15, 2020, Maui Council became the first council in the United States to have such a plan. Understanding themselves as the "Feminist Covid-19 Response Team", the group consisted of Native women and immigrant women, with Jabola-Carolus specifically inviting people into the team "whose working status or economic attainment normally keeps them out from engaging in policy formation and implementation", as stated in an article reporting on Hawai'i's Post-Covid recovery plan in the *yesmagazine* in July 2020. The plan's key recommendations include one to "diversify and reshape the economy" by moving away from tourism and the military and investing more in "subsistence living and the perpetuation of land- and sea-based practices traditional to Hawai'i's ecological and food system."⁵⁴ There is a particular focus on care, demanding at once to build the state's social infrastructures of childcare, education and healthcare, to focus on midwifery and maternal health services, to introduce a universal basic income—which is seen as particularly relevant to combating sexual violence against women, with economic dependencies increasing the exposure to violence—and to "fully incorporate gender-based violence prevention in the immediate response and long-term recovery."⁵⁵ The plan calls into question the presumed neutrality of economic recovery stimulus funds and renders such neutrality legible as one of the instruments of power violence in unequal societies, insisting that a recovery plan need to "tie in gender with race, indigeneity, and class."⁵⁶ Viewing policy as a means to effect "deep cultural change", they insist that "response and recovery" has to necessarily include "repair and revival" in order to address historical violence and revive "place-based practices and knowledge."⁵⁷

Building Bridges, Not Walking on Backs is the title of the Hawaiian feminist economic recovery plan. This seems to be an unusually poetic title for a policy document, the language of which is widely held to be bureaucratic or dry. Its metaphorical and literary quality is an indication that this feminist economic recovery plan understands changes in economy and politics to be necessarily part of larger processes of cultural transformation that are deeply connected to imaginaries. The title speaks to infrastructural consciousness and evokes images of feminized physical exertion, pain, exploitation, and even breakage. Forcing human backs to make up for missing bridges is an act of infrastructural violence and harm. It also raises the question who will walk and who will be walked on. This speaks to societal and political violence in the form of economies of inequality, with some enabled to walk while others become their system of support and are walked on. The title also places the feminist recovery plan in the larger cultural context of feminist writing as it is evocative of the seminal anthology *The Bridge Called My Back: Writings by Radical Women of Color*, edited jointly by Cherrie Moraga and Gloria E. Anzaldúa in 1981. Here, "the bridge" placed alongside spaces and infrastructures—which include roads, paths, tables, beds, and streets which can hold women back, which in the aftermath of colonial, racist, and sexist patriarchy can become sites of violence, exploitation, harm, and even death—is used as a powerful metaphor for liberation. In "Acts of Healing", placed at the beginning of the volume *The Bridge Called My Back*, feminist and queer cultural theorist Gloria Anzaldúa writes: "We carry this bridge inside us, the struggle, the movement toward liberation. No doubt all of us have found by now that you don't build bridges by storming walls – that only puts people's backs up."⁵⁸ Bridges for liberation, carried inside, have to be translated into material bridges for liberation understood as real infrastructures of support and care. The struggles, and ethics, of decolonial, indigenous, and feminist-of-color politics are acknowledged and honored in the recovery plan's title. This underlines that this plan consciously builds on legacies of feminist liberation and understands its aims as part of the ongoing process of liberation, which is the very process of recovery from colonial racial patriarchy. Viewing the title for the feminist economic recovery plan as a programmatic declaration, a feminist manifesto and an acknowledgment of earlier feminisms, I also identify a distinct perspective here, which I view as feminist infrastructural consciousness-raising. The title speaks to infrastructural imaginaries. If infrastructure is lacking or failing, then bodies are obliged to make up for this and, at the same time, are imperiled, endangered, put at risk and exhausted more through forms of extractivism that require bodies to make up for lacking or failing essential infrastructures, in terms of both material-technological as well as human resources. Considering bodies as living infrastructure, in particular gendered and racialized bodies as well as bodies marked by class or caste, is constitutive of colonial racial patriarchy. Addressing gender, class, caste, ethnicity, race, and indigeneity as discriminatory and violent dimensions of infrastructure and working toward a distinctly feminist infrastructure politics makes explicit the crucial importance of infrastructure to both recovery and liberation. The enormity of violent planetary infrastructural penetration and the inequity and harm caused by lack of infrastructure, in particular the exclusion of the most vulnerable populations from access to infrastructural equity, requires thinking with the close, even intimate connection between bodies, environments, and infrastructures, which the title suggests. This situates infrastructure, as I argue, at the crucial intersection of social and environmental justice and makes socio-environmental and bio-material interdependencies central to infrapolitical accountability and responsibilities. Heightened infrastructural awareness motivated by the vulnerabilities that result from the compounded effects of pandemic and climate catastrophe requires conceiving of infrapolitics in terms of infrastructural intimacy, acknowledging that this "intimacy ... poses a question of scale that links the instability of individual lives to the trajectories of the collective."⁵⁹ Connecting backs and bridges is a powerful way of introducing historical infrastructural harm and the need for recovery as well as repair, revitalization and liberation beyond Covid-19.

"The road to economic recovery should not be across women's backs."[60] This is the opening sentence of the Hawaiian Feminist Economic Recovery Plan. Policy advice, here, begins by stating what economic recovery should not be. The sentence was widely quoted, as the Hawaiian feminist recovery plan drew much attention in the context of feminist policy making, administration, and economics and provided strong inspiration and a model for feminists in many different parts of the world. It was also included in a new *Handbook on Gender and Public Administration* in the latter's chapter on gender-responsive budgeting.[61] Across women's backs is a captivating metaphor, not an idiom per se, but evocative of idiomatic expressions and other metaphors which foreground body and materiality. Across—movement across—women's backs makes one think of a long line of women: it is, perhaps, even evocative of the frontline. There are other images that come to mind: that each single woman's back, from one side to the other, is exposed to a heavy burden or weight causing pain and suffering, as though the paving of the road to recovery were repressing them and running across their backs rather than providing infrastructures of support. Across women's backs evokes their bodies, labors and strength, but also the pains caused them by too much weight. It invokes the dangers of exhaustion and of breaking. It makes one think of extremely arduous and exhausting labor, of hard physical efforts, with dictionary examples of how the word back is used often associated with the military, as in digging trenches. One may also think of the context of construction, where strongbacks running across joists are secondary support members to existing structures, and, interestingly enough, are also referred to as formwork soldiers—another indication of how deep-reaching such military imaginaries are, as they have informed literal and figurative language in many different contexts. Placing the formulation of 'across women's backs' next to familiar idioms including 'behind one's back', 'watch one's back' or 'have one's back', one realizes that this phrasing is strongly associated with watchfulness and carefulness. Doing something behind one's back means that it is done without someone's knowledge, most often to the person's disadvantage. To watch one's back means that one has to be very alert to what danger is happening. To have one's back means that this person is willing to look out for someone, to help, to be of assistance. The first sentence of the recovery plan seems to suggest, therefore, that women have to be most watchful that a hegemonic economic recovery plan does not run them over, does not hit them, while at the same time it is a recommendation to be very careful that such plans are not made behind women's backs, that is without their involvement and their knowledges in plural, that come from their histories, biographies, and their care worlds. Raising awareness of women's past exclusion from writing economic recovery plans after economic crises, environmental disasters, or wars also explains that, in the past, such recovery plans have silenced the essentiality of care, as they knowingly placed extra burdens on women's backs.

Highly critical of "capitalism, white supremacy and systemic sexism", the feminist recovery plan demonstrates that policy can be used as an instrument in order to build bridges between grassroots activism and government as well as between the needs and interests of different women and act as a vehicle for "women's liberation".[62] Viewing policy as a means of effecting wider cultural change beyond the economy, this feminist recovery plan encourages "a deep structural transition to an economy that better values the work we know is essential to sustaining us" and stipulates a requirement to "recognize and value all members of our communities beyond their value to economic production in capitalism."[63] Jabola-Carolus, who initiated the plan, stressed the following: "I'm an anti-imperialist feminist. I am a transnational feminist, and I'm also a bureaucrat. I get to occupy this space because I had built up a sisterhood around me and that sisterhood existed before me, built by other women", as she emphasized that planning and working for feminist recovery is "a manifestation of the women's movement in Hawai'i."[64] This makes visible the importance to bureaucracy of anti-imperialist, transnational, and liberatory feminism: and there needs to be assurance that bureaucracy will not become an instrument in the hands of "femocrats", but truly works for liberation, in alliance and close collaboration with grassroots feminisms, activists, and researchers.[65] The Hawaiian plan sparked other feminist recovery plans on national as well as international levels. Feminist planning for recovery in pandemic times and beyond can thus be viewed as a manifestation of the contemporary transnational women's movement, which seeks to recover from the wounds of patriarchal violence and the harms of historical and mainstream white-centric feminism as care is placed at the center of political and economic organizing and cultural imaginaries.

African Feminist Post-COVID-19 Economic Recovery Statement

In July 2020, the NAWI Afrifem Macroeconomics Collective, which had been launched earlier the same year to work intersectionally and transformatively on macroeconomic policies, wrote the *African Feminist Post-COVID-19 Economic*

Recovery Statement, which was signed by 340 African feminists from different places across the African continent. The statement was sent as a letter to Ngozi Okonjo-Iweala, Donald Kaberuka, Tidjane Thiam, Trevor Manuel, and Abderrahmane Benkhalfa, the Special Envoys mandated by the African Union to mobilize international support in order to address the Covid-19 pandemic across the African continent. Writing from a perspective of Pan African liberation, the collective argues against economic orthodoxy and compulsory neoliberalism and connects a macroeconomic perspective to a human rights lens in order to foreground the centrality of a different economy, not based on profit and the exploitation of lands, resources, and care. They critically point out that the "gender dimensions of prevailing policies" are not well understood and that the pandemic crisis has exposed women's economic and "fiscal precarity" and that women's unpaid care and domestic work continually subsidizes economic profits.[66] They strongly recommend that states reorient their economies to the "popular or horizon economy", with "almost all of the agricultural sector in Africa, 97.7 percent" informal and thus invisibilized. Further, they demand debt cancellation and argue for the right of African communities, who are "the custodians of the land and environment", to veto finance or development projects.[67] The *African Feminist Post-COVID-19 Economic Recovery Statement* places care at the center, stating that "no turnaround in Africa's socio-economic fortunes will happen without recognizing the economic, social, political and cultural value of the care economy", that states have harmed care as they withdrew from their international human rights obligations and that the "time is well overdue for policies that recognize the centrality of care work for health systems and the economy."[68]

A Feminist Economic Plan for Recovery in Canada

The YWCA in Canada, which is Canada's largest, and oldest, women's multi-service organization, diagnosed that the
"COVID-19 pandemic has deepened a trio of interlocking crises that threaten women and girls around the world: spiking levels of gender-based violence, steep losses in employment and an unmanageable increase in unpaid care work", which also led to establishing its #GenderEquityDuringAPandemic virtual series featuring online town hall discussions and open space resource sharing."[69] In July 2020, *A Feminist Economic Plan for Recovery in Canada* was released, co-written by the YWCA. The homepage of the website, which offers

the key recommendations along with the full plan document, states that "there *is* no recovery if we leave women, Two-Spirit, and gender-diverse people behind."⁷⁰ This reveals what hegemonic understandings of economic recovery choose to ignore. If there were a return to so-called normal, the bodies, minds, energies, spirits, and lives of those left behind would never be supported and enabled to recover, because of lack of health, housing, education and income. The precarious economic actualities of the majority of people around the world would worsen, if global recession, rising debt, and job loss were not counteracted with transition to a different economic model that places the care for humans and all other living and non-living beings and their shared planetary environments at the center. The plan's opening sentence clearly states the brutal reality that recovery is no recovery at all if the majority—who, in all countries around the world, are populations who have historically been made vulnerable and marginalized—are left behind again and are not considered central to how economic recovery is defined and organized. Such leaving out and leaving behind are characteristics of structural carelessness and uncaring policies.

The Canadian feminist economic plan for recovery, which was the first national plan of its kind, was led by innovation scholar and founding Director of the Institute for Gender and the Economy at Toronto's Rotman School of Management at the University of Toronto Sarah Kaplan and by social worker and CEO of YWCA Canada Maya Roy, who, in 2019, had been a member of Canada's official delegation to the United Nations Commission on the Status of Women. The two report authors are Anjum Sultana, who focuses on public health, gender equity, civic engagement, and public policy and serves as the National Director of Public Policy and Strategic Communications at YWCA Canada, and Carmina Ravanera, whose research focuses on feminism, equity, and social and economic justice and who is a research associate at the Institute for Gender and Economy at the University of Toronto. Acknowledging that the two institutions at which the people behind the feminist plan are based have "benefited from colonial policy" and expressing that "Canada's economic prosperity is rooted in the appropriation and theft of indigenous lands and resources", the objective of the feminist plan is to support "policies, which enable the decolonization and indigenizing of Covid-19 recovery efforts."⁷¹ Observing that there is growing public understanding that feminized and racialized labor is essential to the production of public health and well-being and that this is owed to the caring labors of women, "especially women of color and recent immigrants", who are leading the current response to the pandemic crisis and are actively preventing further fallout, the report suggests that there is actually a larger paradigm shift underway that recognizes the centrality of care.[72] According to the Canadian feminist plan, public policy for recovery should be built on the following eight pillars: intersectionality, analysis of the root causes of systemic racism, care work as essential work, investment in good jobs, fighting sexual violence, bolstering small businesses, strengthening infrastructure, and political change through diverse voices in decision-making.[73]

Covid-19 Feminist Recovery Plan: Women's Policy Group in Northern Ireland

July 2020 also witnessed the release of the Covid-19 Feminist Recovery Plan by the Women's Policy Group in Northern Ireland. Much like the Hawaiian feminist plan, this one was a collaborative process, which provides evidence for women's capacity to organize in pandemic times, as feminists in public policy, labor and health organizing, community mobilization, advocacy, activism, civic society organizations, and research have long been cultivating exchanges and collaborations before the pandemic. One could say that feminists were prepared to respond to the hegemonic response prompted by the pandemic crisis. Drawing on years of feminist organizing and bringing together on this platform perspectives and knowledge from trade unions, grassroots activism, women's networks, campaigning organizations, LGBT+ organizations, migrant groups, support service providers, NGOs as well as human rights and equality organizations, they explicitly acknowledge the Hawaiian plan as a source of inspiration and also refer to their 2019 Women's Policy Group NI Manifesto. Highlighting the detrimental effects of the austerity measures following the economic/financial crisis of 2008 on the economic situation and the lives of women, the report draws on the evidence of the pandemic, which, again, disproportionately impacted on women, who had already been suffering for over a decade. Resting on four pillars—economic justice, health justice, social justice, and cultural justice, which refers to women and girls in the media, hate crimes and online abuse, rape culture, violence against women, and to education and training—their recommendations are aligned with the Purple Pact, a 2020 initiative by the European Women's Lobby that proposes feminist economics for "peace and wellbeing for all on a healthy planet", seeking to reconcile economic, social and environmental justice, the infrastructures needed for a universal social care system, and a labor market that focuses on care, social protection, and equality.[74]

Covid-19 Feminist Recovery Plan to Achieve Substantive Gender Equality-Center for Women's Global Leadership at Rutgers

In 2021, the Center for Women's Global Leadership at Rutgers, a public research university in the United States, published its policy recommendations as part of the 2021 *Covid-19 Feminist Recovery Plan to Achieve Substantive Gender Equality*. These recommendations are written from the perspectives of macroeconomics as well as women's rights as human rights. The Center for Women's Global Leadership at Rutgers, which is behind the plan, was founded in 1989 and is active in international policy and United Nations monitoring as well as being a contributor to transnational campaigning and mobilizing, as exemplified, among others, by the making of the campaign *16 Days of Activism Against Gender-Based Violence*. The feminist report was written by former faculty director at the Center for Women's Global Leadership at Rutgers and president of the International Association for Feminist Economics Radhika Balakrishnan, and by women's rights advocate Melissa Upreti and social anthropologist Camila Belliard. Based on the rights approach, they share the following diagnosis of the UN Working Group on discrimination against women and girls:

> there has been a systemic failure to properly integrate the biological function of reproduction and the gendered function of unpaid caring into macroeconomic policy in a holistic, effective and coherent way, to ensure that reproduction and caring go hand-in-hand with the overall economic empowerment of women.[75]

Their policy recommendations follow not only from a literature review on "care work, feminist macroeconomics, human rights and Covid-19 recovery reports" but also from additional online exchanges with people from different parts of the world over a period of three months in the fall of 2020, in particular with the New Zealand Human Rights Commission. The feminist plan of the Center for Women's Global Leadership specifically recommends a "purple economy" with its focus on the centrality of unpaid caring labor and a broad understanding of care across human care needs and environmental care needs.[76] According to their recommendations, the purple economy should be "organized around sustainability of caring labor through a redistributive internationalization of the costs of care into the workings of an economic system" and they advocate access to universal social care services, labor market regulation for a work-life balance for all regardless of their gender, ecologically sound infrastructure, in particular for rural communities, and a macroeconomic environment that enables decent employment.[77] They strongly emphasize that it is important to "work to transform the international economic system" for "caring economies across the world."[78]

Feminist Recovery Plan Project at the University of Warwick

One example of fostering transnational exchange at grassroots, policy, and academic levels for the purpose of writing policies and plans for feminist recovery during and after the Covid-19 pandemic was an event hosted online by the University of Warwick in June 2021.[79] The event brought together the following people, who had been working on feminist recovery in different parts of the world: Khara Jabola-Carolus, women's sector lobbyist; Rachel Powell from the Women's Policy Group NI, WRDA Northern Ireland, who published a Feminist Recovery Plan in July 2020; Constanza Pauchulo from the International Women's Rights Action Watch Asia Pacific in Malaysia (IWRAW AP has Special Consultative status with the Economic and Social Council of the United Nations); and Anita Gurumurthy, who works at the nongovernmental organization IT for Change in Bengalaru, India and focuses on how Covid-19 has exacerbated the existing disadvantages for women in the digital economy, particularly for women in rural contexts. Further, the event brought together Beatrice Karore, community mobilizer and founder of the Wanawake Mashinani (grassroots women) Initiative in Mathare in Kenya's capital, Nairobi, who works with survivors of abuse and violence and was joined by Nairobi-based activist Felogene Anumo, who is with the Association for Women's Rights in Development, a movement-support organization dedicated to gender justice and women's human rights; Enrica Rigo, Teresa Maisano, and Michela Pizzicanelle, from the Non Una di Meno movement Roma in Italy, who focused on the Covid-related rise of femicides in Italy; social scientist and leader of Ni Una Menos Argentina, Verónica Gago, and sociologist and Ni Una Menos activist, Lucí Cavallero, who co-authored *A Feminist Reading of Debt*; and Rocío Rosero Garcés and Silvana Tapia Tapia, who focus on violence against women, from the Coalicion Nacional de Mujeres del Ecuador.[80] I have listed here, in detail, the speakers brought together by this workshop, which was organized by socio-legal scholar Serena Natile in order to emphasize how transnational organizing not only kept alive, but in fact invigorated feminism in Covid-19 times and how these feminist approaches specifically address economies and politics that result in violence, injustices, and increased inequality that puts lives and labors under deadly pressures.

Concerned with structural transformation, this gathering also exemplifies how expertise and expert findings generated across sectors in politics and across fields in academia need to converge, because the body that experiences a lack of care, burdens of care, pressures of debt, and violent attacks is the same body that suffers from being split into sectors or fields when these very much needed specializations in these sectors and fields fail to come together and listen to one another. This is one way in which feminist organizing and knowledge-making counteracts the legacies of epistemologies of separation. Understanding the university, here, to offer a platform for listening and learning with grassroots activism inspires hope that unlearning patriarchy is, in fact, possible. This event demonstrated that plans for feminist recovery can bring together activism, community mobilization, policy, research, scholarship, and theory from university institutions in order to respond to the catastrophic conditions of the real world. The resulting report, written by Serena Natile at the University of Warwick and titled *Towards feminist recovery plans for Covid-19 and beyond*, is a policy brief aimed at national and transnational levels. It was published by the Centre for Law, Regulation & Governance of the Global Economy, GLOBE, as part of their Policy Brief Series dedicated to matters of public interest and contemporary concerns. Natile describes systematically, and methodologically, the differences between hegemonic recovery plans and feminist recovery plans, making it clear that the so-called normal of top-down policy-making, which assumes a self-contained, neutral subject and gender equality and is only of interest when viewed from the perspective of profit and growth, can be counteracted by policy based on grassroots expertise, listening and learning from and with marginalized and jeopardized subjects, and on redistributive measures against global injustice and for long-term wellbeing.[81] This emergent feminist understanding of recovery addresses "global injustice" in its locally specific contexts and is highly aware of infrastructural violence, income injustices and debt violence, and the devaluation of caring labors. Concerned, at the same time, with how policies, and politics, should be made in the future and how economies should operate, the recommendations include transnational labor standards and enforcement mechanisms by community and grassroots groups, universal basic income, social services connected to infrastructure, reparation by means of cancelling countries' external debt, food and land rights, and digital technology useful to reparation and redistribution.[82]

UN Women: Beyond Covid-19

In September 2021, UN Women published a close to hundred pages long feminist plan, which has the title *Beyond Covid-19. A Feminist Plan for Sustainability and Social Justice*. With the support of expert advisors as well as in consultation with a large group of people from organizations around the world—among them NAWI, who had written the Pan-African feminist recovery recommendations, or Rhadika Balakrishnan, who had worked on the plan at the Center for Women's Global Leadership at Rutgers—the plan acknowledged the expertise of others who had already worked on feminist economic recommendations for public policy. Highlighting that the feminist plan is written from the perspective of "diverse feminists" and drawing attention to the long history of Black and Indigenous activists resisting the idea of a universal woman subject based on notions of Whiteness and class privilege, the feminist recovery plan is based on the concept of intersectionality, as developed in legal terms by civil rights advocate and scholar of critical race theory Kimberlé Crenshaw.[83] During the pandemic, Crenshaw hosted the podcast *Intersectionality Matters!* which is available at the website of the African American Policy Forum and foregrounds how the pandemic has laid bare intersectional vulnerabilities.[84] Intersectional politics, in the context of this plan, advocates the recognition of historically produced injustices arising from colonialism, which also enforced compulsory heteronormativity and gender binarity on the plurality of lived sexualities and multiple genders, as well as an understanding that feminist struggles are linked with other social and environmental justice movements.[85] The plan argues that the acute pandemic crisis has revealed a "livelihood crisis", which increases the vulnerability of the majority of people, along with a "care crisis", which leaves those in need of care, in particular children and adults, who are dependent upon care, without support while, at the same time, "imposing hard choices and enormous costs on women and girls". To these two crises, they add a third the "environmental and climate crisis", which poses new threats to social justice and in particular to gender equality.[86] The recommendations and proposals include focusing on social protection, care-led recovery and building a new care economy, producing more data on care, and a green recovery with gender-responsive and gender-just transitions in energy and agriculture and more data on the gender and environment nexus.[87] Perhaps one sees here, in the language of policy and perspectives on human rights and macroeconomics, a coming together of a politics of intersectionality and a politics of interdependencies of bodies and natures, which has long been the focus of ecofeminist analysis and struggles—and, perhaps, that often criticized project of examining together the state of women and the state of nature will be revitalized by the real actualities of social and environmental catastrophe.

Broadly speaking, these different feminist economic recovery plans, whether aiming their recommendations at local, state, or international contexts, demonstrate the capacity of feminists to organize in times of crises. I argue here that this feminist preparedness made manifest in reply to the acute crisis provoked by the way many governments and economies responded to the pandemic and moved toward recovery as back to normal is owed to the fact that the histories, and practices, of feminisms can be understood as a continuously transforming response to changing conditions of crises, with the actualities of each crisis different, but the structural dimensions of crisis under patriarchy continuous. While it may appear reductive to understand feminism through its very capacity to respond to crisis, since this might suggest that feminism does not act, but simply re-acts to the given, I see feminism's special, and intimate, relation to crisis as its strength, in its capacity to never give up and to continue to work for liberation, emancipation, and just transformation precisely when liberation, emancipation, and just transformation come to seem impossible. The structural crisis of care has long been understood by feminist activism and scholarship and much spoken and written about by, among others, Margaret Prescod, Silvia Federici, Selma James, Nancy Fraser, or Françoise Vergès. Feminist philosopher and critical political theorist Nancy Fraser, a seminal diagnostician of this crisis, explains that "the gendered separation of social reproduction from economic production constitutes the principal institutional basis for women's subordination in capitalist societies."[88] With the pandemic exposing the essentiality of care, the structural and pre-existing crisis of care, which extends beyond human care and includes the planetary care needs of all living and non-living beings and their shared environments, became highly visible.

Building on decades and centuries of feminist legacies that have all—albeit in different ways, with different emphases or even very different arguments—argued for the centrality of care for bodies, minds, spirits, and natures, feminist economic recovery plans began to envision a present and a future which will make care the center of economic and political organization.[89] These plans used the tools and language of public policy for care. Acknowledging the violent, and deadly dimensions of pandemic conditions, and the economic and mental pressures on care, these conditions were also viewed as a moment to bring the uncaringness to light and to work for a transition to a just organization of livelihoods that cares for humans and environments. In the pandemic crisis, writing public policy became an articulation, and an instrument, of feminism. The way in which the feminist plans and their recommendations are written demonstrates that this feminist policy is informed by grassroots activism as well as feminist theories, in particular transnational, multidimensional, race critical, indigenous, gender-critical, decolonial, ecological, and environmental feminist theories, and that thinking and writing policy is understood through horizontal, collaborative, and transversal feminist politics. In the Hawaiian feminist economic recovery plan, the choice of language continued traditions of feminist theorizing through metaphor as expressions of materially lived actualities and articulations of hope for liberation and transformation.

The feminist plans for recovery and their policy recommendations for caring economies and infrastructures, and the care feminism of the twenty-first century more broadly, suggest that the need for a new international care order is held to be central.[90] In March 2020, Oxfam, the British-founded and Nairobi-headquartered confederation of twenty-one charitable organizations that focuses on poverty eradication, disaster relief, and policy research, released a briefing titled "Coronavirus does not discriminate, but inequality does. Beating the pandemic means dealing with inequality". They state that "our fates are not predestined" and that "Coronavirus shows us the raw outlines of the system in which we live, the inequality that we had hoped to ignore, and the urgent need to revalue and strengthen our sense of what is public, common, and collective."[91] Writing in 2020, diagnosing the pandemic situation in the United States of America, health activist and epidemiologist of microbial diseases Gregg Gonsalves and legal scholar Amy Kapczynski, who specializes on health justice and political economy, share an observation that goes beyond their geographical context and is of global relevance:

> We must build, in short, a new infrastructure of care to protect us all – a new order that, instead of perpetuating the virulent inequality and exploitation

of late twentieth-century capitalism, makes health justice and care a core feature of our democracy.[92]

A new global international care order is, indeed, needed. The Global Alliance for Care argues for recognizing "care as human right".[93] In what follows I will examine more closely the notion of the right to care, placing it in historical relation to how care was framed and defined through the two central international economic and human rights frameworks that were established in response to traumatic experience of war and crisis in the twentieth century. Thinking expansively on what care feminism is and does, I place the present-day feminist plans for recovery, in particular the notions used by the Global Alliance for Care, not only in relation to the historical modern international care order, but also adjacent to emergent developments around the rights of nature, asking how there are imaginaries and articulations of care feminism that are moving beyond the separation of humans from all other living and non-living beings.

The Modern International Care Order: Gross Domestic Product and Universal Human Rights

In the twentieth century, the crises of economic depression and of genocidal war became the defining moments of how care has been defined through a new international order in economic, legal, and political terms. Understanding that the definition, and thus the economic and legal conditions of care are not naturally given, but historically produced, leads to better understanding of the original conflict and the persistent contradiction between economic values and human rights. The impact of the economic meltdown that followed the 1929 Great Depression upon the global economy and upon how lives can be lived, and conditions of life in the aftermath of mass death and genocidal murder after World War II, gave rise to the establishment of two international frameworks which still determine, today, how economic values and human rights are understood. These frameworks are the measurement of national economies through the Gross Domestic Product GDP, which was internationally accepted after the Bretton Woods Conference in 1944, and the Universal Declaration of Human Rights, which was adopted in 1948. Placing these two frameworks in dialogue with each other allows a much clearer understanding of the structural causes behind the care dilemma that arises from the prevailing and, if anything, deepening contradiction between the economy and politics. The Great Depression, which Gita Gopinath, the chief economist of the International Monetary Fund, compares with the economic shock caused by the Great Lockdown in pandemic times, shattered the world economies after the stock market collapsed in October 1929.[94]

The Great Depression endured throughout the 1930s. In response to the experience of the crash in 1929, governments felt that they needed to have much better data on the state of their economies in order to be better prepared for future economic crises. Governments wanted an early warning system to be in place so that economic crisis would not hit so unexpectedly. This led to the first such statistical account measuring the economy of the United States in 1934 and, subsequently, to the adoption of this model of measuring their gross domestic product by other countries ten years later, in 1944. Measuring the economy was firmly tied to the organizational model of the nation state. In 1934, statistician Simon Kuznets produced, in the United States, the first such set of data, which is widely understood to mark the beginning of what is called the GDP.[95] During the process of economists, statisticians, and policy makers deliberating and eventually deciding on what counts as valuable to the economy and therefore needs to be measured, the exclusion of unpaid care work was a "deliberate decision".[96] The economist and advisor to public finance and public administrations Paul Studensky observed in his 1958 *The Income of Nations* that the "omission of unpaid services of housewives from national income computation distorts the picture" and that even though "unpaid work in the home should be included in the GDP", it was not.[97] In her book *GDP A Brief But Affectionate History*, which was first published in 2014, the economist and expert on public policy Diane Coyle, who also conducts research and advises on new measures for the economy in the twenty-first century beyond the GDP, explains that the main reason provided in hegemonic economic views to justify "not counting unpaid housework as part of the 'economy'" is "the difficulty of measuring it."[98] How can it be that what keeps economies alive and is essential to them is too difficult, too time-consuming to measure? What does this tell us about such hegemonic economic ways of seeing? Why is it so much easier to exclude from economic viewing angles the complex ways in which caring labors are obliged to view the world? How can it be that the productivity of the *oikos*—the ancient Greek word for household—from which emanates a specific *nomos*, the ancient Greek for a habit of social and political behavior (that is the etymology behind economy) was actually excluded from hegemonic economy? We can view this establishment of twentieth-century statistical silencing as a distinct form of classed, gendered, and racialized data violence as well as economic violence, at the level of state economies. As activist and journalist Caroline Criado Perez observes, "what governments do and what businesses do came to be seen as the definition of the economy".[99] Everything else, even though understood to be essential to the economy, has been divested of any economic value. One of the founding figures of feminist economics and expert in public policy, Marilyn Waring, elucidates in her book *Counting for Nothing: What Men Value and What Women are Worth* that the GDP is "used to monitor rates and patterns of growth to measure 'economic welfare'" and that all the activities outside of the "production boundary"—the "great bulk of labour performed by women in an unpaid capacity" in all the nations around the world—"are excluded from the GDP."[100] Coyle explains that in the historical fixation on productivity, the "production boundary" can be understood as an "imaginary line" that divides the productive from the unproductive.[101] Following Waring, everything outside of production is "economic inactivity".[102] One can see, here, that the diagnosis by the International Monetary Fund's director Georgieva of the standstill of the world economy is, in fact, a continuation of this historic production boundary, with its imperative of growth and of ignoring what is held to be economic inactivity. This distinction between so-called economic activity and so-called economic inactivity is also an effect of epistemologies of separation. What is of interest, here, in tracing the formation of the international care order—along with its potential transformation, in its historical lineage, which continues to powerfully and lastingly shape economic realities just as much economic imaginaries—is how closely related to war measurement of the economy and of what, today, is understood as the GDP actually is. National accounting, as Coyle explains in her history of the GDP, is linked to the history of war and emerges from the need of England and Wales to understand the "resources to fight a conflict and finance it through taxes" during the seventeenth-century Anglo-Dutch wars.[103]

With the 1929 Great Depression, as stated earlier, leading to the modern idea of data on the state's economy-relevant government, the development of the GDP in the decades that followed was, in fact, based on the idea of a war economy, with states needing information so they could "see the economic potential for war production". Instead of welfare, which is what statistician Kuznet had had in view when collecting data on the state of the economy, warfare became the economy's defining objective.[104] Better statistics were needed for preparedness for the war effort.[105] Better statistics for understanding economies from the viewpoint of care, and through the lens of hours needed to provide for care in order to sustain and continue life in social and environmental terms, could have been an approach to the economy in general, but they were not—for the obvious reasons of masculinist and militarist values. Interestingly enough, subsistence economies became crucially relevant and women's labor needed for producing food and care was visibly harnessed for the war effort at the time the new standard for measuring the GDP was being developed. As now, in pandemic times, when the centrality of care is highly visible and the pandemic gaze celebrates this centrality through visual forms of care militancy and care heroism, there was a comparable visual mobilization not only of women's paid labor in the war workforce (as in the iconic image of Rosy the Riveter, who became the poster girl for women who worked in factories and shipyards for the war effort of the United States during World War II)—the poster images of Victory Gardens, which showed women as agricultural workers and therefore nurturers of the nation on the home front, were equally iconic.[106] This specific hinterland economy, essential to the functioning of the war economy, lent high visibility to women's labor—in particular, also, to their unpaid labor in the nation's war gardens—while denying this labor economic value. Visual visibility of care should not be mistaken for economic visibility or acknowledgment in data. Yet the data collection methods for visualizing women's unpaid hours of caring labors would have been readily available at the time. In scholarly terms, the statistical tools for collecting data on unpaid caring labors actually predate the development of measuring the GDP of states.

During the 1920s, political scientist and economist Käthe Leichter introduced statistics and time-use surveys in order to gather data on working women's conditions of work and life in Vienna. In the context of the establishment of the Chamber of Labour, introduced by law in Austria in 1920, socialist women demanded a special Department for Women's Affairs. Leichter became the first spokesperson of this department and immediately set out to organize the collection of data. Mobilizing the context of the organized labor movement, thousands of women workers, including domestic servants and homeworkers, were interviewed on their hours of work, housework, and childcare. Combining in the survey what came to be known as the double shift, that is working women's economic condition of having to do paid and unpaid work, Leichter's development of time surveys was aligned with the "battle for the rights of working women" and aimed at "equal pay for equal work" as well as "protection for working mothers."[107] Even though working class women's political demands, at the time, were not focused on pay for housework or on how unpaid caring labors could be more equally shared, but, rather, on the equality of pay for work performed in the factories, as domestics, or as homeworkers, the specific political struggles of women within the working-class labor movement led to Leichter establishing a scientific method of collecting extensive information on how the economy actually works. Interestingly, we can see in her approach a practice and a politics of what I suggest calling data pedagogies. In her books and publications, Leichter employed the new graphic design method for the visualization of complex data as they were developed at the time, which was devised by Otto Neurath and Marie Neurath, née Reidemeister. These statistics in visual form, which later became well known as isotypes—International System of Typographic Picture Education—, are icons that aim to translate statistical data collected through sociological research into easily graspable imagery. This approach of making data visible and thus more easily accessible and useful to those who are being represented via the data, speaks at once to political socialist activism, research ethics, and a nascent form of data pedagogies. I therefore see Leichter's work as an early twentieth-century contribution not only to feminist economy, social research, and policy, but also to innovative feminist data pedagogies which developed ways of making care visible, thus counteracting the systemic invisibilization of women's caring labors. In particular, the method provides evidence of the time needed for and invested in these labors.

Today, we are still faced with a persistent data gap when it comes to statistical data on the number of hours women invest in doing unpaid work. According to British journalist and campaigner Caroline Criado Perez, "the failure to measure unpaid household services is perhaps the greatest gender data gap of all", with estimates "that unpaid care work could account for up to 50% of GDP in high-income countries, and as much as 80% of GDP in low- income countries."[108] With unpaid caring labors trapped in global economic invisibility, viewing care as inactivity and unproductive has, of course, largely impacted on ways of seeing paid caring labor. Far from organizing measurement of the economy from the viewpoint of the centrality of care, care was erased from what is officially viewed as counting as the economy. Referring to John Maynard Keynes, Waring states that "much of the economic discipline is a matter of perception", as she concludes from this that "what does or does not constitute production" depends on "the way you see the world."[109] As a cultural theorist, I am particularly interested in this emphasis on ways of seeing, as this underlines how hegemonic economic imaginaries of what counts as production and what does not have had far-reaching consequences beyond the economy and impacted largely not only on the economic status of people, but impacted on their bodies, minds and spirits in epistemic, emotional, and affective ways of how they came to think of their own ways of seeing and knowing the world and their political subjectivities. The production binary, that is the imaginary line that divides what is held to be productive from what is held to be unproductive, and the realities and imaginaries of war informed the economic order, in which care was devalued in economic terms, a phenomenon which has to be placed in relation to epistemological, cultural, social, and political devaluation. What patriarchal economy has taken from the ways in which the world is seen is the value of care. Such hegemonic imaginaries can exhaust, dry up, and kill off people's collective cultural and social imaginaries and also threaten individual people's capacity to imagine care differently and to become able to have, again, ways of seeing care outside of the economic policing of the production boundary, which is governed today by punitive, and compulsory, neoliberal capitalism.

So far, I have examined the establishment of the GDP as one of the two frameworks that defined the new international care order in the twentieth century. I will now turn to the second framework, the Universal Declaration of Human Rights. Just one year after the global standard for measuring the economy was adopted internationally in the Bretton Woods Conference, representatives of the Allies of World War II including China, France, the United Kingdom, and the United States came together for a conference in San Francisco in 1945 that led to the Charter of the United Nations, which is the foundational treaty of the United Nations. At this meeting, human rights were not even on the official agenda. Yet the very recent experience of having lived through enormous pressures on human rights on account of the hardships suffered during the Great Depression and during World War II, the trauma of the Holocaust, and also the incipient struggles for liberation from colonial oppression, led many to argue for the inclusion of human rights on the agenda of the United Nations. Following from the political understanding that human rights are central to the postwar transition and to working toward peace, in 1946 a nine-person commission with members from Norway, Belgium, France, Peru, China, the Soviet Union, Yugoslavia, India, and the United States was appointed. The group began to work on what ultimately became the international document of the Universal Declaration of Human Rights. The commission was chaired by the US Delegate to the United Nations, Eleanor Roosevelt, a political activist and social reformer with ties to the civil rights movement and to the women's movement. Historian Allida M. Black has pointed out that Roosevelt's understanding of what human rights are was shaped not only by her learning about the Holocaust and the life conditions of survivors of Nazi concentration camps, which has often been emphasized as central to Roosevelt's active engagement for basic human rights, but also by the experience of the Great Depression, which impacted disproportionately the lives of African Americans and other disenfranchised and marginalized communities with the increase in racialized violence and injustice caused by the economic meltdown.[110] Roosevelt's awareness of these traumatic historical contexts led to her insistence that political rights were real only in the concrete actualities and practices of everyday life.

Human rights do not exist as abstract ideas or ideals. Consequently, owed to Roosevelt's insistence, such basic needs for human life and survival, including food, shelter, clothing, or health—which are, of course, all essential to care—have been written into the universal declaration of human rights. Realizing that it was, in fact, one person's understanding of what centrally matters to human life and survival, along with this person's insistence, that led to including these rights to food, shelter, clothing, and health—in short, care—makes this a crucial moment, which allows a realization, in historical hindsight, that the hegemonic patriarchal view, the epistemologies of separation and mastery, could have easily led to forgetting, silencing, and excluding what is essential for human life from human rights—in the way that caring labors were excluded from the hegemonic framework of the GDP, which was internationally adopted at the same time. One can identify, here, a moment in which the presence and insistence of one woman's perspective did make a change. This also leads to understanding how important it is to feminist policy-writing in today's pandemic times that policy is written together by advocates, bureaucrats, activists, researchers, and many other perspectives: this necessarily changes the knowledge perspectives on what matters and how rights are viewed and defined.

I will now quote, in full length, Article 25 of the Universal Declaration of Human Rights, in order to show how the rights to care, even though they were not called rights to care, were defined as part of human rights in 1948:

> (1) Everyone has the right to a standard of living adequate for the health and well-being of himself and of his family, including food, clothing, housing and medical care and necessary social services, and the right to security in the event of unemployment, sickness, disability, widowhood, old age or other lack of livelihood in circumstances beyond his control. (2) Motherhood and

childhood are entitled to special care and assistance. All children, whether born in or out of wedlock, shall enjoy the same social protection.[111]

In a 1953 speech to the UN, Eleanor Roosevelt highlighted the realities of rights:

> Where, after all, do universal human rights begin? In small places, close to home – so close and so small that they cannot be seen on any map of the world. Yet they *are* the world of the individual person: The neighborhood he lives in; the school or college he attends; the factory, farm, or office where he works. Such are the places where every man, woman, and child seek equal justice, equal opportunity, equal dignity without discrimination. Unless these rights have meaning there, they have little meaning anywhere. Without concerted citizen action to uphold them close to home, we shall look in vain for progress in the larger world.[112]

Such an understanding of human rights in actual material realities foregrounds that conditions of everyday life are defined by access to what these rights are intended to guarantee. Reading her description of the everyday sites and spaces in which human rights are enacted (where lives have rights to live or to assert that their rights are being violated, harmed, or infringed upon), one cannot help but notice the omission of the home, which is of course a central, essential site for human rights. For human rights as they were conceptualized at the time after World War II, and for the newly emerging notion of a right to care today to be substantive, one has to think of rights everywhere in order to understand more fully the enormity of their absence. The global international care order created by those two frameworks—the measurement of the Gross Domestic Product and the Universal Declaration of Human Rights—manifests how care was being torn up through this split that separates economy from politics. I see this as one central expression of an epistemology of separation, as it is translated into economic and political realities. This separation, with care absent from economic imaginaries and frameworks yet present in legal ones, resulted in the creation of a global international care dilemma. This care dilemma is faced with an economy that does nothing to uphold the rights to care but demands everything in order to provide for care. This care dilemma is caused by a political world order that recognizes human rights as legally binding, yet does very little to actually guarantee that these rights, including the rights to care, are upheld in lived concrete realities. A different politics in and for the economy is needed in order to reconcile this dilemma. I see this politics embodied and practiced in care feminism, which can offer the basis for imagining a new global international care order around a new economic framework that defines the value of everything and, most importantly, the value of care differently.

These two twentieth-century frameworks have become dominant. They have not only shaped political, social, and legal realities, but they have also informed people's ideas and imaginaries of what economies and human rights are and are therefore hugely influential on ways of seeing care. Here, we see how care has been placed outside the active economy and inside what matters to human rights-bearing subjects. Since the universal declaration of human rights, the idea of universality has been the reason for deep unease, profound questioning, and, in my own reading, feminist worry. The title of the declaration does not proclaim universal human rights, but, rather, makes their declaration universal, which is a strong indication that these are Man-made laws, made by Men, who wielded power to declare that their declaration is universal. Yet critiques and contestations of universality in relation to human rights have elided the discussion of the universality of the declaration, and focused on the universality of rights. Who is the human who was thought to have universal rights? Who is represented in this notion of the human as bearer of universal rights and can therefore claim legal representation through this idea? To make this even clearer: Whose ideas and whose epistemic understandings defined historically who counts as human and who does not?

The violent histories of racist and sexist colonialism, the philosophical and political ideas of who counts as a citizen which are behind the modern institution of citizenship as well as more recent critical understandings of the supremacist violence inherent in speciesism, provide plenty of grounds for feminist worry in relation to this notion of universality. In 1948, the very year of the Universal Declaration of Human Rights, South Africa introduced and implemented the system of apartheid. At the very inception of any substantive universality, the aftermath of conquest, the annihilation of indigenous life, and the afterlife of slavery globally, but particularly in settler colonial contexts—as, for example, across the Americas and the Pacific or in the context of Northern colonialism in Europe or Russian colonialism, with the Soviet Union's territories based on the imperial conquests of Tsarist Russia—would have required practices of reparation, restitution, and recovery to be enshrined in such a universal declaration of human rights. There would have been the need to acknowledge and account for the historical violence with its epistemologies of separation, which rendered some of the humans human while denying other humans their humanity. Racist and anti-Semitic science produced death-making realities and supported extinction imaginaries, mass violence—including exploitation through slavery—, and genocide. But rather than confronting these violent legacies of defining who counts as human, modern supremacist Man informed the ideology behind the universality of rights—as decolonial and anti-colonial thinkers have tirelessly pointed out. At the time the universal declaration was written, philosophical and legal imaginaries of who counts as human were still keeping the violent expressions of the epistemologies of separation very much alive and present.

Following decolonial thought traditions, as first developed by psychiatrist and political philosopher Frantz Fanon, writer and cultural theorist Sylvia Winter, whose focus is on the overrepresentation of Man, observes the following on how human rights are delimited by what constitutes being human:

> The struggle of our new millennium will be one between the ongoing imperative of securing the well-being of our present ethnoclass (i.e. Western Bourgeois) conception of the human, Man, which over represents itself as if it were the human itself, and that of securing the well-being, and therefore the full cognitive and behavioural autonomy of the human species itself/ourselves.[113]

Feminist legal studies and decolonial citizenship studies have produced critical analyses of the exclusionary philosophical and political ideas of class, gender, and race. Such epistemologies of separation of who counts as Man, as Citizen, and, finally, as human were foundational to the legal concepts of first the Declaration of Rights of Man and of the Citizen in 1789 and then the Universal Declaration of Human Rights in 1948. Following the analysis of legal historian William Rogers Brubaker, the "ideology of national citizenship", which was developed during the French Revolution, became the paradigm for modern citizenship and central to the formation of Western political imaginaries of universalism and human rights, based in liberty, equality, and fraternity.[114] This ideology of citizenship is tied to the power of the nation state that grants and regulates the status of citizenship. At the same time, it is necessary to consider the global patriarchal impact of this ideology, which defined Man as citizen and citizen as Man and therefore the only one who is fully human and the bearer of rights. Gender historian Joan Wallach Scott observed that "slaves, wage-earners and women were initially ruled out of active citizenship."[115] The citizen was fundamentally based on the idea of privileged White Man, that is on racist and sexist modern ideas of supremacy that had been shaped by Enlightenment philosophy and were most influential on the formation of institutionalized disciplines of modern science, including deadly scientific racism and sexism. Epistemologies of separation and necro-epistemics, with their politics of life and death boundaries, separated those whose lives mattered to protection and care from those whose lives did not count. Frantz Fanon, uncovering the "imperial humanism" of citizenship that was so hugely influential on both understanding human rights as rights of the individual and defining who counts as a universal model for this individual, extends the anticolonial struggle to peoples. Wynter has diagnosed that this universal humanism is actually a monohumanism: "The larger issue is [...] the incorporation of all forms of human being into a single homogenized descriptive statement that is based on the figure of the West's liberal mono-humanist Man." [116] These deadly wrongs to humans who were excluded through mono-humanism need to be most care-fully accounted for when beginning to think of new rights today, such as the right of nature or the right to care. Rights only become realities in relations. Even if granted to individuals, rights come to life through social, material, infrastructural, and technological relations of interdependencies, in which they are embedded and through which they are made real and can or cannot be lived. Care, which is always understood through interdependencies and relationalities, therefore offers a very helpful interpretative lens in order to understand the violent and deadly impact of exclusionary mono-humanism. How the planet and all its beings will recover from the afterlife of mono-humanism, the accelerated hyper-individualization, and the hubris of speciesism which became the dominant ideology in the decades following the universal declaration of human rights is the central question for feminist recovery in the present and the future.

Demanding a new "social contract", the UN Women feminist recovery plan uncovers the interconnected impacts of mono-humanism that underlie the 1948 declaration of universal human rights and the exclusion of caring labors from the measurement of the gross domestic product of nation states. This plan states that the old social contract "never fully included women" as it was based on a model of "universal citizenship" that reinforced pre-existing hierarchies and led to demanding from women "so-called solidarity" in the form of their unpaid or underpaid work without, in return, providing "protection against economic risks and physical and emotional harm".[117] The UN Women feminist recovery plan critically observes that the old social contract was focused on "the relationships between states and markets, workers and capital, while ignoring relationships that fall outside of these requirements but are required for social reproduction and the preservation of global ecosystems."[118] In short, the old social contract was care-less, uncaring and threatening to annihilate care for humans and environments. The UN Women plan inspires hope. It emphasizes that it is actually possible that a new feminist social contract can come out of the "wreckage of the pandemic".[119] In their words, the new social contract needs to be based on the recognition of multiple discriminations, under the acknowledgement that "no one is safe until everyone is safe".[120] This resonates with my diagnosis that a "new care feminism for postpandemic futures not only has to rely on the broadest concept of care possible" but also "has to start from the premise that global care is only as good as the worst kind of care available for those who need it the most."[121]

Planetary Imagination Beyond Epistemologies of Separation

Perhaps quite unexpectedly for such an international policy document, UN Women state in their plan that recovery needs "imagination".[122] Such an appeal to the capacities of the imagination, to the powers of the mind, intellect, creativity, and spirit that make imagination come into the world, reveals both feminist worry and feminist hope. The realities of punitive neoliberalism, forcible authoritarianism, austerity extractivism, and chains of debt can erode the capacity to imagine a different politics of care. The pandemic declaration of war on the virus and the conscription of care into the global frontline of care put further pressure on the realities and imaginaries of care. Invoking imagination is, in my understanding, also an expression of feminist hope. Crisis can lead to recovery. Recovery needs care, time, and imagination. Imagination then becomes a form of care. How recovery is imagined, how care is imagined is a distinct articulation of ideas held about care. Such ideas, as we have seen in the historical realities of frameworks such as the gross domestic product or human rights, are influential and agential, they produce agency. Imagination, therefore, is crucially agency for care and empowerment of care. That the imagination was limited through epistemologies of separation is painful. It raises troubling concerns and questions that hurt: How was it possible that imaginaries—such as the one that envisages Man as separate, and independent, from nature, when every breath of air most deeply connects human bodies to the earth's atmosphere—became foundational to dominant Western thought traditions? How can anyone think or feel that the human mind can exist separately from, that is independently of, the human body?

Epistemologies of separation are harmful to relations of interdependencies, as they fill these relations with unequal hierarchies and the violence of classism, racism, sexism, and speciesism. What are new imaginaries for the rights to care in relation to the historical necro-epistemologies of separation? International humanitarian law researcher Anamika Misra has thought about reimagining. Misra writes that "reimagining the human as a verb that is alterable and dynamic, existing as a living form within asymmetrical relationships can introduce a reciprocity and care for humanity and other living and non-living beings." [123] Imagination is needed to actually imagine, that is grasp, the vast historical ruination and mass genocidal and ecocidal violence of the necro-political and necro-economic impacts of epistemologies of separation. Imagination is needed for caring and lively epistemologies in order to envision recovery from the wounds caused by this history.

Today, there is the imagination provided by new care feminism, which, while extending across such epistemologies of separation, remains marked, and impaired, by their legacies. Rights are central to the work of re-imagining living with an infected planet. Rights of humans are constantly being expanded and fought for to be understood more expansively as human rights as disability rights, as human rights as children's rights, as human rights as LGBTQIA+ rights, as human rights as trans rights, or as human rights as women's rights. There is also the emergence of a new understanding of rights of nature, not the old version of humans having a right to nature and to preserved and protected environments for their own good, but the rights of nature understood also through the realities of human-nature interdependence. In 2008, Ecuador became the first country globally to recognize the rights of nature in its constitution. Pacha Mama, as nature is known in the Quichua and Aimara indigenous languages, is acknowledged in all its life forms. Article 71 one of the Ecuadorian Constitution reads as follows: "Nature, or Pacha Mama, where life is reproduced and occurs, has the right to integral respect for its existence and for the maintenance and regeneration of its life cycles, structure, functions and evolutionary processes."[124]

Placing, now, the demands made by the Global Alliance for Care in relation to the Rights of Nature and a planetary understanding of care, I argue here that imaginaries of care and a new imagination of the rights to care will need to extend beyond the notion of human rights. Medical physician and public health expert Nadine Gasman Zylbermann, who is the President of INMUJERES, the National Institute of Women in Mexico, stresses that for a new global care agenda it is necessary, on "International Human Rights Day", to "make visible the double dimension of the concept of care: care is at the same time a right that people should have access to, but also the act of caring is a key function for the reproduction of society."[125] I interpret this to refer to the different semantic interpretations of what the "right to" can mean—one can have a right to something as well as a right to *do* something. In relation to care, this means that there is the right to have access to care infrastructures and necessary provisions as well as the right to give care, to perform care, and to have a political say in both how care infrastructures are shaped and how care can be given. The Global Alliance for Care views care as "a public good" and calls for the responsibility of the state as "the main sponsor of care."[126] Its commitments include the following: to develop and increase care services, involving actions by states, families, communities, and the private; public policies to reconcile personal, family, and work life with flexible hours; recognition of the rights of care providers and recipients; transformative actions for joint responsibility for care; investment in social and physical care to meet various needs under equal conditions; and more extensive data, research, and dissemination of practices in care work through an experience exchange platform and the creation of a fiscal space for the financing of a universal and sustainable care system.[127] Other local initiatives around care include, for example: the Bündnis Sorgearbeit Fair Teilen, the alliance for balancing unpaid care work by the Federal Ministry for Family Affairs, Senior Citizens and Youth in Germany, and the association ISS, the Institute for Social Work and Social Pedagogy; the activist organization of the Congress for Care in Berlin; or the network Mehr für Care Wirtschaften fürs Leben, More for Care Economies for Life, which resulted from a 2021 event organized by Femme Fiscale in Austria together with other feminist platforms.[128] Globally, there is much feminist organizing for what can be understood as the right to care, with a particular focus on the economic realities of care, the responsibility of the state, and the infrastructural dimensions of care. While I absolutely agree with "the right to care as a human right", as stated by expert in law and social science and UN Women Regional Director for Latin America and the Caribbean, María Noel Vaeza, at the UN Women event co-convened by the Government of Mexico, through its National Institute of Women (INMUJERES), and UN Women (and I agree, equally, with all the other initiatives for improving care and the economic conditions of care work, with some of them mentioned here), I do think that reducing the right to care to a human right not only follows from the logic of epistemologies of separation, but actually still follows them.[129] We need imagination for the infected planet to heal from these epistemologies in order for there to be true recovery.

The legacies of human exceptionalism and speciesism, which are fundamental expressions of the epistemologies of separation, are continued if the right to care remains human-centric. The legacies of hierarchies and selection are still not unsettled if some mountains, some rivers, some forests are protected through environmental personhood and others are not. I argue, here, that death-making separations and all forms of speciesist hierarchies, which formed the political imaginaries of human exceptionalism, need to be overcome for there to be truly caring imaginaries for the right to care. Such androcentric human exceptionalism, which is the deep structure for speciesism, led to a political economy that was based on subjugating land and nature, with Man taking the position of God who has the power to decide over life and death. Feminist recovery needs to regain what has been lost on account of such violent separations. Connecting legal imaginaries of rights to economic, political, and social imaginaries, and the realities in which they are deeply embedded, one comes to understand that a right to care can only be substantive if the international care order changes fundamentally, to the effect that *care counts at all levels and at all scales*. I also want to point out again, here, that the existing declaration of human rights, even though the ideologies behind it are penetrated and shaped by fundamental racism and sexism, in fact already contains many dimensions that can be useful to mobilizing around care as a human right, as human rights include the rights to food, shelter, health, and education. With the pandemic exposing the interconnected infra-political crises of public health and the climate, of care and the environment, with systemic vulnerabilization resulting in interlocking and mutually reinforcing forms of violence against humans and other living and non-living beings, the UN Women's feminist plan, unlike the Global Alliance for Care, addresses the structural conditions shared by care and the environment: "Like the care economy, ecosystems and natural resources are a critical foundation for the economy but are taken for granted and treated as though their supply is limitless and their use costless."[130] The plan foregrounds the accountability of states and their responsibility to counteract these conditions. Reporting on the UN Women Feminist Plan, the editorial team of the Gender & Covid-19 website observe the importance of the local community level and women's leadership for ecological care.

> Women leaders in local communities are spearheading innovative approaches to promote gender-just green transitions in key sectors, for exam-

ple in sustainable energy in Nigeria, South Africa, Uganda and Tanzania; and in agroecology in Brazil, Cuba and Nicaragua, efforts that protect local ecosystems based on Indigenous knowledge.[131]

The Recovery Will Be Green and Feminist or it Will Not Be

Reporting on Chile's new constitution in May 2022, which is perhaps the "world's first green and feminist constitution", international human rights expert and former United Nations Special Rapporteur on extreme poverty and human rights Magdalena Sepúlveda Carmona states what is at stake when one speaks of recovery: "the post-pandemic recovery will be green and feminist, or it will not be."[132] I read this to be the expression of hope and of worry, of insistentialism and doubt. It will be. But, there is the very real danger that it won't be at all, if those conditions for its coming into being are not there. If those conditions do not even form part of how it is imagined, then surely, it will never be at all. Stating that it will be—indicative, declarative, and affirmative—, but only if—conditional, doubtful, and questioning—is an appeal to the imagination. The imagination becomes the condition based on which different realities—always imperfect, always in need of improvement, but still changed for the better—can and could come into being. Only if there is this imagination of recovery in the first place can recovery then be green and feminist. This does not mean that the path from imagination to reality is ever smooth or even guaranteed. But without imagination, the path does not even appear, it cannot even be imagined to exist.

Arguing that there is a new care feminism necessarily has to acknowledge that social reproduction theory, care ethics, and ecofeminism, which are specific traditions of transnational and Western feminism at once, are all essential to how care has been understood as shaped by hegemonic politics and economies. At the same time, today's feminist movements, as they take shape in transnational exchange and with deep local roots everywhere in the twenty-first century world, have begun to move beyond the specific care boundaries that are particular to modern traditions of feminist activism and thought, as these often inherently reproduced epistemologies of separation by way of introducing new, and also violent, epistemologies of opposition. Ultimately, oppositionality follows the binary logic of war and competition. Today, the imagination supplied for life-making and feminist recovery of care is articulated in many different imaginaries and articulations by multidimensional feminist perspectives, in particular by previously marginalized worldviews. Imagination extends across imaginaries and realities and becomes manifest and public in articulations. I have shown here that such articulations can importantly include collective feminist policy writing. Expanding and deepening imaginaries of care is as important to care feminism as is working on material, infrastructural, technological, and labor conditions of and for care.

With many arguing that a new global international care order is paramount for life and survival and that this order should emerge through notions of rights and a right to care, I have shown the importance of international frameworks to ordering care, not just in economic and political realities, but in terms of the imagination. The impacts of international frameworks that ordered care in the aftermath of genocidal trauma and economic collapse after World War II, which still largely define the global international care order today, have to be better understood. This includes studying how they shaped deep-rooted cultural imaginaries and social ontologies of care that are based on epistemologies of separation. At the same time, this requires studying where there are points of departure for reimagining such frameworks today. In our times of ecocide and pandemicide, it is crucial to re-imagine rights to care in order to heal the deep wounds and splits that have resulted from the logic of separation with its hierarchical and violent structure of boundaries and oppression, and ultimately notions of disposable life and environments of extraction and extinction. While any care feminism based on the idea of rights to care has, of course, to be centrally concerned with the fundamental essentials such as food, housing, and healthcare and the economic and political rights of the global care workforce, it is equally important not to repeat the violence of epistemologies of separation, which underpinned the deep structure of the international frameworks in the twentieth century by splitting human rights from the rights of all other living and non-living beings, known as nature.[133] Postcolonial environmental humanities scholar Graham Huggan and postcolonial and literary animal studies scholar Helen Tiffin state that "the righting of wrongs in relation to all living creatures, as well as to the extra-human environments cannot be accomplished as long as we continue to treat these issues as discrete".[134] A new framework of care and rights to care needs to include epistemic, mental, emotional, spiritual, social, cultural, economic, and political recovery from the aftermath of the old frameworks. There is hope. There can be recovery. But, there is a very clear warning. The recovery will not be, unless the right to care extends across humans and all other living and non-living beings. Only if political, and economic, life are finally organized in such a way that their aims are to "support care" will it become possible to collectively take care of the world so all living and non-living beings can recover together with their infected planet.[135] Feminist recovery means learning how to breathe again carefully, aware of the fundamental interconnectedness of all living and non-living beings with the air and the planet and overcoming the patriarchal supremacist violence of reducing beings and the planet to subservience to human life; and doing this without reducing care to a service reserved for some humans but not for the majority of all the other humans. Feminist recovery is an expression of the hope that recovery is, and will be, possible. Feminist recovery is, at the same time, an expression of worry that recovery will only happen if there is a different care for care. Feminist recovery is, and will be, the continued laborious process of healing from the fundamental theft, neglect, and loss caused by the war of patriarchy that has infected, damaged, and wounded the planet. Feminist recovery will be planetary or it will not be. Some days I feel that a right of care can be imagined, not a right to care, but care having a right to be with the planet.

Conclusion: We Care Therefore We Are

Living with others means that we are never living alone. Human bodies are, always, living with others, which range from tiny organisms called microbiota, to other humans, to the earth's atmosphere. Conceiving of planetary existence as living with others foregrounds interdependency and raises awareness of the fact that relating to others always means relating to interdependencies. How relations to interdependencies are imagined emotionally, epistemologically, ethically, and spiritually is central to the economic, infrastructural, material, and political realities of how these relations are defined and how interdependencies can be lived.

By writing this book under the conditions of living with an infected planet, my aim was to provide a feminist cultural analysis of keywords, keymetaphors, and keyimages that articulated the politics of the response to the pandemic catastrophe in the early months of the pandemic in March and April 2020. The extreme health emergency led to full lockdown mandates and, at the same time, introduced essential work orders. Using as my study material political oratory, in particular at the level of supranational organizations, but also at the level of the nation state, policy frameworks, and globally circulating media imagery—such as cover images of magazines or popular public art—, my analysis shows that the terminology and visuality of war articulated the emergence of a new militarized care essentialism and compulsory heroism expected of those conscripted to the global frontlines of care. Declarations of war in the name of care and the militarization of care in response to the pandemic produced new frontline ontologies that organize interdependencies as class antagonism between the caring classes, who have to fight, and those who depend on them, so we can survive. The terms war and frontline present us with the patriarchal symptomatology of the pandemic.

Troubled by the hegemonic political response to the pandemic, I started to research if there was a distinctly feminist response to how hegemonic politics and economy dealt with the pandemic, placing my particular focus on dimensions of care in policy as articulated in the feminist recovery plans for Covid-19 and beyond. The longer I engaged with the rhetoric of war in political speeches and the normalized terminology of war, as expressed in the term frontline in policy documents, the more I came to understand that not only did the pandemic result in an acute crisis of care, but the political response to the pandemic revealed a deep lack of public and political imaginaries of care. This poverty of imaginaries of care is the aftermath of the historical silencing and invisibilization of care, a lasting effect of exploitative care extractivism. The structural devaluation of care was at once corporeal, material, economic, epistemic, and spiritual. Colonial sexist and racist capitalism and patriarchal modernity have not only foreclosed care as knowledge but also eroded the capacity of developing public and political imaginaries of care. Therefore, I read the idea of feminist recovery, in and beyond policy, as a proposal for finding ways of living as recovery from the historical and present-day onslaught on care. As one possible way of contributing to making recovery real, I developed in this book an epistemic intervention, namely feminist worry and feminist hope as analytics that are derived from care as knowledge.

Care as knowledge starts from acknowledging that living is always living with others in interdependencies. Responses to living with interdependencies need to be based on care. Feminist analysis of how these responses are articulated, with my particular interest in the material implications of metaphors and the power of metaphors as public and political imaginaries, begins to change when worry and hope are recognized and used as analytical tools. Recovery can be slow, very slow even, but it can be. Recovery from colonial capitalist patriarchy can seem impossible. Therefore, recovering the capacity of developing imaginaries, in particular new public and political imaginaries of care, is necessary. The extension of recovery to imaginaries counteracts both the depletion and the erosion of the capacity to imagine collectively which occur under the conditions of compulsory neoliberal capitalism and in the aftermath of historical patriarchal imaginaries of independence, war, enmity, heroism, and competition; as imaginaries constantly change, adapt, and evolve in response to the present.

In the midst of pandemic mass death, ongoing Covid-19 mutations, and constant work overload for care workers, my thoughts were devoted equally to a feminist recovery which eschews hegemonic economic and political care regimes and to hegemonic epistemic traditions that have excluded care from knowledge. The legacy of Cartesian modernity and its philosophical principle

I think therefore I am is still powerful. The imperative of the cogito was the premise for the formation of the modern subject, that is, modern Enlightenment Man who made Himself at once a universal and exceptional figure. The absence of a historical legacy based on the principle we care therefore we are is felt most painfully. This absence has given rise to the lack of public and political imaginaries of care just as much as the exploitative economic violence against all those from whom care is extracted, historically as well as in the present. Recognizing care as knowledge is central to today's care feminism and to beginning to work for new public and political imaginaries of care. While feminist worry is always concerned with the conditions of possibilities (that is, with the conditions that make new public and political imaginaries of care possible), feminist hope works toward new imaginaries of care even if the conditions for them are not there yet, and insists on making them possible. Hope and worry can work together to care-think, to not split caring from thinking and thinking from caring.

Hope and worry speak to living with the infected planet as recovering with the planet. Some days I believe that we can arrive at a point where it is possible for us to think: we care therefore we are.

Bibliography

Aboulnaga, Mohsen M., Mona F. Badran, and Mai M. Barakat. *Resilience of Informal Areas in Megacities – Magnitude, Challenges, and Policies. Strategic Environmental Assessment and Upgrading Guidelines to Attain Sustainable Development Goals.* Cham: Springer, 2021.

Abrell, Elan. *Saving Animals: Multispecies ecologies of rescue and care.* Minneapolis, MN: University of Minnesota Press, 2021.

Agamben, Giorgio. *Where Are We Now? The Epidemics as Politics.* Translated by Valeria Dani. Lanham, Boulder: Rowman & Littlefield, 2021.

Ahmed, Sara. *What's the Use?* Durham, NC and London: Duke University Press, 2019.

Anzaldúa, Gloria, and the Gloria Anzaldúa Trust. *This Bridge Called My Back. writings of radical women of color.* Edited by Cherrie Moraga and Gloria Anzaldúa. Albany, NY: State University of New York Press, 2015.

Arendt, Hannah. *The Human Condition.* Chicago, IL: University of Chicago Press, 1958.

Arruzza, Cinzia, Tithi Bhattacharya, and Nancy Fraser. *Feminism for the 99%. A Manifesto.* London: Verso, 2019.

Balakrishnan, Radhika, Melissa Upreti, and Camila Belliard. *A Covid-19 Feminist Recovery Plan to Achieve Substantive Gender Equality.* Rutgers Center for Women's Global Leadership 2021. Accessed July 22, 2022. https://cwgl.rutgers.edu/blog-details/644-a-covid-19-feminist-recovery-plan-to-achieve-substantive-gender-equality.

Bartov, Omer. "Man and the Mass: Reality and the Heroic Image in War." *History and Memory* 1, no. 2 (Fall-Winter 1989): 99–122.

Bayramoğlu, Yener, and María do Mar Castro Varela. *Post/Pandemisches Leben. Eine neue Theorie der Fragilität.* Bielefeld: transcript, 2021.

Barnes-Ceeney et al. "Recovery After Genocide: Understanding the Dimensions of Recovery Capital Among Incarcerated Genocide Perpetrators in

Rwanda." *Frontiers in Psychology* 10, Article 637 (April 6, 2019). Accessed July 22, 2022, doi: 10.3389/fpsyg.2019.00637. eCollection 2019.

Bean, Richard. "War and the Birth of the Nation State." *The Journal of Economic History* 33, no. 1 (March 1973): 203–221.

Berger, John. *Ways of Seeing*. London: Penguin Books, 1972.

Berlant, Lauren. "Intimacy: A Special Issue." *Critical Inquiry* 24, no. 2 (Winter 1998): 281–288.

Bhattacharya, Tithi, ed. *Social Reproduction Theory: Remapping Class, Recentering Oppression*. London: Pluto Press, 2017.

Brand, Ulrich, and Markus Wissen. *The Imperial Mode of Living. Everyday Life and the Ecological Crisis of Capitalism*. Translated by Zachary King. London: Verso, 2021.

Brubaker, William Rogers. "The French Revolution and the Invention of Citizenship." *French Politics and Society* 7, no. 3 (1989): 30–49.

Butler, Judith. *Precarious Life. The Powers of Mourning and Violence*. London and New York: Verso, 2004.

Butler, Judith. *Frames of War. When is Life Grievable?* London and New York: Verso, 2009.

Butler, Judith, and Athena Athanasiou. *Dispossession: The Performative is Political*. Cambridge: Polity Press, 2013.

Butler, Judith. *The Force of Nonviolence. An Ethico-Political Bind*. London and New York: Verso, 2020.

Butler, Judith. *What World Is This? A Pandemic Phenomenology*. New York: Columbia University Press, 2022.

Campt, Tina M. *Listening to Images*. Durham, NC and London: Duke University Press, 2017.

Casid, Jill H. "Handle with Care." *The Drama Review* 56, no. 4 (Winter 2012): 121–135.

Code, Lorraine. *Ecological Thinking: The Politics of Epistemic Location*. Oxford and New York: Oxford University Press, 2006.

Collins, Patricia Hill. *Black Feminist Thought: Knowledge, Consciousness, and the Politics of Empowerment*. New York: Routledge, 1991.

Colomina, Beatriz. *Domesticity at War*. Cambridge, MA and London: MIT Press, 2007.

Coyle, Diane. *GDP. A Brief but Affectionate History*. Princeton, NJ and Oxford: Princeton University Press, 2015.

Crary, Jonathan. *24/7. Late Capitalism and the Ends of Sleep*. London: Verso, 2014.

Crenshaw, Kimberlé. "Demarginalizing the Intersection of Race and Sex: A Black Feminist Critique of Antidiscrimination Doctrine, Feminist Theory and Antiracist Politics." *University of Chicago Legal Forum* no. 1 (1989): 139–167.

Crenshaw, Kimberlé, and Daniel Hosang. *Under the Blacklight: The Intersectional Vulnerabilities that the Twin Pandemics Lay Bare.* Chicago, IL: Haymarket Books 2023.

Criado-Perez, Caroline. *Invisible Women: Exposing Data Bias in a World Designed for Men.* New York: Ballantine Books, 2020.

Crutzen, Paul J. and Eugene F. Stoermer. "The 'Anthropocene'." *Global Change Newsletter* 41 (May 2000): 17–18.

de la Bellacasa, María Puig. *Matters of Care. Speculative Ethics for More than Human Worlds.* Minneapolis, MN: University of Minnesota Press, 2017.

de Waal, Alex. "New Pathogen, Old Politics." In *Thinking in a Pandemic. The Crisis of Science and Policy in the Age of Covid-19*, edited by Deborah Chasman and Joshua Cohen, 10–48. Boston, MA: Boston Review; London: Verso, 2020.

de Waal, Alex. *New Pandemics, Old Politics: Two Hundred Years of War on Disease and its Alternatives.* Cambridge: Polity, 2021.

Dowling, Emma. *The Care Crisis: What Caused It and How Can We End it?* London and New York: Verso, 2021.

Dowling, Emma et al., eds. *Caring in Times of a Global Pandemic, Historical Social Research HRS* vol. 46 no. 178 (2021).

Dworkin, Andrea. "Antifeminism" In *Right-wing Women*, 195–238. New York: Perigee Books, 1983.

Ehrenreich, Barbara. "Maid to Order: The Politics of Other Women's Work." *Harper's Magazine* (April 2000): 59–70.

Enloe, Cynthia. *Maneuvers. The International Politics of Militarizing Women's Lives.* Berkeley, CA: University of California Press, 2000.

Enloe, Cynthia. *The Curious Feminist. Searching for Women in a New Age of Empire.* Berkeley, CA: University of California Press, 2004.

Fals Borda, Orlando. *Una sociología sentipensante para América Latina.* Bogota: Clacso and Siglo de Hombre Editores, 2009.

Farris, Sarah. *In the Name of Women's Rights: The Rise of Femonationalism.* Durham, NC and London: Duke University Press, 2017.

Federici, Silvia. "Undeclared War against Women." *Artforum International* 55, no. 10 (Summer 2017). Accessed July 22, 2022. https://www.artforum.com/contributor/silvia-federici.

Federici, Silvia. *Revolution at Point Zero: Housework, Reproduction, and Feminist Struggle.* Oakland, CA: PM Press, 2020.

Feminist Analysis of Covid-19. Special Issue. *Feminist Studies* 46 no. 3 (2020). Accessed July 22, 2022. http://www.feministstudies.org/issues/vol-40-49/46-3.html.

Feminists Theorize Covid-19: A Symposium. *Signs. Journal of Women in Culture and Society*. Accessed July 22, 2022. http://signsjournal.org/covid/.

Ferguson, Richard Brian. "Masculinity and War." *Current Anthropology* 62, no. S23 (2021). Accessed July 22, 2022. https://www.journals.uchicago.edu/doi/full/10.1086/711622#_i18.

Ferguson, Susan. *Women and Work. Labour and Social Reproduction*. London: Pluto Press, 2019.

Fine, Michael, and Joan Tronto, eds. *Care, caring and the global Covid-19 pandemic. International Journal of Care and Caring* 6, no. 1–2 (February 2022).

Fitz, Angelika, and Elke Krasny, eds. *Critical Care. Architecture and Urbanism for a Broken Planet*. Boston, MA: MIT Press, 2019.

Foote, Stephanie, and Jeffrey Jerome Cohen, eds. *The Cambridge Companion to Environmental Humanities*. Cambridge: Cambridge University Press 2021.

Foro Generación Igualdad. "Global Alliance for Care: An Urgent Call to Action." June 28, 2021. Accessed July 22, 2022. https://forogeneracionigualdad.mx/7740-2/?lang=en.

Fraser, Nancy. "Feminism, Capitalism and the Cunning of History." *New Left Review* 56 (March 2009): 97–117.

Fraser, Nancy. "Contradictions of Capital and Care." *New Left Review* 100 (July/August 2016): 99–117.

Fraser, Nancy interviewed by Sarah Leonhard. "Capitalism's Crisis of Care." *Dissent Magazine* (Fall 2016). Accessed July 22, 2022. https://www.dissentmagazine.org/article/nancy-fraser-interview-capitalism-crisis-of-care.

Gaugele, Elke, and Elke Krasny. "Von Figurationen der Verfolgung. *Der Sklavenmarkt* von Jean-Léon Gérôme (1866) im rechtsextremen Wahlkampf der AfD." In *Rechte Angriffe – toxische Effekte. Umformierungen extrem Rechter in Mode, Feminismus und Popkultur*, edited by Elke Gaugele and Sarah Held, 129–159. Bielefeld: transcript, 2021.

Gender & Covid-19. "Beyond Covid-19: A Feminist Plan for Sustainability and Social Justice." March 8, 2022. Accessed July 22, 2022. https://www.genderandcovid-19.org/editorial/beyond-covid-19-a-feminist-plan-for-sustainability-and-social-justice/.

Gender and Development Network. "Lessons for a feminist Covid-19 economic recovery: multi-country perspectives." March 2022. Accessed July 22, 2022. https://gadnetwork.org/gadn-resources/covid-economic-recovery.

Geuskens, Isabelle. "Introduction." In *Gender and Militarism. Analyzing the Links to Strategize for Peace*, edited by Isabelle Geuskens, Merle Gosewinkel, and Sophie Schellens, 3–6. (The Hague: Women Peacemakers Program, 2014).

Gonsalves, Gregg, and Amy Kapczynski. "The Politics of Care." In *The Politics of Care. From Covid-19 to Black Lives Matter*, edited by Deborah Chasman and Joshua Cohen, 11–43. Boston, MA: Boston Review; London: Verso, 2020.

Graeber, David. *Bullshit Jobs: A Theory*. London: Simon & Schuster, 2019.

Graziano, Valeria et al. *Rebelling with Care. Exploring open technologies for commoning healthcare*. WeMake: 2019.

Greenhalgh, Trisha. "Will Evidence-Based Medicine Survive Covid-19." In *Thinking in a Pandemic. The Crisis of Science and Policy in the Age of Covid-19*, edited by Deborah Chasman and Joshua Cohen, 136–146. Cambridge, MA: Boston Review; London: Verso Books, 2020.

Guterres, António. "Declare War on this Virus – UN Chief on the Coronavirus Covid-19." Speech, UN Video, March 13, 2020. https://videos.un.org/en/2020/03/13/declare-war-on-this-virus-u-n-chief-on-the-coronavirus-covid-19-13-march-2020/.

Hall, Stuart. "A 'Reading' of Karl Marx Introduction to the Grundrisse," *Centre for Cultural Studies*, 1–20. Birmingham: University of Birmingham 1973,

Hall, Stuart. "Race, articulation and societies structured in dominance." In *Sociological theories: race and colonialism*, edited by UNESCO, 305–45. UNESCO, 1980.

Haraway, Donna J. *When Species Meet*. Minneapolis, MN and London: University of Minnesota Press, 2008.

Haraway, Donna J. "SF: Science fiction, speculative fabulation, string figures, so far." *Ada: A Journal of Gender, New Media, and Technology* 3 (2013). Accessed July 22, 2022. https://adanewmedia.org/2013/11/issue3-haraway/.

Haraway, Donna J. *Staying with the Trouble. Making Kin in the Chthulucene*. Durham, NC and London: Duke University Press, 2016.

Harvey, Rowan. "The Ignored Pandemic. The Dual Crisis of Gender-Based Violence and Covid-19." In the Oxfam Digital Repository. November 2021. Accessed July 22, 2022. https://oxfamilibrary.openrepository.com/bitstream/handle/10546/621309/bp-ignored-pandemic-251121-en.pdf.

Higgins, David. "Apocalypse/Extinction." In *The Cambridge Companion to Environmental Humanities*, edited by Jeffrey Jerome Cohen and Stephanie Foote, 114–127. Cambridge: Cambridge University Press, 2021.

Hilton, Carol Ann. "Indigenomics." *Site Magazine* (2020). Accessed July 22, 2022. https://www.thesitemagazine.com/covid19provisions.

Hilton, Carol Ann. *Indigenomics: Taking a Seat at the Economic Table*. Gabriola Island: New Society Publishers, 2021.

Hirsch Ballin, Ernst, Huub Dijstelbloem, and Peter de Goede. "The Extension of the Concept of Security." In *Security in an Interconnected World. Research for Policy*, edited by Ernst Hirsch Ballin, Huub Dijstelbloem, and Peter de Goede, 13–39. Cham: Springer 2020.

hooks, bell. *Talking Back: Thinking Feminist, Thinking Black*. London and New York: Routledge, 2014.

Huggan, Graham, and Helen Tiffin. *Postcolonial Ecocriticism: Literature, Animals, Environment*. London: Routledge, 2010.

Iheka, Cajetan. "Rights." In *The Cambridge Companion to Environmental Humanities*, edited by Jeffrey Jerome Cohen and Stephanie Foote, 26–38. Cambridge: Cambridge University Press.

Ilkkaracan, Ipek. "Four things to know about the purple economy." IWRWA Asia Pacific, Kuala Lumpur: International Women's Rights Action Watch Asia Pacific, 2018. Accessed July 22, 2022. https://www.iwraw-ap.org/wp-content/uploads/2018/10/Four-Things-to-Know-about-the-Purple-Econ omy.pdf.

Ilkkaracan, Ipek. "A Feminist Alternative to Austerity. The purple economy as a gender-egalitarian strategy for employment generation."In *Economics and Austerity in Europe: Gendered impacts and sustainable alternatives*, edited by Hannah Bargawi, Giovanni Cozzi, and Susan Himmelweit, 27–39. London and New York, Routledge, 2017.

Illner, Peer. *Disasters and Social Reproduction. Crisis Response between the State and Community*. London: Pluto Press, 2020.

Jabola-Carolus, Khara and members of the community. *Building Bridges, Not Walking on Backs. A Feminist Economic Recovery Plan for Covid-19*. Honolulu: Hawai'i State Commission on the Status of Women, 2020). Accessed July 22, 2022. https://humanservices.hawaii.gov/wp-content/uploads/2020/0 4/4.13.20-Final-Cover-D2-Feminist-Economic-Recovery-D1.pdf.

Jacobs, Susie, Ruth Jacobson, and Jen Marchbank. "Wars Against Women: Sexual Violence, Sexual Politics and the Militarised State." In *States of Conflict: Gender, Violence, and Resistance*, 45–65. London: Zed Books, 2000.

Kabeer, Naila, Shahra Razavi, and Yana van der Meulen Rodgers. *A Special Issue on Feminist Economic Perspectives on the Pandemic. Feminist Economics* 27 (2021). Accessed July 22, 2022. https://www.tandfonline.com/toc/rfec20/27/1-2.

Karpf, Anne. *How Women Can Save the Planet*. London: Hurst Publishers, 2021.

Katzmann, David. *Seven Days a Week*. Chicago, IL: University of Illinois Press, 1981.

Kirton, John R. *G20 Governance for a Globalized World*. London and New York: Routledge, 2016.

Krasny, Elke. "Care Feminism for Living with an Infected Planet." Academy of Fine Arts Vienna. April 2020. Accessed July 22, 2022. https://www.academia.edu/43164537/Care_Feminism_for_Living_with_an_Infected_Planet

Krasny, Elke. "In Sorge Bleiben: Care Feminismus für einen infizierten Planeten." In *Die Corona-Gesellschaft. Analysen zur Lage und Perspektiven für die Zukunft*, edited by Michael Volkmer and Karin Werner, 405–414. Bielefeld: transcript, 2020.

Krasny, Elke. "Staying with the Crisis. A Feminist Politics of Care for Living with an Infected Planet." *Escritura e Imagen* 16 (2020): 307–326

Krasny, Elke. "Living with a Wounded Planet: Infrastructural Consciousness Raising." In *Broken Relations. Infrastructure, Aesthetics, and Critique*, edited by Beatrice von Bismarck et al., 67–76. Leipzig: Spector Books, 2022.

Kretzer, Joshua. *Resolve in International Politics*. Princeton, NJ: Princeton University Press, 2016.

Lakoff, George and Mark Johnson. *Metaphors We Live By*. Chicago, IL: University of Chicago Press, 2003.

Lehtinen, Matthias, and Tuukka Brunila. "A Political Ontology of the Pandemic: Sovereign Power and the Management of Affects through the Political Ontology of War." *Frontiers in Political Science* (July 28, 2021). Accessed July 22, 2022. https://doi.org/10.3389/fpos.2021.674076.

Lewis, Jill. "Mobilising Working Women in Red Vienna: Käthe Leichter and the Vienna Arbeiterkammer." *L'homme: Zeitschrift für feministische Geschichtswissenschaft* 26 (2015): 151–159.

Loucaides, Darren, Alessio Perrone, and Josef Holnburger. "How Germany became ground zero for the Covid infodemic." *openDemocracy* (March 31, 2021). Accessed July 22, 2022. https://www.opendemocracy.net/en/germany-ground-zero-covid-infodemic-russia-far-right/.

Macchiavello, Carla. "Caring, Curiosity and Curating. Beyond the End." *Seismopolite. Journal of Art and Politics* (July 1, 2015). Accessed July 22, 2022, http://www.seismopolite.com/caring-curiosity-and-curating-beyond-the-end.

MacMillan, Margaret. *War: How Conflict Shaped Us*. London: Profile Books, 2020.

Majewska, Ewa. "Weak Resistance." *Krisis. Journal for contemporary philosophy* 2 (2018). Accessed July 22, 2022. https://archive.krisis.eu/weak-resistance/.

Maouyo, Rachel, Bridget Noon, Barbara Hobilla, Hojung Kim, and Karen Roush. "A Message from Frontline Nurses: Let's Keep the Real Enemy in Sight." *AJN American Journal of Nursing* 120, no. 8 (August 2020). Accessed July 22. 2022. https://journals.lww.com/ajnonline/fulltext/2020/08000/a_message_from_frontline_nurses__let_s_keep_the.29.aspx.

Marks Rubin, Marilyn, and John R. Bartle. "Gender-responsive budgeting: a global perspective." In *Handbook on Gender and Public Administration*, edited by Patricia M. Shields and Nicole M. Elias, 133–148. Cheltenham: Edward Elgar Publishing, 2022.

Marx, Karl. *Capital: A Critique of Political Economy*, vol. 1. Translated by Ben Fowkes. New York, Penguin Books, 1976.

Mbembe, Achille. "Necropolitics." *Public Culture* vol. 15 no. 1 (2003): 11–40.

Mbembe, Achille. "The society of enmity." *Radical Philosphy* (Nov/Dec 2016). Accessed July 22, 2022. https://www.radicalphilosophy.com/article/the-society-of-enmity?fbclid=IwAR0Ty4cfy-DgS_oRazPdKhYdPxdpKrERkk48WJ-bIi32HRED5xGHqnGl1-k.

Mbembe, Achille. *Necropolitics*. Durham, NC and London: Duke University Press, 2019.

MacKenzie, Debora. *Covid-19. The Pandemic that Never Should Have Happened, and How to Stop the Next One*. London: The Bridge Street Press, 2020.

Merchant, Carolyn. *The Death of Nature. Women, Ecology, and the Scientific Revolution*. San Francisco, CA: Harper & Row, 1980.

Misra, Anamika. "Humanity's Catastrophe: Following Sylvia Wynter in the Age of Coronavirus." *Critical Legal Thinking* (April 10, 2020). Accessed July 22, 2022. https://criticallegalthinking.com/2020/04/10/de-prioritising-humanity/.

Mitchell, Gemma. "Clap for Heroes: Nurses say they do not want return of applause" *Nursing Times* (January 7, 2021). Accessed July 22, 2022. https://www.nursingtimes.net/news/coronavirus/clap-for-heroes-nurses-say-they-do-not-want-return-of-applause-07-01-2021/.

Mitropoulos, Angela. *Pandemonium. Proliferating Borders of Capital and the Pandemic Swerve*. London: Pluto Press, 2020.

Mlambo-Ngcuka, Phumzile for UN Women, "COVID-19: Women front and centre." March 20, 2020, accessed July 22, 2022. https://www.unwomen.org/en/news/stories/2020/3/statement-ed-phumzile-covid-19-women-front-and-centre.

Mlambo-Ngcuka, Phumzile for UN Women, "Op-ed: Women Working on the Frontline." December 23, 2020. Accessed July 22, 2022. https://www.unwo

men.org/en/news/stories/2020/12/op-ed-ed-phumzile-women-working-on-the-front-line.

Morris, Madeline. "By force of arms: rape, war, and military culture." *Duke Law Journal* 45, no. 4 (1996): 651–781.

Moses, Julia. "Social Citizenship and Social Rights in an Age of Extremes: T.H. Marshall's Social Philosophy in the Longue Durée." *Modern Intellectual History* 16, no. 1 (April 2019): 155–184.

Musu, Constanza. "War metaphors used for Covid-19 are compelling, but also dangerous." *The Conversation* (April 8, 2020). Accessed July 22, 2022. https://theconversation.com/war-metaphors-used-for-covid-19-are-compelling-but-also-dangerous-135406.

Myers, Ella. *Worldly Ethics. Democratic Politics and Care for the World.* Durham, NC and London: Duke University Press, 2013.

Nakate, Vanessa. *A Bigger Picture: My Fight to Bring a New African Voice to the Climate Crisis.* Boston, MA: Mariner Books, 2021.

Natile, Serena. "Towards feminist recovery plans for Covid-19 and beyond." Globe Centre Policy Brief Series. February 2022. Accessed July 22, 2022. https://warwick.ac.uk/fac/soc/law/research/projects/feminist-recovery-plan/towards_feminist_recovery_plans_for_covid-19_and_beyond_-_serena_natile.pdf, 1.

Nixon, Rob. *Slow Violence and the Environmentalism of the Poor.* Cambridge, MA: Harvard University Press, 2011.

OECD Policy Responses to Coronavirus (COVID-19). *Women at the core of the fight against Covid-19 crisis.* April 1, 2020. Accessed July 22, 2022. https://www.oecd.org/coronavirus/policy-responses/women-at-the-core-of-the-fight-against-covid-19-crisis-553a8269/.

Oxfam Briefing. "Coronavirus Doesn't Discriminate, But Inequality Does. Beating the pandemic means dealing with inequality." In the Oxfam Digital Repository. March 2020. Accessed July 22, 2022. https://oi-files-d8-prod.s3.eu-west-2.amazonaws.com/s3fs-public/2020-04/Coronovirus%20doesn´t%20discriminate%2C%20but%20inequality%20does%20-%20Brief.pdf.

Povinelli, Elizabeth. *Geontologies. A Requiem to Late Liberalism.* Durham, NC and London: Duke University Press, 2016.

Prattes, Riikka. "'I don't clean up after myself': epistemic ignorance, responsibility and the politics of the outsourcing of domestic cleaning." *Feminist Theory* 21, no 1 (2020): 25–45. Accessed July 22, 2022. https://doi.org/10.1177/1464700119842560.

Prattes, Riikka. "Learning through Care: Decentering Dominant Epistemologies to Theorize Caring Men at the 'Center'." In *Decentering Epistemologies and Challenging Privilege: Critical Care Ethics Perspectives*, edited by Sophie Bourgault, Maggie FitzGerald, and Fiona Robinson. New Brunswick, NJ: Rutgers University Press, 2023.

Romero, Mary. "An Intersection of Biography and History: My Intellectual Journey." In *Mapping the Social Landscape*. Ninth Edition, edited by Susan Ferguson, 18–30. Thousand Oaks, CA: Sage Publications, 2021.

Quammen, David. *Spillover. Animal Infections and the Next Human Pandemic*. New York and London: W.W. Norton & Company, 2013.

Roosevelt, Eleanor. *Courage in a Dangerous World. The Political Writings of Eleanor Roosevelt*. Edited by Allida M. Black. New York: Columbia University Press 2000.

Salzani, Carlo. "Covid-19 and State of Exception: Medicine, Politics and the Epidemic State." The Paris Institute for Critical Thinking, March 12, 2021. Accessed July 22, 2022. https://parisinstitute.org/depictions-article-covid-19-and-state-of-exception-medicine-politics-and-the-epidemic-state/.

Santana, María Cristina. "From Empowerment to Domesticity: The Case of Rosie the Riveter and the WWII Campaign." *Frontiers in Sociology* 1 (2016). Accessed July 22, 2022. https://www.frontiersin.org/articles/10.3389/fsoc.2016.00016/full.

Schiebinger, Londa. "Why Mammals are Called Mammals: Gender Politics in Eighteenth-Century Natural History." *The American Historical Review* 98, no. 2 (April 1993): 382–411.

Schmitt, Carl. *Political Theology: Four Chapters on the Concept of Sovereignty*. Translated by George Schwab. Chicago, IL: University of Chicago Press, 2005.

Scott, Joan Wallach "French Universalism in the Nineties." In *Women and Citizenship*, edited by Marilyn Friedman, 35–51. Oxford: Oxford University Press, 2005.

Segato, Rita Laura. "A Manifesto in Four Themes." Translated by Ramsey McGlazer. *EuroNomade* (October 2013). Accessed July 22, 2022, http://www.euronomade.info/wp-content/uploads/2018/03/A-Manifesto-in-Four-Themes.pdf.

Service, Robert F. "You may be able to spread coronavirus just by breathing, new report finds." *Science* (April 2, 2020). Accessed July 22, 2022. https://www.science.org/content/article/you-may-be-able-spread-coronavirus-just-breathing-new-report-finds.

Sjoberg, Laura. *Gendering Global Conflict. Toward a Feminist Theory of War.* New York: Columbia University Press, 2013.

Skeggs, Beverley. "Necroeconomics: How Necro Legacies Help Us Understand the Value of Death and the Protection of Life During the COOVID-19 Pandemic." *Historical Social Research HRS* vol. 46 no. 178 (2021): 123–142.

Smiler, Andrew. *Is Masculinity Toxic?* London: Thames & Hudson, 2019.

Snowden, Frank M. *Epidemics and Society: From the Black Death to the Present.* New Haven, CT and London: Yale University Press, 2020.

Sontag, Susan. *Illness as Metaphor.* London: Penguin Books, 1991.

Soszyńska-Budny, Joanna. *Analysis of Critical Infrastructure: Impact of Operation Processes and Climate Change.* Cham: Springer, 2021.

Srinivasan, Amia. *The Right to Sex.* London: Bloomsbury, 2021.

Steiner, Henriette, and Kristin Veel. *Touch in the Time of Corona. Reflections of Love, Care and Vulnerability in the Pandemic.* Berlin and Boston, MA: De Gruyter, 2021.

Steinert, Heinz. "The Indispensable Metaphor of War: On Populist Politics and the Contradictions of the State's Monopoly of Force." *Theoretical Criminology* (August 1, 2003). Accessed July 22, 2022. https://doi.org/10.1177/13624806030073002.

Sultana, Anjum, and Carmina Ravanera. *A Feminist Economic Recovery Plan for Canada: Making the Economy Work for Everyone.* The Institute for Gender and the Economy (GATE) and YWCA Canada. July 28, 2020. Accessed July 22, 2022. https://static1.squarespace.com/static/5f0cd2090f50a31a91b37ff7/t/5f205a15b1b7191d12282bf5/1595955746613/Feminist+Economy+Recovery+Plan+for+Canada.pdf, 1.

Tapscott, Rebecca. "Militarized masculinity and the paradox of restraint: mechanisms of social control under modern authoritarianism." *International Affairs* 96, no. 6 (November 2020): 1565–1584. https://doi.org/10.1093/ia/iiaa163.

The Care Collective. *The Care Manifesto.* London and New York: Verso, 2020.

The Pirate Care Project. Accessed July 22, 2022. https://pirate.care/pages/concept/#fn-6.

Titunik, Regina. "The myth of the macho military." *Polity* 40, no. 2 (2008): 137–63.

Tolleson, Jeff. "Why deforestation and extinctions make pandemics more likely." *Nature* (August 7, 2020). Accessed July 22, 2022. https://www.nature.com/articles/d41586-020-02341-1.

Tronto, Joan, and Berenice Fisher. "Toward a Feminist Theory of Caring." In *Circles of Care: Work and Identity in Women's Lives*, edited by Emily K. Abel and Margaret K. Nelson, 35–62. Albany, NY: State University of New York Press 1990.

Tronto, Joan. *Who Cares? How to Reshape a Democratic Politics*. Ithaca, NY and London: Cornell University Press, 2015.

Tronto, Joan. *Caring Democracy. Markets, Equality, and Justice*. New York and London: New York University Press, 2013.

Tsing, Anna. "Earth Stalked by Man." *The Cambridge Journal of Anthropology* 34. no. 1 (2016): 2–16.

Tsomou, Margarita. "Care and Regeneration Work in the Paradigm of Ecological Catastrophes." In *Empowerment. Art and Feminisms*, edited by Andreas Beitin, Katharina Koch, and Uta Ruhkamp, 176–183. Wolfsburg: Kunstmuseum Wolfsburg, 2022.

Una Voce di Agamben. Accessed July 22, 2022. https://www.quodlibet.it/una-voce-giorgio-agamben.

United Nations Office for the Coordination of Humanitarian Affairs. *Global Humanitarian Response Plan COVID-19. United Nations Coordinated Appeal April-December 2020*, March 28, 2020. Accessed July 22, 2022. https://www.unocha.org/sites/unocha/files/Global-Humanitarian-Response-Plan-COVID-19.pdf.

United Nations Secretary General, "Transcript of the Secretary General's virtual press encounter on the appeal for global ceasefire." United Nations, March 23, 2020. Accessed July 22, 2022. https://www.un.org/sg/en/content/sg/press-encounter/2020-03-23/transcript-of-the-secretary-generals-virtual-press-encounter-the-appeal-for-global-ceasefire.

UNICEF Education Covid-19 Response. "Issue Brief: Covid-19 and Girls' Education in East Asia and Pacific." October 2020. Accessed July 22, 2022. https://www.unicef.org/eap/media/7146/file/Issue_Brief%3A_Issue_Brief%3A_COVID-19_and_Girls'_Education_in_East_Asia_and_Pacific.pdf.

UNHCR The UN Refugee Agency. *Figures at a Glance*. June 16, 2022. Accessed, July 22, 2022. https://www.unhcr.org/figures-at-a-glance.html.

UN General Assembly. "Universal Declaration of Human Rights." (Paris 1948). Accessed July 22, 2022. https://www.un.org/en/universal-declaration-human-rights/.

UN Women. "The Shadow Pandemic: Violence against women during Covid-19." May 27, 2020. Accessed July 22, 2022. https://www.unwomen.o

rg/en/news/in-focus/in-focus-gender-equality-in-covid-19-response/violence-against-women-during-covid-19.

UN Women. "In Photos: Women on the front lines of COVID-19 in India." August 17, 2021. Accessed July 22, 2022. https://www.unwomen.org/en/digital-library/multimedia/2021/8/photo-essay-women-on-the-front-lines-of-covid-19-in-india.

UN Women. "Care Work. Increased burdens for women. Covid-19. Rebuilding for Resilience." Accessed July 22, 2022. https://www.unwomen.org/en/hq-complex-page/covid-19-rebuilding-for-resilience/care-work.

UN Women, *Beyond Covid-19: A Feminist Plan for Sustainability and Social Justice*, ed. Tina Johnson, (New York: UN Women, 2021). Accessed July 22, 2022. https://www.unwomen.org/sites/default/files/Headquarters/Attachments/Sections/Library/Publications/2021/Feminist-plan-for-sustainability-and-social-justice-en.pdf.

UN Women. "Recognize care as a human right, urge leaders of the Global Alliance for Care." December 14, 2021. Accessed July 22, 2022. https://www.unwomen.org/en/news-stories/news/2021/12/recognize-care-as-a-human-right-urge-leaders-of-the-global-alliance-for-care.

U.S. Department of Homeland Security. "Advisory Memorandum on Ensuring Essential Critical Infrastructure Workers' Ability to Work during the Covid-19 Response." August 10, 2021. Accessed July 22. 2022. https://www.cisa.gov/sites/default/files/publications/essential_critical_infrastructure_workforce-guidance_v4.1_508.pdf.

Van Paassen, Barbara. "Why we need feminist leadership for climate justice." *OpenDemocracy* (May 5, 2022). Accessed July 22, 2022. https://www.opendemocracy.net/en/changemakers/climate-change-justice-feminist-leaders-rebuilding-world/.

Vergès, Françoise. *Un féminisme décolonial*. Paris: La fabrique 2019.

Vergès, Françoise. *A Decolonial Feminism*. London: Pluto Press, 2021.

von Clausewitz, Carl. *On War*. Edited and translated by Michael Howard and Peter Paret. Princeton, NJ: Princeton University Press, 1989.

Waring, Marilyn. *Counting for Nothing: What Men Value and What Women are Worth*. Toronto: University of Toronto Press, 1999.

Wibben, Annick T.R. "Introduction: Feminists study war." In *Researching War: Feminist Methods, Ethics and Politics*, edited by Annick T.R. Wibben, 1–16. New York and London: Routledge, 2016.

Wichterich, Christa. "Protection and Protest by 'Voluntary' Community Health Workers: Covid-19 Authoritarianism in India." *Historical Social Research HRS Forum Caring in Times of a Global Pandemic* 46, no. 178 (2021): 163–188.

Williams, Raymond. *Keywords. A Vocabulary of Culture and Society*. London: Fontana Press, 1976.

Willis, Don E., and Pearl A. McElfish. "Racial disparities in the COVID-19 response affecting the Marshall Islands diaspora, United States of America." *Bulletin of the World Health Organization* 99, no. 9 (September 1, 2021): 680–681. Accessed July 22, 2022, doi:10.2471/BLT.20.277855.

Wynter, Sylvia. "Unsettling the Coloniality of Being/Power/Truth/Freedom: Towards the Human, After Man, Its Overrepresentation–An Argument." *New Centennial Review* 3, no. 3 (Fall 2003): 257–337.

Wynter, Sylvia, and Katherine McKittrick. "Unparalleled Catastrophe for Our Species? Or, to Give Humanness a Different Future: Conversations." In *Sylvia Wynter: On Being Human as Praxis*, edited by Katherine McKittrick, 9–89. Durham, NC: Duke University Press, 2015.

Witteven, Dirk, and Eva Velthorst. "Economic hardship and mental health complaints during Covid-19." *Proceedings of the National Academy of Sciences of the United States of America PNAS* 117, no. 44 (October 12, 2022). Accessed October 30, 2022. https://www.pnas.org/doi/10.1073/pnas.2009609117.

Women's Budget Group. "Crises Collide: Women and Covid-19. Examining gender and other equality issues during the Coronavirus outbreak." April 2020. Accessed July 22, 2022. https://wbg.org.uk/wp-content/uploads/2020/04/FINAL.pdf.

Women's International League for Peace and Freedom. "WILPF's approach: Feminist Peace." *Women's International League for Peace and Freedom*. Accessed July 22, 2022. https://www.peacewomen.org/why-WPS/solutions/integrated-approach.

World Bank. "Girls' Education." February 10, 2022. Accessed July 22, 2022. https://www.worldbank.org/en/topic/girlseducation.

World Health Organization. "Covid-19: physical distancing." Accessed July 22, 2022. https://www.who.int/westernpacific/emergencies/covid-19/information/physical-distancing.

World Health Organization. "Infodemic." Accessed July 22, 2022. https://www.who.int/health-topics/infodemic#tab=tab_1.

World Health Organization. "WHO Director General's remarks at the G20 Extraordinary Leaders' Summit on Covid-19 – 26 March 2020." March 26, 2020. Accessed August 19, 2021. https://www.who.int/director-general/sp

eeches/detail/who-director-general-s-remarks-at-the-g20-extraordinary-leaders-summit-on-covid-19---26-march-2020.

World Health Organization. "The Seventy-Fourth World Health Assembly closes." May 31, 2021. Accessed July 22, 2022. https://www.who.int/news/item/31-05-2021-the-seventy-fourth-world-health-assembly-closes.

World Health Organization. "The impact of COVID-19 on health and care workers: a closer look at deaths." September 2021. Accessed July 22, 2022. https://apps.who.int/iris/handle/10665/345300.

Whorton, James. *Before Silent Spring. Pesticides and Public Health in Pre-DDT America*. Princeton, NJ: Princeton University Press, 1974.

YWCA Canada and the Institute for Gender and the Economy. *A Feminist Recovery Plan for Canada*. July 20, 2020. Accessed July 22, 2022. https://www.feministrecovery.ca/about-us.

Zine, Jasmin. "Reading Muslim Women and Muslim Women Reading Back: Transnational Feminist Reading Practices, Pedagogy and Ethical Concerns." *Intercultural Education* 18, no.4 (2007): 271–280.

Notes

Introduction: Worry and Hope

1. United Nations, "Academic Impact. #WorkforUN: Language Professionals," no date, accessed July 22, 2022, https://www.un.org/en/academic-impact/work4un-language-professionals; United Nations, *Declare War on this Virus – UN Chief on the Coronavirus Covid-19*. Speech by António Guterres, UN Video (March 13, 2020), accessed July 22, 2022, https://videos.un.org/en/2020/03/13/declare-war-on-this-virus-u-n-chief-on-the-coronavirus-covid-19-13-march-2020/.
2. World Health Organization, "About WHO," no date, accessed July 22, 2022, https://www.who.int/about; World Health Organization, "WHO Director-General's opening remarks at the media briefing on COVID-19 – 11 March 2020," March 11, 2020, accessed July 22, 2022, https://www.who.int/director-general/speeches/detail/who-director-general-s-opening-remarks-at-the-media-briefing-on-covid-19---11-march-2020.
3. United Nations Office for the Coordination of Humanitarian Affairs, *Global Humanitarian Response Plan COVID-19. United Nations Coordinated Appeal April-December 2020*, March 28, 2020, accessed July 22, 2022, https://www.unocha.org/sites/unocha/files/Global-Humanitarian-Response-Plan-COVID-19.pdf.
4. Susan Sontag, *Illness as Metaphor* (London: Penguin Books, 1991), 67.
5. Debora MacKenzie, *Covid-19. The Pandemic that Never Should Have Happened, and How to Stop the Next One* (London: Bridge Street Press, 2020), 217.
6. Alex de Waal, "New Pathogen, Old Politics," in *Thinking in a Pandemic. The Crisis of Science and Policy in the Age of Covid-19*, eds. Deborah Chasman and Joshua Cohen (Cambridge, MA: Boston Review; London: Verso, 2020), 47.
7. Sara Ahmed, *What's the Use?* (Durham, NC and London: Duke University Press, 2019), 3; John Berger, *Ways of Seeing* (London: Penguin Books, 1972).

8   Raymond Williams, *Keywords. A Vocabulary of Culture and Society* (London: Fontana Press, 1976), 15 and 14.
9   Lakoff, George and Mark Johnson, *Metaphors We Live By* (Chicago, IL: University of Chicago Press, 2003), 159–160.
10 Judith Butler, *The Force of Nonviolence. An Ethico-Political Bind* (London and New York: Verso, 2020), 16. Judith Butler's book on the pandemic came out in November 2022, when this book was in the final stages of production. The book description on the publisher's website states that the book explores how the pandemic compels us to ask fundamental questions about our place in the world and that it offers an account of interdependency. See: Judith Butler, *What World Is This? A Pandemic Phenomenology* (New York: Columbia University Press, 2022).
11 Butler, 16.
12 Judith Butler and Athena Athanasiou, *Dispossession: The Performative is Political* (Cambridge: Polity Press, 2013), xi.
13 Butler and Athanasiou, 40.
14 On the concept and method of listening to images see: Tina M. Campt, *Listening to Images* (Durham, NC and London: Duke University Press, 2017).
15 Butler and Athanasiou, 40.
16 Donna J. Haraway, *When Species Meet* (Minneapolis, MN and London: University of Minnesota Press, 2008), 4; Donna J. Haraway, "SF: Science fiction, speculative fabulation, string figures, so far," *Ada: A Journal of Gender, New Media, and Technology* 3 (2013), (2013), accessed July 22, 2022, https://adanewmedia.org/2013/11/issue3-haraway/.
17 See: bell hooks, *Talking Back: Thinking Feminist, Thinking Black* (London and New York: Routledge, 2014). See also: Jasmin Zine, "Reading Muslim Women and Muslim Women Reading Back: Transnational Feminist Reading Practices, Pedagogy and Ethical Concerns," *Intercultural Education* 18, no. 4 (2007): 271–280.
18 Joan Tronto and Berenice Fisher, "Toward a Feminist Theory of Caring," in *Circles of Care: Work and Identity in Women's Lives*, eds. Emily K. Abel and Margaret K. Nelson (Albany, NY: State University of New York Press 1990), 40.
19 See for example: Hannah Arendt, "Man: A Social or Political Animal," in *The Human Condition* (Chicago, IL and London: University of Chicago Press 1998 [1958]), 22–28.
20 Tronto and Fisher, 40.

21 Nancy Fraser, "Contradictions of Capital and Care," *New Left Review* 100 (July/August 2016), 99. Fraser was one of the many critical voices on the left who spoke publicly about care in pandemic times and brought a perspective rooted in social reproduction theory to the public discussion. See for example: Nancy Fraser, "The Left and the Pandemic," podcast, September 22, 2020, accessed July 22, 2022, https://mosaik-blog.at/the-left-and-the-pandemic-nancy-fraser/. *Mosaik*, operating out of Vienna, is a blog based on solidarity counteracting the turn to right-wing politics and authoritarianism. Contributors come from civil society organizations, social movements, political parties, science, and culture. *Mosaik* is funded solely through reader donations.

22 Robert F. Service, "You may be able to spread coronavirus just by breathing, new report finds," *Science* (April 2, 2020), accessed July 22, 2022, https://www.science.org/content/article/you-may-be-able-spread-coronavirus-just-breathing-new-report-finds. *Science* dates back to 1880 and was originally started with seed money from Thomas Edison and later financial support from Alexander Graham Bell. In 1944, ownership was transferred to the *American Association for the Advancement of Science*.

23 I first introduced the idea of new global international care order in my essay "Care Feminism for Living with an Infected Planet", which was published as part of a 2020 series of corona essays, offered to the public on the website of Academy of Fine Arts Vienna and then further elaborated on this idea in two more essays published the same year. See: Elke Krasny, "Care Feminism for Living with an Infected Planet," Academy of Fine Arts Vienna (April 2020), accessed July 22, 2022, https://www.academia.edu/43164537/Care_Feminism_for_Living_with_an_Infected_Planet; Elke Krasny, "Staying with the Crisis. A Feminist Politics of Care for Living with an Infected Planet," *Escritura e Imagen* 16 (2020): 307–326; Elke Krasny, "In Sorge Bleiben: Care Feminismus für einen infizierten Planeten," in *Die Corona-Gesellschaft. Analysen zur Lage und Perspektiven für die Zukunft*, eds. Michael Volkmer and Karin Werner (Bielefeld: transcript, 2020), 405–414.

24 I am grateful to conversations with feminist scholar of care Riikka Prattes and her untiring commitment to and insistence on care as knowledge.

25 I follow the notion of "the Enlightenment figure Man" as introduced by feminist anthropologist Anna Tsing. Anna Tsing, "Earth Stalked by Man," *The Cambridge Journal of Anthropology* 34, no. 1 (2016): 3.

26 World Health Organization, "14.9 million excess deaths associated with the Covid-19 pandemic in 2020 and 2021," May 5, 2020, accessed July 22, 2022, https://www.who.int/news/item/05-05-2022-14.9-million-excess-deaths-were-associated-with-the-covid-19-pandemic-in-2020-and-2021.
27 Haraway, *When Species Meet*, 3.
28 Haraway, 71.
29 Donna J. Haraway, *Staying with the Trouble. Making Kin in the Chthulucene* (Durham, NC and London: Duke University Press, 2016), 2.

Chapter 1: We Are at War

1 United Nations, "Declare War on this Virus – UN Chief on the Coronavirus Covid-19," speech by António Guterres, in the UN Video Repository, March 13, 2020, accessed July 22, 2022, https://videos.un.org/en/2020/03/13/declare-war-on-this-virus-u-n-chief-on-the-coronavirus-covid-19-13-march-2020/.
2 United Nations, "Declare War on this Virus," March 13, 2020.
3 United Nations Secretary General, "Transcript of the Secretary General's virtual press encounter on the appeal for global ceasefire," March 23, 2020, accessed July 22, 2022, https://www.un.org/sg/en/content/sg/press-encounter/2020-03-23/transcript-of-the-secretary-generals-virtual-press-encounter-the-appeal-for-global-ceasefire.
4 United Nations Secretary General, "Transcript," March 23, 2020.
5 United Nations Secretary General, "Transcript," March 23, 2020.
6 Alex de Waal, *New Pandemics, Old Politics: Two Hundred Years of War on Disease and its Alternatives* (Cambridge: Polity, 2021), 2.
7 Stephanie Foote and Jeffrey Jerome Cohen, "Introduction: Climate Change/Changing Climates," in *The Cambridge Companion to Environmental Humanities*, eds. Stephanie Foote and Jeffrey Jerome Cohen (Cambridge: Cambridge University Press 2021), 2.
8 Cynthia Enloe, *The Curious Feminist. Searching for Women in a New Age of Empire* (Berkeley, CA: University of California Press, 2004) 3, quoted in Annick T.R. Wibben, "Introduction: Feminists Study War," in *Researching War: Feminist Methods, Ethics and Politics*, ed. Annick T.R. Wibben (New York and London: Routledge, 2016), 4.

9 António Guterres, "Remarks at 2019 Climate Action Summit," September 23, 2019, accessed July 22, 2022, https://www.un.org/sg/en/content/sg/speeches/2019-09-23/remarks-2019-climate-action-summit.
10 Guterres, "Remarks," September 23, 2019.
11 In December 2013, Emile Ouamouno, a small child who lived in a village in the forests of southeast Guinea, died of Ebola after playing in the hollow of a fruit tree which was home to fruit bats, from which the zoonotic virus can be transmitted to humans. Ouamouno is considered the first victim of the 2013–2016 Ebola epidemic. Frank M. Snowden, historian of medicine with a particular focus on epidemics, explains that the spillover had a "complex gestation", which we have to understand as part of the Anthropocene condition. Contrary to the common media portrayal of the "forested region" where Ouamouno played in a tree close to his home, as "virgin forest" or "remote", these forests had been thoroughly globalized and were "deeply integrated into world markets from the closing decades of the twentieth century through thick and overlapping networks of trade, investment, mining, logging, and agrobusiness." Snowden explains that the "areas where Ebola outbreaks have occurred since 1976 map perfectly onto the geography of deforestation in Central and West Africa." Before the arrival of agrobusiness, which after excessive land grabbing and deforestation transformed the land into large-scale oil palm plantations, the "bats normally roosted high in the forest canopy, far from human activities." Because of capitalist forestry, the bats' homes, humans, and bats were forced into closer proximity to one another. See: Frank M. Snowden, "SARS and Ebola," in *Epidemics and Society: From the Black Death to the Present* (New Haven, CT and London: Yale University Press, 2020), 474–481.
12 I capitalize "Man" and "His" following feminist anthropologist Anna Tsing, who introduced this strategy of capitalization of Man as a feminist analytic to mark patriarchal dominance under the banner of modern Enlightenment. The latter represents the materialization of power through the hegemony of the idea of Man and the realities of colonial sexist and racist capitalism that were created and supported by Enlightenment modernity. See: Anna Tsing, "Earth Stalked by Man," *The Cambridge Journal of Anthropology* 34, no. 1 (2016): 3. *The Cambridge Journal of Anthropology* was started in 1973 at the Department of Social Anthropology at Cambridge University. Since 2020, the journal is Open Access as part of the BerghahnOpenAnthro initiative. Berghahn books is a global publisher of academic books

founded by Marion Berghahn in 1994 and operates out of New York and Oxford.
13   United Nations, *Declare War on this Virus*, March 13, 2020.
14   Steven Erlanger, "Macron Declares France 'at War' With Virus, as E.U. Proposes 30-Day Travel Ban," *New York Times*, March 16, 2020, accessed July 22, 2022, https://www.nytimes.com/2020/03/16/world/europe/coronavirus-france-macron-travel-ban.html. For a political theoretical analysis see: Matthias Lehtinen and Tuukka Brunila, "A Political Ontology of the Pandemic: Sovereign Power and the Management of Affects through the Political Ontology of War," *Frontiers in Political Science* (July 28, 2021), accessed July 22, 2022, https://doi.org/10.3389/fpos.2021.674076. *Frontiers in Political Science* is a peer-reviewed interdisciplinary journal with a focus on the theory and practice of governments and political systems. It provides open access to all of its research publications. It is part of *Frontiers Media*, operating out of Lausanne since 2007.
15   As stated in the introduction, the formation of international organizations, institutions of global political and economic governance, institutions of international law as well as intergovernmental fora almost always took place in response to conditions of crisis. The history of the G20, which focuses on global economic growth and the global financial system, perfectly illustrates that this intergovernmental forum is a crisis-response institution. The G20 was formed in response to the global economic crisis in the late 1990s. Over the 1990s, a series of deep crises affected a number of countries including Finland, Sweden, Mexico, Thailand, Indonesia, Hong Kong, Laos, Malaysia, the Philippines, Singapore, South Korea, Taiwan, Vietnam, Japan, Russia, Brazil, and Turkey. In 1999, the intergovernmental forum of the G7 Group of Seven including Canada, France, Germany, Italy, Japan, the United Kingdom, and the United States, which had been founded in response to the economic crisis of the 1970s oil shock, decided to expand its forum to 20 members. The G20 Group of Twenty includes the following countries: Argentina, Australia, Brazil, Canada, China, France, Germany, India, Indonesia, Italy, Japan, the Republic of Korea, Mexico, Russia, Saudi Arabia, South Africa, Turkey, the United Kingdom, and the United States, along with the European Union. The 2008 global financial crisis escalated the G20 to summit level. For a detailed chronological account and theoretical analysis of the international relations in this informal forum that presents a new model of global crisis response and governance through leader

level summits, see: John R. Kirton, *G20 Governance for a Globalized World* (London and New York: Routledge, 2016).

16 World Health Organization, "WHO Director General's remarks at the G20 Extraordinary Leaders' Summit on Covid-19 – 26 March 2020," accessed August 19, 2021, https://www.who.int/director-general/speeches/detail/who-director-general-s-remarks-at-the-g20-extraordinary-leaders-summit-on-covid-19---26-march-2020.

17 Interpressnews, "WHO Director-General: We are at war with a virus that threatens to tear us apart," *Interpressnews*, March 27, 2020, accessed July 22, 2022, https://www.interpressnews.ge/en/article/106515-who-director-general-we-are-at-war-with-a-virus-that-threatens-to-tear-us-apart-if-we-let-it/. InterPressNews was founded in 2000 in Georgia with the stated aim of providing accurate, balanced and objective information.

18 John Cadham, "Covid-19 and Climate Change," *Center for International Governance Innovation* August 24, 2020, accessed July 22, 2022, https://www.cigionline.org/articles/covid-19-and-climate-change/. The Canada-based Center for International Governance Innovation was founded in 2001 and created through a $30-million endowment, including $20 million from Jim Balsillie and $10 million from Mike Lazaridis, co-CEOs of Research in Motion (BlackBerry). Two years later, this think-tank received match funding from the Canadian Department of Foreign Affairs and International Trade. This independent Center for International Governance Innovation produces peer-reviewed research with the aim of providing a basis for policy innovation in global issues at the intersection of technology and international governance.

19 The moving of viruses from one species to another is called a spillover event or spillover infection. In 2013, science writer David Quammen, who warns that ecological disruption causes spillover, published a book-length investigation on how human diseases originate in animals. See: David Quammen, *Spillover. Animal Infections and the Next Human Pandemic* (New York and London: W.W. Norton & Company, 2013).

20 The founding of this global health organization in 1948 responded to the aftermath of World War II. Its constitution had been adopted by the International Health Conference held in New York in 1946.

21 Deutsche Welle, "World Health Assembly: UN chief says globe is 'at war' with COVID," *Deutsche Welle*, May 24, 2021, accessed July 22, 2022, https://www.dw.com/en/world-health-assembly-un-chief-says-globe-is-at-war-with-covid/a-57638308. Deutsche Welle is a German, state-owned

international broadcaster, which was founded in 1953. Deutsche Welle broadcasts in 32 languages.
22 World Health Organization, "The Seventy-Fourth World Health Assembly closes," May 31, 2021, accessed July 22, 2022, https://www.who.int/news/item/31-05-2021-the-seventy-fourth-world-health-assembly-closes.
23 Joshua Kretzer, *Resolve in International Politics* (Princeton, NJ: Princeton University Press, 2016), 1.
24 Trisha Greenhalgh, "Will Evidence-Based Medicine Survive Covid-19," in *Thinking in a Pandemic. The Crisis of Science and Policy in the Age of Covid-19*, eds. Deborah Chasman and Joshua Cohen (Cambridge, MA: Boston Review; London: Verso Books, 2020), 145.
25 Carl von Clausewitz, *On War*, eds. and trans. Michael Howard and Peter Paret (Princeton, NJ: Princeton University Press, 1989), 85.
26 Clausewitz, 75.
27 Constanza Musu, "War metaphors used for Covid-19 are compelling, but also dangerous," *The Conversation* (April 8, 2020), accessed July 22, 2022, https://theconversation.com/war-metaphors-used-for-covid-19-are-compelling-but-also-dangerous-135406. *The Conversation* was started in 2011, is available in English, French, Spanish and Indonesian. Operation out of Melbourne, this network of not-for profit media outlets publishes, news, academic research, analysis, and opinion pieces.
28 Alex de Waal, "New Pathogen, Old Politics," in *Thinking in a Pandemic. The Crisis of Science and Policy in the Age of Covid-19*, eds. Deborah Chasman and Joshua Cohen (Cambridge, MA Boston Review; London: Verso, 2020), 47. *Boston Review* is a quarterly that was originally founded as *New Boston Review* in 1975. Operating as a non-profit, the *Boston Review* co-published *Thinking in a Pandemic* with Verso Books, a left-wing publishing house, which was founded in 1970 by the *New Left Review* and has offices in London and New York.
29 Simon Tisdall, "Lay off those war metaphors, world leaders. You could be the next casualty," *Guardian*, March 21, 2020, accessed July 22, 2022, https://www.theguardian.com/commentisfree/2020/mar/21/donald-trump-boris-johnson-coronavirus.
30 Lawrence Freedman, "Coronavirus and the language of war," *New Statesman* (April 11, 2020), accessed July 22, 2022, https://www.newstatesman.com/science-tech/2020/04/coronavirus-and-language-war. *The New Statesman* is a London-based cultural and political journal that dates back

to 1913 and was historically connected to the Fabian Society, a British socialist organization.
31 Constanza Musu, "War metaphors used for Covid-19 are compelling, but also dangerous," *The Conversation* (April 8, 2020), accessed July 22, 2022, https://theconversation.com/war-metaphors-used-for-covid-19-are-compelling-but-also-dangerous-135406.
32 Musu, "War metaphors," (April 8, 2020).
33 Musu, "War metaphors," (April 8, 2020).
34 *Una Voce di Agamben*, accessed July 22, 2022, https://www.quodlibet.it/una-voce-giorgio-agamben. The Italian publishing house Quodlibet was founded in Macerata in 1993 by a group of students of Giorgio Agamben with a focus on philosophy.
35 Carl Schmitt, *Political Theology: Four Chapters on the Concept of Sovereignty*, trans. George Schwab (Chicago, IL: University of Chicago Press, 2005), 7
36 Schmitt, *Political Theology*, 13.
37 Giorgio Agamben, *Where Are We Now? The Epidemics as Politics*, trans. Valeria Dani (Lanham, MA: Rowman & Littlefield, 2021), 9.
38 Agamben, 49 and 41. I am well aware of the historical imperial, colonial, fascist, racist, and sexist violence of Western medicine, which forms part of a cruel hierarchy of bodies and can be understood as one expression of the ongoing war on the marginalized and disenfranchised. My argument here is concerned with an emergent ideology of freedom as a new-old ethics of supremacist carelessness and reckless hyper-individualism.
39 Agamben, 49 and 41.
40 Agamben, 49 and 41.
41 World Health Organization, "Infodemic," accessed July 22, 2022, https://www.who.int/health-topics/infodemic#tab=tab_1.
42 Carlo Salzani, "Covid-19 and State of Exception: Medicine, Politics and the Epidemic State," The Paris Institute for Critical Thinking, March 12, 2021, accessed July 22, 2022, https://parisinstitute.org/depictions-article-covid-19-and-state-of-exception-medicine-politics-and-the-epidemic-state/. The Paris Institute for Critical Thinking was founded in 2018. This non-profit and volunteer-run organization pushes back against the massification and corporatization of university education and aims to create a public space for education in the humanities and arts. Seeking ultimately to make access to their educational offers free by having a membership-based structure, their enrollment fees go directly to their instructors to ensure fair payment.

43 Salzani, March 12, 2021.
44 Darren Loucaides, Alessio Perrone, and Josef Holnburger, "How Germany became ground zero for the Covid infodemic," *openDemocracy*, March 31, 2021, accessed July 22, 2022, https://www.opendemocracy.net/en/germany-ground-zero-covid-infodemic-russia-far-right/. *openDemocracy* is a UK-based political website that seeks to foster and promote democratic debate. Its funding is provided by the Charles Stewart Mott Foundation, the Open Society Foundation, the Ford Foundation, and the Joseph Rowntree Charitable Trust, among others.
45 Lydia Gall, "Hungary's Orbán Uses Pandemic to Seize Unlimited Power," *Human Rights Watch*, March, 23, 2020, accessed July 22, 2022, https://www.hrw.org/news/2020/03/23/hungarys-orban-uses-pandemic-seize-unlimited-power. Human Rights Watch was founded in 1978. This international non-governmental organization with headquarters in New York refuses any government funding. It currently comprises 450 people of over 70 nationalities.
46 Council of Europe, "Secretary General writes to Viktor Orbán regarding Covid-19 state of emergency in Hungary, Council of Europe," March 24, 2020, accessed July 22, 2022, https://www.coe.int/en/web/portal/-/secretary-general-writes-to-victor-orban-regarding-covid-19-state-of-emergency-in-hungary-.
47 Council of Europe, "Secretary General writes to Viktor Orbán," 2020.
48 ICNL and ECN L, *Covid-19 Civic Freedom Tracker*, accessed July 22, 2022, https://www.icnl.org/covid19tracker/.
49 Arendt, *The Human Condition*, 199.
50 Sontag, *Illness as Metaphor*, 59.
51 Lyndon Baines Johnson, *"First State of the Union Address,"* delivered January 8, 1964, accessed July 22, 2022, https://www.americanrhetoric.com/speeches/lbj1964stateoftheunion.htm.
52 Sontag, 59.
53 de Waal, "New Pathogen, Old Politics", 31.
54 See: Hirsch Ballin, Ernst, Dijstelbloem, and Huub, de Goede, Peter, "The Extension of the Concept of Security," in *Security in an Interconnected World. Research for Policy*, eds. Ernst Hirsch Ballin, Huub Dijstelbloem, and Peter de Goede (Cham: Springer 2020), 19.
55 Snowden, *Epidemics and Society*, 467 and 469.
56 Omer Bartov, "Man and the Mass: Reality and the Heroic Image in War," *History and Memory* 1, no. 2 (Fall-Winter 1989), 99. The double-blind peer-

reviewed journal *History and Memory. Studies in Representation of the Past* is edited by the School of Graduate Historical Studies at Tel Aviv University. Founded in 1989, it covers the study of historical consciousness and collective memory and has counted Saul Friedländer and Dan Diner among its editors.

57 Jill H. Casid, "Handle with Care," *The Drama Review* 56, no. 4 (Winter 2012): 125. *The Drama Review* was founded in 1955 and, since 2021, the quarterly journal is published by Cambridge University Press. Promoting an expanded understanding of drama, the journal includes analyses of performance and ritual in relation to politics and everyday life. Richard Schechner has been highly influential to the direction of the journal.

58 Carla Macchiavello, "Caring, Curiosity and Curating. Beyond the End," *Seismopolite. Journal of Art and Politics* (July 1, 2015), accessed July 22, 2022, http://www.seismopolite.com/caring-curiosity-and-curating-beyond-the-end. *Seismopolite* is a Norwegian-English quarterly. It was launched in 2011 and is published by the Arts Council Norway. The focus is on art-making worldwide, with a specific interest in how artists respond to local political situations.

59 Haraway, *When Species Meet*, 36.

60 Erin Manning, "Review of Posthuman and Political Care Ethics for Reconfiguring Higher Education Pedagogies," accessed July 22, 2022, https://www.routledge.com/Posthuman-and-Political-Care-Ethics-for-Reconfiguring-Higher-Education/Bozalek-Zembylas-Tronto/p/book/9780367619060.

61 Heinz Steinert, "The Indispensable Metaphor of War: On Populist Politics and the Contradictions of the State's Monopoly of Force," *Theoretical Criminology* (August 1, 2003) accessed July 22, 2022, https://doi.org/10.1177/13624806030073002. The journal *Theoretical Criminology* was established in 1997 and focuses on criminological theorization based in empirical and theoretical approaches in relation to developments in social, cultural, and political theory. It is published by the global academic publisher SAGE publications.

62 PBS News Hour, "WHO report finds nearly 15 million deaths associated with Covid-19 worldwide," May 5, 2022, accessed July 22, 2022, https://www.pbs.org/newshour/show/who-report-finds-nearly-15-million-deaths-associated-with-covid-19-worldwide.

63 Women's International League for Peace and Freedom, "WILPF's approach: Feminist Peace," accessed July 22, 2022, https://www.peacewom

en.org/why-WPS/solutions/integrated-approach. The beginnings of the Women's International League for Peace and Freedom can be traced back to the International Congress of Women held in The Hague in 1915. The name was chosen in 1919, and today this non-profit non-governmental organization, which has a United Nations Office in New York, works for permanent peace. WILPF presents one of many examples of feminist activism within the structures of the United Nations. See: Wikipedia: "Women's International League for Peace," Wikipedia, last edited July 30, 2021, https://en.wikipedia.org/wiki/Women%27s_International_League _for_Peace_and_Freedom.

64 Andrew Smiler, *Is Masculinity Toxic?* (London: Thames & Hudson, 2019). Smiler's book is part of the London-based publisher Thames and Hudson's series The Big Ideas. The books in this series are described as primers for the 21st century, offering introductions to some of the most complex and densest concerns of our time and intended for a general audience. Themes addressed include capitalism, democracy, gender, and space.

65 Smiler, 13.

66 Julia Moses, "Social Citizenship and Social Rights in an Age of Extremes: T.H. Marshall's Social Philosophy in the Longue Durée," *Modern Intellectual History* 16, no. 1 (April 2019): 155–184. The journal *Modern Intellectual History* is published by Cambridge University Press and focuses on the history of ideas through analysis of the context and reception of texts published since the mid-seventeenth century.

67 Joan Tronto, *Caring Democracy. Markets, Equality, and Justice* (New York and London: New York University Press, 2013), 26.

68 Tronto, 25.

69 See: Richard Bean, "War and the Birth of the Nation State," *The Journal of Economic History* 33, no. 1 (March 1973): 203–221, accessed July 22, 2022, https://www.cambridge.org/core/journals/journal-of-economic-histo ry/article/abs/war-and-the-birth-of-the-nation-state/420A5525071101 201C94B49FB7ABE8DA. *The Journal of Economic History* was founded in 1941. It is published by Cambridge University Press and characterized by quantitative and statistical approaches.

70 De Waal, "New Pathogen, Old Politics," 33.

71 María Cristina Santana, "From Empowerment to Domesticity: The Case of Rosie the Riveter and the WWII Campaign," *Frontiers in Sociology* 1 (2016), accessed July 22, 2022, https://www.frontiersin.org/articles/10. 3389/fsoc.2016.00016/full. *Frontiers in Sociology* is part of an interdisci-

plinary, community-based publishing platform founded in 2007 by the two neuroscientists Henry and Kamila Markram. Based on a model of private investment and article processing charges, *Frontiers* provides an open access model. In 2016, *Frontiers in Sociology* was launched as the first social-sciences journal of the Frontiers open science platform.
72   Wikipedia, "Home front during World War I," *Wikipedia*, last edited July 17, 2021, https://en.wikipedia.org/wiki/Home_front_during_World_War_I.
73   Isabelle Geuskens, "Introduction," in *Gender and Militarism. Analyzing the Links to Strategize for Peace*, eds. Isabelle Geuskens, Merle Gosewinkel, and Sophie Schellens (The Hague: Women Peacemakers Program, 2014), 4.
74   Judith Butler, *Precarious Life. The Powers of Mourning and Violence* (London and New York: Verso, 2004), xii. Ella Myers focuses on the questions of ethics and the ontological dimensions of vulnerability in her chapter on "Levinasian Ethics, Charity, and Democracy". See: Ella Myers, *Worldly Ethics. Democratic Politics and Care for the World* (Durham and London: Duke University Press, 2013), 85–110.
75   Judith Butler, *Frames of War. When is Life Grievable?* (London and New York: Verso 2009), 43.
76   Butler, *Precarious Life*, 31.
77   Butler, *Frames of War*, 43.
78   Tronto, *Caring Democracy*, 72.
79   Achille Mbembe, "The society of enmity," *Radical Philosophy* (Nov/Dec 2016), accessed July 22, 2022, https://www.radicalphilosophy.com/article/the-society-of-enmity?fbclid=IwAR0Ty4cfy-DgS_oRazPdKhYdPxdpKrERkk48WJ-bIi32HRED5xGHqnGl1-k. Radical Philosophy is a left-wing journal that began as a self-publishing endeavor in Britain in 1972. The bimonthly academic journal continues to operate outside of corporate publishing and appears three times per year in print form, but also makes freely available online all its content including all its back issues.
80   On the erosion of sleep see, for example: Jonathan Crary, 24/7. *Late Capitalism and the Ends of Sleep*. (London: Verso, 2014). Rob Nixon has provided an example of lack of sleep combined with lack of access to light for studying at night: Niger Delta villages where children, for decades, had no access to electricity for studying at night, while above their communities Shell's gas flares created toxic nocturnal illumination. Too dark for education, too bright for sleep: modernity's false dawn. Rob Nixon, *Slow Violence and*

the *Environmentalism of the Poor* (Cambridge, MA: Harvard University Press, 2011), 42.
81 Anna Tsing, "Earth Stalked by Man," *The Cambridge Journal of Anthropology* 34, no. 1 (2016): 3.
82 See: Elizabeth Povinelli, *Geontologies. A Requiem to Late Liberalism* (Durham, NC and London: Duke University Press, 2016), 18.
83 Povinelli, 48.
84 In the context of living with an infected planet caused by the historical consequences of Man's exceptionalism, which define the hierarchical scale of care, it is relevant that Povinelli observed that the virus precisely draws into question the distinction between "Life" and "Nonlife". See: Povinelli, *Geontologies*, 19.
85 See: Anna Tsing, "A Feminist Approach to the Anthropocene: Earth Stalked by Man" (Helen Pond McIntyre '48 Lecture at Barnard College, November 10, 2015), accessed July 22, 2022, https://vimeo.com/149475243; Carolyn Merchant, *The Death of Nature. Women, Ecology, and the Scientific Revolution* (San Francisco, CA: Harper & Row, 1980).
86 Tsing, "A Feminist Approach to the Anthropocene" (November 10, 2015).
87 Merchant, 271.
88 See: Merchant, 1980.
89 Paul J. Crutzen and Eugene F. Stoermer, "The 'Anthropocene'," *Global Change Newsletter* 41 (May 2000): 17–18. The *Global Change Newsletter* is the quarterly newsletter of the International Geosphere-Biosphere Programme, IGBP, which is sponsored by the International Council for Science. In 2009, it changed its name to *Global Change Magazine*.
90 Jeff Tolleson, "Why deforestation and extinctions make pandemics more likely," *Nature* (August 7, 2020), accessed July 22, 2022, https://www.nature.com/articles/d41586-020-02341-1. Nature is a peer-reviewed British weekly scientific journal, which was started in 1869. The focus of the articles is on science and technology.
91 Ella Myers, *Worldly Ethics. Democratic Politics and Care for the World* (Durham, NC and London: Duke University Press, 2013), 6.

Chapter 2: Serving at the Frontlines

1 Concurrently with the pandemic outbreak and pandemic developments, researchers began to collect and collate data comparing policy responses

and measures taken by governments to slow the spread of the virus around the world. One such example, ongoing at time of writing, is the *Covid-19 Government Response Tracker* by the Blavatnik School of Government and the University of Oxford. Covering more than 180 countries to provide information on data to decision-makers and citizens, the project's aim is "aiding efforts to fight (sic!) the pandemic." See: Covid-19 Government Response Tracker, accessed July 22, 2022, https://www.bsg.ox.ac.uk/research/research-projects/covid-19-government-response-tracker.

2   Kristalina Georgieva, "Transcript of Kristalina Georgieva's Participation in the World Health Organization Press Briefing," *International Monetary Fund*, April 3, 2020, accessed July 22, 2022, https://www.imf.org/en/News/Articles/2020/04/03/tr040320-transcript-kristalina-georgieva-participation-world-health-organization-press-briefing. The International Monetary Fund is a United Nations specialized agency and an international financial institution. It was funded at the Bretton Woods Conference in July 1944. The aim of this conference was to regulate the international monetary and financial order in the aftermath of World War II.

3   Chris Giles, "Global economy set for sharpest reversal since Great Depression," *Financial Times*, April 3, 2020, accessed July 22, 2022, https://www.ft.com/content/19d2e456-0943-42fc-9d2d-73318eee0f6ab; Associated Press, Deccan Chronicle "Coronavirus pandemic has brought world economy to a standstill: IMF," *Deccan Chronicle*, (April 3, 2020), accessed July 22, 2022, https://www.deccanchronicle.com/business/economy/030420/coronavirus-pandemic-has-brought-world-economy-to-a-standstill-imf.html. *The Financial Times* is a British daily newspaper, which was established in 1888. Operating out of London, it is owned by Nikkei Inc. and The Financial Times Group. Nikkei Inc. is a Japanese media company focusing on newspaper publishing. It dates back to 1876. The Financial Times Group publishes news on business. This media company dates back to 1888. *The Deccan Chronicle* is an Indian English-language daily newspaper, which dates back to the 1930s and is currently owned by Samagrah Commercial Pvt Limited, an Indian Non-Government Company, which was registered in 2018.

4   Ahmed Gurhan Kartal, "World on Standstill: Covid-19 deals major blow to life as we know it," *Anadolu Agency*, March 23, 2020, accessed July 22, 2022, https://www.aa.com.tr/en/health/world-on-standstill-covid-19-de

als-major-blow-to-life-as-we-know-it/1775711. *Anadolu Agency* is a Turkish state-run news agency operating out of Ankara. It was established in 1920.

5   See for example: Amelia Cheatham et al., "The Year the Earth stood still," *Council on Foreign Relations*, December 7, 2020, accessed July 22, 2022, https://www.cfr.org/article/2020-year-earth-stood-still-covid-19. The Council on Foreign Relations is a membership organization operating out of New York. This think tank and publisher was founded in 1921. In the 1930s, the Ford Foundation and the Rockefeller Foundation began to largely fund the Council of Foreign Relations.

6   Williams, *Keywords*, 15.

7   Among many others: International Domestic Workers Federation, https://idwfed.org; International Council of Nurses, https://www.icn.ch; Nurses International, https://nursesinternational.org; Território Domestico, https://www.facebook.com/territoriodomestico/; Women's Global Strike, http://womensglobalstrike.com; women strike – Transnational Social Strike, https://www.transnational-strike.info/article/tag/women-strike/.

8   UN Women, "Care Work. Increased burdens for women. Covid-19. Rebuilding for Resilience," accessed July 22, 2022, https://www.unwomen.org/en/hq-complex-page/covid-19-rebuilding-for-resilience/care-work.

9   Karl Marx, *Capital. A Critique of Political Economy. Volume 1: The Process of Capitalist Production* (London: Swan Sonnenschein, Lowrey & Co, 1887), xix.

10 Marx, *Capital*, 1887, 412–13, quoted in Mark Dickman, "Marx's Metaphor," *Redwedge* (November 12, 2014), accessed July 22, 2022, http://www.redwedgemagazine.com/essays/marxs-metaphor. *Redwedge* magazine is a socialist publication with a focus on the intersection of art and political struggle from a radical perspective. It was started in 2012 by comrades of the ISO, International Socialist Organization –US, which was dissolved in 2019.

11 Marx, 549.

12 Laura Sjoberg, *Gendering Global Conflict. Toward a Feminist Theory of War* (New York: Columbia University Press, 2013), 171.

13 Sjoberg, 171.

14 The notion of sentipensar, feeling-thinking, was described by Colombian sociologist Orlando Fals Borda as part of Indigenous epistemologies of communities in the Caribbean coastal region of Colombia. See: Orlando

Fals Borda, *Una sociología sentipensante para América Latina* (Bogota: Clacso and Siglo de Hombre Editores, 2009).
15 For keyimage as an analytical concept see: Elke Gaugele and Elke Krasny, "Von Figurationen der Verfolgung. Der *Sklavenmarkt* von Jean-Léon Gérôme (1866) im rechtsextremen Wahlkampf der AfD," in *Rechte Angriffe – toxische Effekte. Umformierungen extrem Rechter in Mode, Feminismus und Popkultur*, eds. Elke Gaugele and Sarah Held (Bielefeld: transcript, 2021), 129–159.
16 This book is interested in the pandemic gaze and the politics of pandemic vision under Covid-19 conditions, but the analytical framework of the pandemic gaze is, of course, useful to analyzing the visuality of other pandemics and endemics.
17 On the concept of the working classes as the caring classes see: David Graeber, "Caring too much. That's the curse of the working classes," *Guardian*, March 26, 2014, accessed July 22, 2022, https://www.theguardian.com/commentisfree/2014/mar/26/caring-curse-working-class-austerity-solidarity-scourge.
18 Stuart Hall, "A 'Reading' of Karl Marx Introduction to the Grundrisse," *Centre for Cultural Studies* (Birmingham: University of Birmingham 1973), 7.
19 Hall, 7.
20 Londa Schiebinger, "Why Mammals are Called Mammals: Gender Politics in Eighteenth-Century Natural History," *The American Historical Review* 98, no. 2 (April 1993): 382–411. *The American Historical Review* is an academic journal, which was founded in 1895 and is published by the American Historical Association.
21 Schiebinger, 409.
22 Care scholar Riikka Prattes focuses her feminist inquiry on questions of care, masculinity and knowledge. Riikka Prattes, "'I don't clean up after myself': epistemic ignorance, responsibility and the politics of the outsourcing of domestic cleaning," *Feminist Theory* 21, no 1. (2020): 25, accessed July 22, 2022, https://doi.org/10.1177/1464700119842560. *Feminist Theory* is a peer-reviewed journal in the field of women's studies. Initiated in the year 2000, the journal is published by Sage Publications, a global academic publisher, founded in 1965 in New York, and currently operating out of California.
23 Tronto, *Caring Democracy*, 72ff. According to Tronto, the military protection of the nation as the duty of men gives men what she calls the protec-

tion pass so they do not have to perform care, which was historically seen as the sole responsibility of women.

24   Margaret MacMillan, *War. How Conflict Shaped Us* (London: Profile Books, 2020).

25   Teaching and Research Resources, "Maneuvers: The International Politics of Militarizing Women's Lives by Cynthia Enloe, 2000," *Critical Military Studies*, accessed July 22, 2022, https://www.criticalmilitarystudies.org/critical-military-studies-resources. See also: Cynthia Enloe, *Maneuvers. The International Politics of Militarizing Women's Lives* (Berkeley, CA: University of California Press, 2000). *Critical Military Studies* is a peer-reviewed academic journal, which was established following a 2011 conference on Military methodologies at Newcastle University. The journal focuses on interdisciplinary approaches to military power and is published by Taylor & Francis. Taylor & Francis is an international company. This global academic publisher operates out of England and dates back to 1852.

26   Madeline Morris, "By force of arms: rape, war, and military culture," *Duke Law Journal* 45, no. 4 (1996): 701, quoted in Rebecca Tapscott, "Militarized masculinity and the paradox of restraint: mechanisms of social control under modern authoritarianism," *International Affairs* 96, no. 6 (November 2020): 1565–1584, accessed July 22, 2022, https://academic.oup.com/ia/article/96/6/1565/5912451. *International Affairs* is an academic journal on international relations. It was founded in 1922 and is currently published by Chatham House, an independent policy institute, which dates back to 1920. Headquartered in London, the policy institute is also known under the name The Royal Institute of International Affairs.

27   Regina Titunik, "The myth of the macho military," *Polity* 40, no. 2 (2008): 137–63, quoted in Rebecca Tapscott, "Militarized masculinity and the paradox of restraint: mechanisms of social control under modern authoritarianism," *International Affairs* 96, no. 6 (November 2020): 1565–1584, https://doi.org/10.1093/ia/iiaa163. *Polity* is the journal of the Northeastern Political Science Association. It has been published quarterly since 1968 by the University of Chicago Press.

28   Covid-19 lockdowns, accessed July 22, 2022, https://en.wikipedia.org/wiki/COVID-19_lockdowns.

29   See: Falko Schmieder, "A Time-Out for Some Self-critical Reflection. 'All the wheels shall stand still," *Goethe Institut*, accessed July 22, 2022, https://www.goethe.de/prj/sti/en/mit/22780732.html. The Goethe Institut is a non-profit cultural association promoting the study of the German

language and promoting cultural exchange. The first Goethe Institut opened in Athens in 1952. Today, there are 159 institutes worldwide. The refusal of workers to work continues to present a powerful threat to capitalist economies. The refusal to perform paid and unpaid care work has also been understood as a powerful threat, and is, of course, much harder to implement, as those who go on strike simultaneously have to ensure that essential care and vital functions are not at risk. One may think, here, of the historical example of the 1975 Icelandic Women's Strike and of contemporary global women's strikes. As the pandemic lasted, a growing global movement of nurses and health workers engaging in waves of strikes and holding protests emerged. See for example: Sorcha A. Brophy et al., "Heroes on Strike: Trends in Global Health Worker Protests during Covid-19," *Accountability Research Center*, April 2022, accessed July 22, 2022, https://accountabilityresearch.org/publication/heroes-on-strike-trends-in-global-health-worker-protests-during-covid-19/. The Accountability Research Center is an action-research incubator based in American University's School of International Service. It is funded by, among others, the Open Society Foundation, the MacArthur Foundation and EducationOutLoud.

30   See: Jonathan Crary, *24/7. Late Capitalism and the Ends of Sleep* (London: Verso, 2014).

31   Associated Press, Deccan Chronicle, "Coronavirus pandemic has brought world economy to a standstill: IMF," *Deccan Chronicle*, April 3, 2020, accessed July 22, 2022, https://www.deccanchronicle.com/business/economy/030420/coronavirus-pandemic-has-brought-world-economy-to-a-standstill-imf.html.

32   Medline Plus, "Viral Infections," accessed July 22, 2022, https://medlineplus.gov/viralinfections.html.

33   Karl Marx, *Capital: A Critique of Political Economy*, vol. 1, trans. Ben Fowkes (New York, Penguin Books, 1976), 275.

34   Marx, 272.

35   In recent years, social reproduction theory has been reenergized in feminist struggles, in feminist social movements, and in feminist theory. See for example: Cinzia Arruzza, Tithi Bhattacharya, and Nancy Fraser, *Feminism for the 99%. A Manifesto* (London: Verso, 2019); Tithi Bhattacharya, ed. *Social Reproduction Theory: Remapping Class, Recentering Oppression* (London: Pluto Press, 2017).

36 See for example: Susan Ferguson, *Women and Work. Labour and Social Reproduction* (London: Pluto Press, 2019); Peer Illner, *Disasters and Social Reproduction. Crisis Response between the State and Community* (London: Pluto, 2020). Pluto Press is a radical publishing house in London, which was founded in 1969.

37 Marx, *Capital*, 275.

38 Beata Mostafavi, "Moms on the Frontline," *Michigan Health*, May 8, 2020, accessed July 22, 2022, https://healthblog.uofmhealth.org/lifestyle/moms-on-frontline. This blog is run by Michigan Medicine at the University of Michigan.

39 Joanna Soszyńska-Budny, *Analysis of Critical Infrastructure: Impact of Operation Processes and Climate Change* (Cham: Springer, 2021), 52.

40 European Commission, "Critical Infrastructure," accessed July 22, 2022, https://home-affairs.ec.europa.eu/pages/page/critical-infrastructure_en. The European Commission is the executive of the European Union and was founded in January 1958.

41 U.S. Department of Homeland Security, "Advisory Memorandum on Ensuring Essential Critical Infrastructure Workers' Ability to Work during the Covid-19 Response," August 10, 2021, accessed July 22, 2022, https://www.cisa.gov/sites/default/files/publications/essential_critical_infrastructure_workforce-guidance_v4.1_508.pdf. The United States Department of Homeland Security is responsible for public security and was founded in November 2002. It is similar to ministries of the interior in other countries.

42 Debora MacKenzie, *Covid-19. The Pandemic that Never Should Have Happened, and How to Stop the Next One* (London: The Bridge Street Press, 2020), 201–202.

43 Helena Hoffmann and Mina Draganska for the European Parliament, "Revaluation of working conditions and wages for essential workers," January 2022, accessed July 22, 2022, https://www.europarl.europa.eu/RegData/etudes/ATAG/2022/703344/IPOL_ATA(2022)703344_EN.pdf. The European Parliament is one of the legislative bodies of the European Union and was established in March 1958.

44 Lindsay M. Monte and Linda Laughlin for the Social, Economic and Housing Statistics Division at the U.S. Census Bureau, "Essential, Frontline & High Risk: How Covid-19 Prioritized Low-wage Workers while Heightening their Disadvantage" (paper presented at the Population Association of America April 6–9, 2022), accessed July 22, 2022, https://

www.census.gov/content/dam/Census/library/working-papers/2022/demo/sehsd-wp2022-08.pdf. The U.S. Census Bureau, established in 1902, is an agency of the U.S. Federal Statistical System, which is tasked with producing data on the American population and economy.

45 Brad Lander, "New York City's Frontline Workers," March 26, 2020, accessed July 22, 2022, https://comptroller.nyc.gov/reports/new-york-citys-frontline-workers/. The Comptroller of New York City is an office that was established in 1801. The comptroller is the city's chief financial officer and auditor.

46 MacKenzie, 202.

47 MacKenzie, 203.

48 MacKenzie, 203.

49 See: Dirk Witteven and Eva Velthorst, "Economic hardship and mental health complaints during Covid-19," *Proceedings of the National Academy of Sciences of the United States of America PNAS* 117, no. 44 (October 12, 2022), accessed October 30, 2022, https://www.pnas.org/doi/10.1073/pnas.2009609117. The *National Academy of Sciences of the United States of America* is a private non-profit organization of researchers with current members electing new members. It is not funded by the U.S. government. It dates back to 1863 and resulted from an Act of Congress approved by Abraham Lincoln.

50 Department of Defense Dictionary and Associated Terms, (United States Joint Chiefs of Staff: Washington D.C. 1987), 238. The Department of Defense was founded by Harry S. Truman in 1947, it is an executive branch department of the federal government.

51 Adrienne Bernhard, "Covid-19: What we can learn from wartime efforts," *BBC*, May 1, 2020, accessed August 19, 2021, https://www.bbc.com/future/article/20200430-covid-19-what-we-can-learn-from-wartime-efforts. BBC, the British Broadcasting Corporation, is the public owned national broadcaster of the United Kingdom. It was founded in 1922.

52 Rachel Maouyo, Bridget Noon, Barbara Hobilla, Hojung Kim and Karen Roush, "A Message from Frontline Nurses: Let's Keep the Real Enemy in Sight," *AJN American Journal of Nursing* 120, no. 8 (August 2020), accessed July 22, 2022, https://journals.lww.com/ajnonline/fulltext/2020/08000/a_message_from_frontline_nurses__let_s_keep_the.29.aspx. *The American Journal of Nursing* is a monthly peer-reviewed journal that dates back to 1900. It is published by Lippincott Williams & Wilkins, a publisher in journals of medicine and nursing.

53 Deying Hu et al., "Frontline nurses' burnout, anxiety, depression, and fear statuses and their associated factors during the COVID-19 outbreak in Wuhan, China: A large-scale cross-sectional study," *eClinicalMedicine* 24 (July 2020), accessed July 22, 2022, https://www.sciencedirect.com/science/article/pii/S2589537020301681. *eClinicalMedicine* is a peer-reviewed open access journal dedicated to clinical and public health research. It was established in 2018 and is published by *The Lancet*, a peer-reviewed medical journal, which was founded in England in 1823.

54 Growth Engineering, "12 Best Practices for Training your Frontline Staff," *Growth Engineering Engagement Online Learning*, July 20, 2022, accessed September 30, 2022, https://www.growthengineering.co.uk/how-frontline-staff-are-trained-differently-to-other-roles/. Growth Engineering is a UK-based company founded in 2004. They offer learner engagement services.

55 Growth Engineering, "12 Best Practices," 2022.

56 Michael James, "Frontline Employees: Who they are and tips for motivating them," accessed September 30, 2022, https://carreersupport.com/frontline-employees-who-they-are-and-tips-for-motivating-them/.

57 David Higgins, "Apocalypse/Extinction," in *The Cambridge Companion to Environmental Humanities*, eds. Jeffrey Jerome Cohen and Stephanie Foote (Cambridge: Cambridge University Press, 2021), 122.

58 Phumzile Mlambo-Ngcuka for UN Women "Op-ed: Women Working on the Frontline," December 23, 2020, accessed July 22, 2022, https://www.unwomen.org/en/news/stories/2020/12/op-ed-ed-phumzile-women-working-on-the-front-line. UN Women was established in 2010 by the United Nations General Assembly and is the United Nations Entity for Gender Equality and the Empowerment of Women. It is governed by a multi-tiered intergovernmental governance structure.

59 Mlambo-Ngcuka, "Op-ed," 2020.

60 Sanket Jain, "India's healthcare workers are busting misinformation on WhatsApp," *The Verge*, June 17, 2021, accessed June 3, 2022, https://www.theverge.com/22535642/covid-misinformation-india-asha-whatsapp; See also: The Model Micro Plan for containment of local transmission of Covid 19 by the Indian Government: https://www.mohfw.gov.in/pdf/ModelMicroplanforcontainmentoflocaltransmissionofCOVID19.pdf. *The Verge* is an American technology news website, which was founded in 2011. It is owned by Vox Media. Vox Media Inc. is a mass media company,

founded in 2011 by American businessman James Philip Bankoff and technologist Trei Brundrett.

61 National Health Mission, "About Accredited Social Health Activist (ASHA)," Ministry of Health and Family Welfare Government of India, accessed July 22, 2022, https://nhm.gov.in/index1.php?lang=1&level=1&sublinkid=150&lid=226. The Ministry of Health and Family Welfare in India was established in 1947. Its tasks include health policy and family planning.

62 UN Women, "In Photos: Women on the front lines of COVID-19 in India," August 17, 2021, accessed July 22, 2022, https://www.unwomen.org/en/digital-library/multimedia/2021/8/photo-essay-women-on-the-front-lines-of-covid-19-in-india.

63 India TV Tech Desk, "COVID Warriors: PM Modi introduces website to connect people with local authorities," *India TV News*, April 27, 2020, accessed June 3, 2022, https://www.indiatvnews.com/technology/news-covid-warriors-website-introduced-pm-narendra-modi-see-what-it-is-611717; http://covidwarriors.gov.in. India TV is a Hindi news channel that was established in 2004 by Rajat Sharma and Ritu Dhawan. The channel operates out of Noida in Uttar Pradesh, India.

64 India TV Tech Desk, "COVID Warriors," 2020.

65 Christa Wichterich, "Protection and Protest by 'Voluntary' Community Health Workers: Covid-19 Authoritarianism in India," *Historical Social Research HRS Forum Caring in Times of a Global Pandemic* 46, no. 178 (2021): 165.

66 Express Web Desk, "Virus may be invisible enemy but COVID warriors invincible: PM Modi," *The Indian Express*, June 1, 2020, accessed June 3, 2022, https://indianexpress.com/article/india/virus-may-be-invisible-enemy-but-covid-warriors-invincible-pm-modi-6437117/. *Indian Express* is an English-language national daily published by Indian Express Limited, a news media publishing company that was established in 1932.

67 Vidayshree S, "Women COVID Warriors Struggle to Maintain Work-life balance Amid Home-workplace Stress," *Republic World*, October 3, 2021, accessed June 3, 2022, https://www.republicworld.com/india-news/general-news/women-covid-warriors-struggle-to-maintain-work-life-balance-amid-home-workplace-stress.html. *Republic*, *Republic TV* and *Republic World*, was launched in 2017. According to their website it is India's first independent media tech company, which, as stated there, has nationalism at its core.

68 Vidayshree, 2021.
69 Wichterich, "Protection and Protest," 2021, 163.
70 Wichterich, 164.
71 Wichterich, 164.
72 Mirror online, "Violence, abuse and rude behaviour against frontline workers is not acceptable: PM Modi," June 1, 2020, accessed June 3, 2022, https://mumbaimirror.indiatimes.com/coronavirus/news/violence-abuse-and-rude-behaviour-against-front-line-workers-is-not-acceptable-pm-modi/articleshow/76130615.cms. *Mumbai Mirror* is an Indian English-language newspaper that was established in 2005. Its focus is on local news and healthcare. It is owned by the media company The Times Group.
73 Wichterich, 174.
74 Jugal Purohit, "COVID-19 India health workers' families fight for compensation," *BBC*, September 22, 2021, accessed July 22, 2022, https://www.bbc.com/news/world-asia-india-58621933.
75 Sanket Jain, "The Care Workers of Rural India are Ready to Strike," *Nation*, July 5, 2022, accessed July 22, 2022, https://www.thenation.com/article/world/india-asha-protest-covid/. *The Nation* is an American biweekly magazine that was originally founded by abolitionists in 1865.
76 EngenderHealth, "EngenderHealth Congratulates ASHA Workers for Winning the Global Health Leaders Award-2022," accessed June 3, 2022, https://www.engenderhealth.org/article/engenderhealth-congratulates-asha-workers-for-winning-the-global-health-leaders-award-2022. EngenderHealth is a non-profit organization operating out of Washington DC. It was founded in 1937 and focuses on sexual and reproductive health. EngenderHealth is active in twenty countries in Africa, Asia, and the Americas. Its founder was Marian Stephenson Olden, a eugenics activist, who was active in the sterilization movement.
77 Jagriti Chandra, "WHO honors ASHA workers for their crucial role linking community during Covid-19 pandemic," *Hindu*, May 23, 2022, accessed July 22, 2022, https://www.thehindu.com/news/national/who-honours-asha-workers-for-their-crucial-role-linking-community-during-covid-19-pandemic/article65454223.ece. *The Hindu* is an Indian English-language daily newspaper operating out of Chennai. It was founded in 1878 by Indian journalist and freedom fighter Ganapathy Dikshitar Subramania Iyer. Today it is owned by Indian publishing company The Hindu Group and Kasturi and Sons Limited, a public limited company.

78 Extractivism is the ideology behind extraction, which satisfies the resource needs of a growth-centric capitalist economy and is one of the main causes of today's climate collapse. Care extractivism is the ideology behind care extraction and can be seen as one of the main reasons behind the total and sometimes even fatal exhaustion of care workers.
79 Priyamvada Kowshik, "Women Warriors versus Covid," *Times of India*, April 23, 2022, accessed July 22, 2022, https://timesofindia.indiatimes.com/india/women-warriors-versus-covid/articleshow/81293316.cms. *The Times of India*, TOI, was founded in 1838. Today, this daily newspaper is the largest selling English-language daily worldwide, with more than 3 million copies sold every day. It has been owned since 1838 by the The Times Group, which is owned by Bennett, Coleman & Co Limited, which is owned by the Sahu Jain family.
80 Rachel Hartigan, "Photos show the world's essential workers serving on the front lines," *National Geographic* (April 23, 2020), accessed July 22, 2022, https://www.nationalgeographic.com/history/article/pictures-essential-workers-serving- world-front-lines-coronavirus. *National Geographic* is a popular American monthly published by the National Geographic Society. Known for its focus on photojournalism, it is held to be one of the most widely read magazines worldwide. It was founded in 1888. Based in Washington D.C., the journal is owned by the National Geographic Society and NG Media National Geographic Partners/Disney Publishing Worldwide.
81 Hartigan, 2020.
82 Alex de Waal, "New Pathogen, Old Politics," in *Thinking in a Pandemic. The Crisis of Science and Policy in the Age of COVID-19*, eds. Deborah Chasman and Joshua Cohen (Boston, MA: Boston Review; London: Verso Books, 2020), 47. The Boston Review is an American quarterly political and literary magazine that dates back to 1975. It publishes both analysis and fiction.
83 Hartigan, "Photos show the world's essential workers," 2020.
84 Berger, 8.
85 Andrea Dworkin, "Antifeminism," in *Right-wing Women* (New York: Perigee Books, 1983), 220.
86 Mary Romero, "An Intersection of Biography and History: My Intellectual Journey," in *Mapping the Social Landscape*. Ninth Edition, ed. Susan Ferguson (Thousand Oaks, CA: Sage Publications, 2021), 29.

87 David Katzmann, *Seven Days a Week* (Chicago, IL: University of Illinois Press, 1981), 269–70, quoted in Romero, "An Intersection of Biography and History," 29.
88 Stuart Hall, "Race, articulation and societies structured in dominance," in *Sociological theories: race and colonialism*, ed. UNESCO (UNESCO, 1980), 341, quoted in Amia Srinivasan, *The Right to Sex* (London: Bloomsbury, 2021), 226.
89 Françoise Vergès, *Un féminisme décolonial* (Paris: La fabrique 2019), 111.
90 Hartigan, 2020.
91 David Graeber, *Bullshit Jobs: A Theory* (London: Simon & Schuster, 2019), 265.
92 *Time* magazine is an American news magazine. It was started as a weekly magazine in 1923 and transitioned to every other week in March 2020. The covers of the *Time* magazine have, since 1927—when they first introduced the new concept of the Man of the Year putting aviator and military officer Charles Lindbergh on their cover—, written world history. Only in 1999 did they change the notion of *Man of the Year* to *Person of the Year*, and in 2018 *Time* magazine broadened the view on who matters to the course of world history and added the new category of *The Guardians*.
93 Jeffrey Kluger and Alice Park, "Guardians of the Year. Dr. Anthony Fauci and Frontline Health Workers," *Time* (December 2020), accessed June 3, 2022, https://time.com/guardians-of-the-year-2020-anthony-fauci-frontline-health-workers. The article was part of the *Time*'s 2020 Person of the Year issue. It invites readers to buy a print of the *Time*'s Anthony Fauci and Frontline Health Workers Guardians of the Year covers.
94 The Time Cover Store offers for purchase art prints of the *Time* covers. The 2020 Guardians of the Year Frontline Healthcare Workers Art Print is for sale online at the Time Cover Store. The image that shows the Frontline Healthcare Workers can be found at: https://timecoverstore.com/featured/2020-guardians-of-the-year-frontline-healthcare-workers-illustration-by-tim-obrien-for-time.html?product=art-print.
95 Kluger and Park, "Guardians of the year," 2020.
96 Kluger and Park, "Guardians of the year," 2020.
97 See: Kluger and Park, "Guardians of the year," 2020.
98 Matt Hunter, "Local Artist Honors Health Care Workers Battling Coronavirus," *Spectrum News 1* (February 3, 2021), accessed June 3, 2022, https://spectrumlocalnews.com/nys/capital-region/coronavirus/2021/02/03/pandemic-portraits-clifton-park-artist#.

99   Hunter, 2021.
100 The notion of the weak self is inspired by feminist philosopher Eva Majewska and in particular by the following essay: Eva Majewska, "Weak Resistance," Krisis. Journal for contemporary philosophy, Issue 2 (2018), accessed July 22, 2022, https://archive.krisis.eu/weak-resistance/. Krisis is a peer-reviewed, open access academic journal with articles in English or in Dutch. It is published by the University of Groningen Press and was established in 2008.
101 Yener Bayramoğlu and María do Mar Castro Varela, Post/Pandemisches Leben. Eine neue Theorie der Fragilität (Bielefeld: transcript, 2021), 23 and 25.
102 See: Steven Morris, "New Banksy piece celebrates superhero health workers," The Guardian (May 6, 2020), accessed July 22, 2022, https://www.theguardian.com/artanddesign/2020/may/06/banksy-artwork-superhero-nurse-nhs-coronavirus-covid-19-southampton-general-hospital. An image of the Banksy piece on display at Southampton general hospital is included in this article. A BBC report by arts editor Will Gompertz titled "New Banksy artwork appears at Southampton Hospital", which was also published on May 6, makes the same image available. See: https://www.bbc.com/news/entertainment-arts-52556544.
103 Poster-Banksy – Real Hero, "Gesellschaftskritische Kunst für Ihre Wände," accessed July 22, 2022, https://www.wall-art.de/poster/Poster-Banksy-Real-Hero.html?listtype=search&searchparam=Banksy&_gl=1*1a6d2vq*_up*MQ..&gclid=CjwKCAiA-8SdBhBGEiwAWdgtcMxe3XG_OlfqJxqPBNGPjkVwawW2TNjNNgNXSfPOsuDFDxtPTSTsVRoCzEAQAvD_BwE.
104 My Art Broker, Banksy, accessed July 22, 2022, https://www.myartbroker.com/artist-banksy/articles/banksys-game-changer-everything-you-need-to-know-about-the-street-artists-gift-to-the-nhs.
105 Radio France Internationale rfi, "Banksy painting sells for €19.4m with proceeds going to fight Covid-19 in the UK," rfi (March 23, 2021), accessed July 22, 2022, https://www.rfi.fr/en/culture/20210323-banksy-art-on-sale-to-support-uk-health-service-in-covid-battle-culture. Radio France Internationale is a state-owned broadcaster. This foreign service department of French radio stations was founded in 1975. Similar to Deutsche Welle, BBC World Service, the Voice of America, China Radio International or Radio Netherlands Worldwide it is one of the most influential and widely listened to international radio stations.
106 Radio France Internationale rfi, "Banksy," March 23, 2021.

107 Richard Brian Ferguson, "Masculinity and War," *Current Anthropology* 62, no. S23 (2021), accessed July 22, 2022, https://www.journals.uchicago.edu/doi/full/10.1086/711622#_i18.

108 HealthCom Media, "American Nurse Heroes Announce Premiere of Multi-Network TV Special," (June 1, 2021), accessed July 22, 2022, https://www.globenewswire.com/news-release/2021/06/01/2239814/0/en/American-Nurse-Heroes-Announces-Premiere-of-Multi-Network-TV-Special.html.

109 Allison Aulds, "Worldwide, People Clapping for Hospital Workers," (April 3, 2020), accessed July 22, 2022, https://www.webmd.com/lung/news/20200403/worldwide-people-clapping-for-hospital-workers.

110 Aulds, 2020.

111 Aulds, 2020.

112 Gemma Mitchell, "Clap for Heroes: Nurses say they do not want return of applause," *Nursing Times* (January 7, 2021), accessed July 22, 2022, https://www.nursingtimes.net/news/coronavirus/clap-for-heroes-nurses-say-they-do-not-want-return-of-applause-07-01-2021/.

113 Mitchell, 2021

114 Mitchell, 2021; The following study on "Clapping for carers in the Covid-19 crisis: Carer's reflections in a UK survey" carried out by Jill Manthorpe and others also provides evidence that clapping was seen to distract from the severity of the pandemic and the lack of resources. See: https://onlinelibrary.wiley.com/doi/10.1111/hsc.13474

115 David Berger, "Please stop calling health care workers 'heroes'. It's killing us," *The Sydney Morning Herald*, July 26, 2020, accessed July 22, 2022, https://www.smh.com.au/national/please-stop-calling-healthcare-workers-heroes-it-s-killing-us-20200723-p55ev2.html.

116 Berger, "Please stop calling health care workers 'heroes'," July 26, 2020.

117 World Health Organization, "The impact of COVID-19 on health and care workers: a closer look at deaths," September 2021, accessed July 22, 2022, https://apps.who.int/iris/handle/10665/345300.

118 Wichterich 175.

119 Wichterich, 183.

120 Elan Abrell, *Saving Animals: Multispecies ecologies of rescue and care* (Minneapolis, MN: University of Minnesota Press, 2021).

121 See: Achille Mbembe, "Necropolitics," *Public Culture* vol. 15 no. 1 (2003): 11–40; Achille Mbembe, *Necropolitics* (Durham, NC and London: Duke University Press, 2019); Beverley Skeggs, "Necroeconomics: How Necro

Legacies Help Us Understand the Value of Death and the Protection of Life During the COVID-19 Pandemic," *Historical Social Research HRS* vol. 46 no. 178 (2021): 123–142. *Public Culture* is a peer-reviewed academic journal in the field of cultural studies. It was established in 1988. It is sponsored by the Department of Media, Culture, and Communication at New York University and published by Duke University Press. *Historical Social Research* is an international peer-reviewed journal. Articles can be published in German or in English. It was established in 1976 and is published by GESIS Leibniz Institut für Sozialwissenschaften in Cologne.

122 Kelley Fearnley and Shaun Peter Qureshi, "Who's Clapping Now? UK health care workers with long Covid have long been abandoned," *Guardian*, July 6, 2022, accessed July 22, 2022, https://www.theguardian.com/commentisfree/2022/jul/06/uk-healthcare-workers-long-covid-abandoned-losing-jobs.

123 Fearnley and Qureshi, "Who's Clapping Now?", 2022.

124 Feminist scholar Riikka Prattes is currently working on dimensions of colonial care with a particular focus on the implications of whiteness. Riikka Prattes's (forthcoming) "Learning through Care: Decentering Dominant Epistemologies to Theorize Caring Men at the 'Center'," in *Decentering Epistemologies and Challenging Privilege: Critical Care Ethics Perspectives*, eds. Sophie Bourgault, Maggie FitzGerald, and Fiona Robinson (New Brunswick, NJ: Rutgers University Press).

125 On the notion of planetary feminism in relation to care see: Margarita Tsomou, "Care and Regeneration Work in the Paradigm of Ecological Catastrophes," in *Empowerment. Art and Feminisms*, eds. Andreas Beitin, Katharina Koch, and Uta Ruhkamp (Wolfsburg: Kunstmuseum Wolfsburg, 2022), 176–183.

Chapter 3: Feminist Recovery

1 World Health Organization, *Covid-19: physical distancing*, accessed July 22, 2022, https://www.who.int/westernpacific/emergencies/covid-19/information/physical-distancing.

2 Ulrich Brand and Markus Wissen, *The Imperial Mode of Living. Everyday Life and the Ecological Crisis of Capitalism*, trans. Zachary King (London: Verso, 2021).

3   Rebecca Solnit, "The Impossible Has Already Happened," *Guardian*, April 7, 2020, accessed July 22, 2022, https://www.theguardian.com/world/2020/apr/07/what-coronavirus-can-teach-us-about-hope-rebecca-solnit.

4   I first introduced the idea of new global international care order in my essay "Care Feminism for Living with an Infected Planet", which was published as part of a 2020 series of corona essays, offered to the public on the website of Academy of Fine Arts Vienna, and then further elaborated on this idea in two more essays published the same year. See: Elke Krasny, "Care Feminism for Living with an Infected Planet," Academy of Fine Arts Vienna (April 2020), accessed July 22, 2022, https://www.academia.edu/43164537/Care_Feminism_for_Living_with_an_Infected_Planet; Elke Krasny, "Staying with the Crisis. A Feminist Politics of Care for Living with an Infected Planet," *Escritura e Imagen* 16 (2020): 307–326; Elke Krasny: "In Sorge Bleiben: Care Feminismus für einen infizierten Planeten", in *Die Corona-Gesellschaft. Analysen zur Lage und Perspektiven für die Zukunft*, eds. Michael Volkmer and Karin Werner (Bielefeld: transcript, 2020), 405–414.

5   On the lack of preparedness for pandemic outbreaks see for example: Debora MacKenzie, "So What do We Do About Disease?" in *The Pandemic that Never Should Have Happened and How to Stop the Next One* (London: The Bridge Street Press, 2020), 141–181.

6   James Whorton, *Before Silent Spring. Pesticides and Public Health in Pre-DDT America* (Princeton, NJ: Princeton University Press, 1974), 248–49; Ben Tarnoff, "How the Internet Was Invented," *Guardian*, July 16, 2016, accessed July 22, 2022, https://www.theguardian.com/technology/2016/jul/15/how-the-internet-was-invented-1976-arpa-kahn-cerf. See also: Beatriz Colomina, *Domesticity at War* (Cambridge, MA and London: MIT Press, 2007).

7   The notion of feminist infrastructural critique was introduced on the occasion of a symposium, which I curated at the Academy of Fine Arts Vienna in 2022. *Feminist Infrastructural Critique. Interdependencies of Bodies, Materials, and Technologies*, Symposium, May 14, 2022, Academy of Fine Arts Vienna, accessed July 22, 2022, https://webportal-live.akbild.ac.at/en/museum-and-exhibitions/Exhibit/exhibitions-events/current-exhibitions/2022/einrichtung-und-gegebenheit-infrastruktur-als-form-und-handlung/feminist-infrastructural-critique. See also: Elke Krasny, "Living with a Wounded Planet: Infrastructural Consciousness Raising,"

in *Broken Relations. Infrastructure, Aesthetics, and Critique*, eds. Beatrice von Bismarck et al. (Leipzig: Spector Books, 2022), 67–76.

8   See: Riikka Prattes "Learning through Care: Decentering Dominant Epistemologies to Theorize Caring Men at the 'Center'," in *Decentering Epistemologies and Challenging Privilege: Critical Care Ethics Perspectives*, eds. Sophie Bourgault, Maggie FitzGerald and Robinson, Fiona (New Brunswick, NJ: Rutgers University Press, 2023). Prattes draws on the work of feminist philosopher and epistemologist Lorraine Code in order to question the epistemology of mastery. See: Lorraine Code, *Ecological Thinking: The Politics of Epistemic Location* (Oxford and New York: Oxford University Press, 2006).

9   Silvia Federici, "Undeclared War against Women," *Artforum International* 55, no. 10 (Summer 2017), accessed July 22, 2022, https://www.artforum.com/contributor/silvia-federici.

10 Rita Laura Segato, "A Manifesto in Four Themes," trans. Ramsey McGlazer, *EuroNomade* (October 2013), accessed July 22, 2022, http://www.euronomade.info/wp-content/uploads/2018/03/A-Manifesto-in-Four-Themes.pdf.

11 See: Susie Jacobs, Ruth Jacobson, and Jen Marchbank, "Wars Against Women: Sexual Violence, Sexual Politics and the Militarised State," in *States of Conflict: Gender, Violence, and Resistance* (London: Zed Books, 2000): 45–65.

12 UN Women, *The Shadow Pandemic. Violence against women during COVID-19*, accessed July 22, 2022, https://www.unwomen.org/en/news/in-focus/in-focus-gender-equality-in-covid-19-response/violence-against-women-during-covid-19.

13 Riikka Prattes "Learning through Care: Decentering Dominant Epistemologies to Theorize Caring Men at the 'Center'" in Bourgault, Sophie, FitzGerald, Maggie and Robinson, Fiona (eds): *Decentering Epistemologies and Challenging Privilege: Critical Care Ethics Perspectives* (New Brunswick, NJ: Rutgers University Press, 2023). Prattes builds on the work of Black feminist social theorist Patricia Hill Collins on epistemologies of separation. See: Patricia Hill Collins: *Black Feminist Thought: Knowledge, Consciousness, and the Politics of Empowerment* (New York: Routledge, 1991).

14 Riikka Prattes, "'I don't clean up after myself': epistemic ignorance, responsibility and the politics of the outsourcing of domestic cleaning," *Feminist Theory* 21, no 1 (2020): 25, accessed July 22, 2022, https://doi.org/10.1177/1464700119842560.

15 See: Prattes, "'I don't clean up after myself'", 2020.
16 Carol Ann Hilton, "Indigenomics," *Site Magazine* (2020), accessed July 22, 2022, https://www.thesitemagazine.com/covid19provisions. See also: Carol Ann Hilton, *Indigenomics: Taking a Seat at the Economic Table* (Gabriola Island: New Society Publishers, 2021).
17 See: Mohsen M. Aboulnaga, Mona F. Badran, and Mai M. Barakat, "Global Informal Settlements and Urban Slums in Cities and the Coverage. Strategic Environmental Assessment and Upgrading Guidelines to Attain Sustainable Development Goals," in *Resilience of Informal Areas in Megacities – Magnitude, Challenges, and Policies. Strategic Environmental Assessment and Upgrading Guidelines to Attain Sustainable Development Goals*. (Cham: Springer, 2021), 1; UNHCR The UN Refugee Agency, *Figures at a Glance*, June 16, 2022, accessed, July 22, 2022, https://www.unhcr.org/figures-at-a-glance.html.
18 Judith Butler, *The Force of Nonviolence*, 50.
19 The COVID racial data tracker. The COVID Tracking Project. *Atlantic* (July 27, 2020) https://covidtracking.com/race, quoted in Don E. Willis and Pearl A McElfish, "Racial disparities in the COVID-19 response affecting the Marshall Islands diaspora, United States of America," *Bulletin of the World Health Organization* 99, no. 9 (September 1, 2021): 680–681, accessed July 22, 2022, doi:10.2471/BLT.20.277855.
20 Census 2021, Updating ethnic contrasts in deaths involving the coronavirus (COVID-19), England: 24 January 2020 to 31 March 2021, *Office for National Statistics*, accessed July 22, 2022, https://www.ons.gov.uk/peoplepopulationandcommunity/birthsdeathsandmarriages/deaths/articles/updatingethniccontrastsindeathsinvolvingthecoronaviruscovid19englandandwales/24january2020to31march2021.
21 Phumzile Mlambo-Ngcuka, "COVID-19: Women front and centre," *UN Women*, March 20, 2020, accessed July 22, 2022, https://www.unwomen.org/en/news/stories/2020/3/statement-ed-phumzile-covid-19-women-front-and-centre.
22 Yeva Aleksanyan and Jason Weinman, "In countries more biased against women, higher COVID-19 death rates for men might not tell an accurate story," *The Conversation*, February 10, 2022, accessed July 22, 2022, https://theconversation.com/in-countries-more-biased-against-women-higher-covid-19-death-rates-for-men-might-not-tell-an-accurate-story-175483.
23 Mlambo-Ngcuka, "Covid-19: Women front and centre," 2020.

24 OECD Policy Responses to Coronavirus (COVID-19), *Women at the core of the fight against Covid-19 crisis*, April 1, 2020, accessed July 22, 2022, https://www.oecd.org/coronavirus/policy-responses/women-at-the-core-of-the-fight-against-covid-19-crisis-553a8269/.
25 Barbara Ehrenreich, "A grubby business. Who cleans up in your house ... a man, a woman ... or a cleaner?" *Guardian*, July 12, 2003, accessed July 22, 2022, https://www.theguardian.com/world/2003/jul/12/gender.book extracts.
26 Henriette Steiner and Kristin Veel, *Touch in the Time of Corona. Reflections of Love, Care and Vulnerability in the Pandemic* (Berlin and Boston, MA: De Gruyter, 2021), 6 and 83.
27 Steiner and Veel, 83.
28 Barbara Ehrenreich, "Maid to Order: The Politics of Other Women's Work," *Harper's Magazine*, (April 2000): 64. *Harper's magazine*, founded in 1850, is the oldest magazine that has been published continuously in the United States of America. This monthly magazine focuses on literature, politics, finance, and culture. The mistress-maid relationship is one of the most profound issues of middle-class White feminism in the context of North America and what was, at the time of the 1970s and 1980s, known as Western Europe in geopolitical terms. Nancy Fraser has also written a seminal piece about the economic shift that took place when feminism was focused on women gaining access to the hegemonic economic and joining its workforce in masses. Fraser has diagnosed this as the cunning of history under capitalism. See: Nancy Fraser, "Feminism, Capitalism and the Cunning of History," *New Left Review* 56 (March 2009): 97–117. For a broader understanding of the public imaginaries of care we are provided with today, the term chore wars, along with the capitalist capture of women's labor power perceived, and even celebrated, as feminist achievement, advancement, and empowerment—at the expense of care being commodified and, perhaps, even more vulnerable to exploitation and devaluation than before—are still useful analytical frames.
29 I want to thank Maddalena Fragnito and Zoe Romano for sharing their activist insights into the condition of domestic workers and care workers, and particularly of vaccine injustice, in their local context of Milan, Italy.
30 Office of the High Commissioner for Human Rights, "Covid 19 and women's rights" (concept note for the annual full-day discussion on the human rights of women, 44th Session of the Human Rights Council), July 14, 2020, accessed July 22, 2022, https://www.ohchr.org/sites/default/fil

es/HRBodies/HRC/RegularSessions/Session44/Documents/CNwomenpanel2COVID.docx.

31 See: *Equal Care Manifest*, February 29, 2020, accessed July 22, 2022, https://equalcareday.de/manifest/.

32 UN Women, *Beyond Covid-19: A Feminist Plan for Sustainability and Social Justice*, ed. Tina Johnson, (New York: UN Women, 2021), 8, accessed July 22, 2022, https://www.unwomen.org/sites/default/files/Headquarters/Attachments/Sections/Library/Publications/2021/Feminist-plan-for-sustainability-and-social-justice-en.pdf.

33 See: Feminists Theorize Covid-19: A Symposium, *Signs. Journal of Women in Culture and Society*, no date, accessed July 22, 2022, http://signsjournal.org/covid/. Feminist Analysis of Covid-19. Special Issue. *Feminist Studies* 46 no. 3 (2020), accessed July 22, 2022, http://www.feministstudies.org/issues/vol-40-49/46-3.html; A Special Issue on Feminist Economic Perspectives on the Pandemic, *Feminist Economics* 27 (2021), accessed July 22, 2022, https://www.tandfonline.com/toc/rfec20/27/1-2; Covid-19 and the Social Politics of Crises Special Issue, Call for Papers, *Social Politics*, accessed July 22, 2022, https://academic.oup.com/sp/pages/call-for-papers.

34 Michael Fine and Joan Tronto, eds., *Care, caring and the global Covid-19 pandemic. International Journal of Care and Caring* 6, no. 1–2 (February 2022).

35 On their website the Gender and Covid-19 Working Group lists the following contributors: Amy Oyekunle, Lokpriy Shrma, Heang-Lee Tan, Mariela Rocha, Samira Karsiem, Anne Ngunijir, Alice Murage, Kate Hawkins, Germaine Furaha, Tahera Ahsan, Sara E. Davies, Chukwuemeka Eluemunor, Huiyun Feng, Karen A. Grépin, Moumita Islam, Naila Kabeer, Selima Sara Kabir, Kelley Lee, Gustavo Matt, Rosemary Morgan, John Mungai, Valerie Mueller, Denise Pimenta, Atonu Rabbani, Sabina F. Rashid, Erica N. Rosse, Julia Smith, and Clare Wenham. See: Gender& Covid 19, The team, acccessed July 22, 2022. https://www.genderandcovid-19.org/team/. The growing list of resources is curated by Rosemary Morgan, whose research focuses on intersectionality, gender inequities, and public health. The Google document can be accessed here: https://docs.google.com/document/d/1_QfLS6Z9ow_1rPM-jdeKC_lQXTcwA8Z4kF8Z5CerZrk/edit#

36 Clare Wenham, Julia Smith, and Rosemary Morgan on behalf of the Gender and Covid-19 Working Group, "Covid-19: the gendered impacts of the outbreak," *The Lancet*, March 6, 2020, accessed July 22, 2022, https://www.thelancet.com/journals/lancet/article/PIIS0140-6736(20)305262/fulltext.

37 Wenham, Smith and Morgan, Covid-19: the gendered impacts of the outbreak, 2020
38 UN Women, "The Shadow Pandemic: Violence against women during Covid-19," May 27, 2020, accessed July 22, 2022, https://www.unwomen.org/en/news/in-focus/in-focus-gender-equality-in-covid-19-response/violence-against-women-during-covid-19.
39 Rowan Harvey, "The Ignored Pandemic. The Dual Crisis of Gender-Based Violence and Covid-19," in the Oxfam Digital Repository, November 2021, accessed July 22, 2022, https://oxfamilibrary.openrepository.com/bitstream/handle/10546/621309/bp-ignored-pandemic-251121-en.pdf.
40 UNICEF Education Covid-19 Response, "Issue Brief: Covid-19 and Girls' Education in East Asia and Pacific," October 2020, accessed July 22, 2022, https://www.unicef.org/eap/media/7146/file/Issue_Brief%3A_Issue_Brief%3A_COVID-19_and_Girls'_Education_in_East_Asia_and_Pacific.pdf
41 World Bank, "Girls' Education," February 10, 2022, accessed July 22, 2022, https://www.worldbank.org/en/topic/girlseducation.
42 UNICEF Education Covid-19 Response, 2020.
43 Jamie Smyth and Sarah Neville, "Covid, burnout and low pay: the global crisis in nursing," *Financial Times*, June 2, 2022, accessed July 22, 2022, https://www.ft.com/content/402df6ca-5098-40ca-9cc8-bae331c39398.
44 Smyth and Neville, 2022.
45 Jenesse Miller, "COVID-19 pandemic has hit women hard, especially working mothers," USC Dornsife, June 18, 2020, accessed July 22, 2022, https://dornsife.usc.edu/news/stories/3234/covid-19-pandemic-has-hit-women-hard-especially-working-mothers/.
46 Kevin Barnes-Ceeney, Lior Gideon, Laurie Leitch and Kento Yasuhara, "Recovery After Genocide: Understanding the Dimensions of Recovery Capital Among Incarcerated Genocide Perpetrators in Rwanda," *Frontiers in Psychology 10*, Article 637 (April 6, 2019), accessed July 22, 2022, doi: 10.3389/fpsyg.2019.00637. eCollection 2019.
47 Brian O'Keeley and Patrick Love, "From Crisis to Recovery. The Causes, Course and Consequences of the Great Recession", in OECD Publishing, 2010, accessed July 22, 2022, https://doi.org/10.1787/9789264077072-en.
48 See for example: Barbara Van Paassen, "Why we need feminist leadership for climate justice," *OpenDemocracy* (May 5, 2022), accessed July 22, 2022, https://www.opendemocracy.net/en/changemakers/climate-change-justice-feminist-leaders-rebuilding-world/.

49 See: Deborah Stone, "Why We Need a Care Movement," *Nation*, March 13, 2000, 13–15; Joan Tronto, *Who Cares? How to Reshape a Democratic Politics* (Ithaca, NY and London: Cornell University Press, 2015); Cinzia Arruzza, Tithi Bhattacharya, and Nancy Fraser, *Feminism for the 99%. A Manifesto* (London and New York: Verso, 2019); The Pirate Care Project, accessed July 22, 2022, https://pirate.care/pages/concept/#fn-6; María Puig de la Bellacasa, *Matters of Care. Speculative Ethics for More than Human Worlds* (Minneapolis, MN: University of Minnesota Press, 2017); Angelika Fitz and Elke Krasny, eds., *Critical Care. Architecture and Urbanism for a Broken Planet* (Boston, MA: MIT Press, 2019); Françoise Vergès, *Decolonial Feminism* (London: Pluto Press, 2021); Emma Dowling, *The Care Crisis: What Caused It and How We Can End It?* (London and New York: Verso, 2021); The Care Collective, *The Care Manifesto.* (London and New York: Verso, 2020); Vanessa Nakate, *A Bigger Picture: My Fight to Bring a New African Voice to the Climate Crisis* (Boston: Mariner Books, 2021); Anne Karpf, *How Women Can Save the Planet* (London: Hurst Publishers, 2021).
50 Judith Butler, *The Force of Nonviolence*, 17.
51 Butler, 43.
52 Judith Butler, "Creating an Inhabitable Earth Means Dismantling Rigid Forms of Individuality," *Time*, April 21, 2021, accessed July 22, 2022, https://time.com/5953396/judith-butler-safe-world-individuality/.
53 UN Women, "Recognize care as a human right, urge leaders of the Global Alliance for Care," December 14, 2021, accessed July 22, 2022, https://www.unwomen.org/en/news-stories/news/2021/12/recognize-care-as-a-human-right-urge-leaders-of-the-global-alliance-for-care.
54 Khara Jabola-Carolus in collaboration with members of the community, *Building Bridges, Not Walking on Backs. A Feminist Economic Recovery Plan for Covid-19* (Honolulu, HI: Hawai'i State Commission on the Status of Women, 2020), accessed July 22, 2022, https://humanservices.hawaii.gov/wp-content/uploads/2020/04/4.13.20-Final-Cover-D2-Feminist-Economic-Recovery-D1.pdf.
55 Jabola-Carolus, 4.
56 Jabola-Carolus, 4.
57 Jabola-Carolus, 17.
58 Gloria Anzaldúa and the Gloria Anzaldúa Trust, "Acts of Healing," in *This Bridge Called My Back. writings of radical women of color*, eds. Cherríe Moraga and Gloria Anzaldúa (Albany, NY: State University of New York Press, 2015), xxviii.

59 Lauren Berlant, "Intimacy: A Special Issue," *Critical Inquiry* 24, no. 2 (Winter 1998), 283.
60 Jabola-Carolus, 1. The quarterly peer-reviewed journal Critical Inquiry has been published by the University of Chicago Press on behalf of the Department of English Language since 1974.
61 See: Marilyn Marks Rubin and John R. Bartle, "Gender-responsive budgeting: a global perspective," in *Handbook on Gender and Public Administration*, eds. Patricia M. Shields and Nicole M. Elias (Cheltenham: Edward Elgar Publishing, 2022), 146.
62 Khara Jabola-Carolus, "A Feminist Recovery Plan for Hawaii, and Beyond, Post-Covid-19," Rosa Luxemburg Stiftung New York City, June 20, 2022, accessed July 22, 2022, https://rosalux.nyc/author/kharajabola-carolus/.
63 Jabola-Carolus, *Building Bridges*, 1 and 17.
64 Megan Wildhood and Ruth Terry, "Hawai'i's Post-COVID Recovery Plan Puts Women First," yesmagazine, July 15, 2020, accessed July 22, 2022, https://www.yesmagazine.org/economy/2020/07/15/hawaii-covid-recovery.
65 Sarah Farris, *In the Name of Women's Rights: The Rise of Femonationalism* (Durham and London: Duke University Press, 2017), 2.
66 Afrifem Macroeconomics Collective, "African Feminist Post-Covid Economic Recovery Statement," July 7, 2020, accessed July 22, 2022, https://www.nawi.africa/the-collective/. The statement was also published on Femnet, https://femnet.org/2020/07/african-feminist-post-covid-19-economic-recovery-statement/.
67 Afrifem Macroeconomics Collective, 2020.
68 Afrifem Macroeconomics Collective, 2020.
69 Anjum Sultana, "Why We Need a Feminist Recovery Plan," YWCA Canada, May 25, 2020, accessed July 22, 2022, https://ywcacanada.ca/news/why-we-need-a-feminist-recovery-plan/.
70 YWCA Canada and the Institute for Gender and the Economy, *A Feminist Recovery Plan for Canada*, July 20, 2020, accessed July 22, 2022, https://www.feministrecovery.ca/about-us.
71 Anjum Sultana and Carmina Ravanera, *A Feminist Economic Recovery Plan for Canada: Making the Economy Work for Everyone*. The Institute for Gender and the Economy (GATE) and YWCA Canada, July 28, 2020, accessed July 22, 2022, https://static1.squarespace.com/static/5f0cd2090f50a31a91b37ff7/t/5f205a15b1b7191d12282bf5/1595955746613/Feminist+Economy+Recovery+Plan+for+Canada.pdf, 1.

72 Sultana and Ravanera, vi.
73 See: Sultana and Ravanera, v.
74 See: Women's Policy Group NI, *Covid-19 Feminist Recovery Plan*, July 2020.
75 UNHR.HN – Human Rights Office of the High Commissioner. Working Group on discrimination against women and girls, OHCHR.UNOG. Discrimination against women in economic and social life, with a focus on economic crisis, A/HRC/26/39 Human Rights Council Twenty-sixth session. (Paragraph 81), 2014, quoted in: Radhika Balakrishnan, Melissa Upreti, and Camila Belliard, *A Covid-19 Feminist Recovery Plan to Achieve Substantive Gender Equality*, Rutgers Center for Women's Global Leadership 2021, accessed July 22, 2022, https://cwgl.rutgers.edu/blog-details/644-a-covid-19-feminist-recovery-plan-to-achieve-substantive-gender-equality, 2.
76 On the purple economy see for example: Ipek Ilkkaracan, "Four things to know about the purple economy," IWRWA Asia Pacific, Kuala Lumpur: International Women's Rights Action Watch Asia Pacific, 2018, accessed July 22, 2022, https://www.iwraw-ap.org/wp-content/uploads/2018/10/Four-Things-to-Know-about-the-Purple-Economy.pdf.; Ipek Ilkkaracan, "A Feminist Alternative to Austerity. The purple economy as a gender-egalitarian strategy for employment generation," in *Economics and Austerity in Europe: Gendered impacts and sustainable alternatives*, eds. Hannah Bargawi, Giovanni Cozzi, and Susan Himmelweit (London and New York, Routledge, 2017): 27–39.
77 Balakrishnan, Upreti and Belliard, 8.
78 Balakrishnan, Upreti and Belliard, 9.
79 Serena Natile, organizer, at the Warwick Social Sciences and School of Law, "Feminist Recovery Plans Workshop," 18 June 2021, accessed July 22, 2022, https://warwick.ac.uk/fac/soc/law/research/projects/feminist-recovery-plan/workshop/.
80 "Feminist Recovery Plans Workshop," 2021, https://warwick.ac.uk/fac/soc/law/research/projects/feminist-recovery-plan/workshop/.
81 Serena Natile, "Towards feminist recovery plans for Covid-19 and beyond," Globe Centre Policy Brief Series, February 2022, accessed July 22, 2022, https://warwick.ac.uk/fac/soc/law/research/projects/feminist-recovery-plan/towards_feminist_recovery_plans_for_covid-19_and_beyond_-_serena_natile.pdf, 1.
82 Natile, "Towards feminist recovery plans," 2022.

83 The concept of intersectionality was first fully developed by Kimberlé Crenshaw, "Demarginalizing the Intersection of Race and Sex: A Black Feminist Critique of Antidiscrimination Doctrine, Feminist Theory and Antiracist Politics," *University of Chicago Legal Forum* no. 1 (1989): 139–167. Black and lesbian feminist activists, like the Combahee River Collective, active in Boston between 1974 and 1980, had already developed such perspectives on multiple and interlocking discriminations before they entered into legal theory.

84 Kimberlé Crenshaw, "Intersectionality Matters!" podcast, *The African American Policy Forum*, accessed July 22, 2022, https://www.aapf.org/imkc-podcast-episodes. Resulting from this series of podcasts, the book by Crenshaw and Daniel HoSang, whose scholarly work focuses on ethnicity, race, and migration, is one on intersectional vulnerabilities and the twin pandemics, which in the context of the United States, are understood as the Covid-19 pandemic and the pandemic of state sanctioned violence against Black people. See: Kimberlé Crenshaw and Daniel HoSang, *Under the Blacklight: The Intersectional Vulnerabilities that the Twin Pandemics Lay Bare* (Chicago: Haymarket Books 2023).

85 UN Women, *Beyond Covid-19. A Feminist Plan for Sustainability and Social Justice*, edited by Tina Johnson, (New York: UN Women, 2021), accessed July 22, 2022, https://www.unwomen.org/sites/default/files/Headquarters/Attachments/Sections/Library/Publications/2021/Feminist-plan-for-sustainability-and-social-justice-en.pdf, 8.

86 UN Women, 8.

87 UN Women, 46 and 58

88 Nancy Fraser interviewed by Sarah Leonhard, "Capitalism's Crisis of Care," *Dissent Magazine* (Fall 2016), accessed July 22, 2022, https://www.dissentmagazine.org/article/nancy-fraser-interview-capitalism-crisis-of-care. *Dissent Magazine*, published since 1954 by the University of Pennsylvania Press on behalf of the Foundation for the Study of Independent Social Ideas, is a quarterly magazine of politics and ideas and, in its own words, a mainstay of the democratic left. It was founded by Irving Howe and Lewis Coser and has published articles by Hannah Arendt, Martha Nussbaum, Roxane Gay, and many others.

89 See also: Gender and Development Network, "Lessons for a feminist Covid-19 economic recovery: multi-country perspectives," March 2022, accessed July 22, 2022, https://gadnetwork.org/gadn-resources/covid-economic-recovery.

90 See: Elke Krasny, "Care Feminism for Living with an Infected Planet," Academy of Fine Arts Vienna, April 2020, accessed July 22, 2022, https://www.academia.edu/43164537/Care_Feminism_for_Living_with_an_Infected_Planet;

91 Oxfam Briefing, "Coronavirus Doesn't Discriminate, But Inequality Does. Beating the pandemic means dealing with inequality," March 2020, accessed July 22, 2022, https://oi-files-d8-prod.s3.eu-west-2.amazonaws.com/s3fs-public/2020-04/Coronovirus%20doesn´t%20discriminate%2C%20but%20inequality%20does%20-%20Brief.pdf.

92 Gregg Gonsalves and Amy Kapczynski, "The Politics of Care," in *The Politics of Care. From Covid-19 to Black Lives Matter*, eds. Deborah Chasman and Joshua Cohen (Boston, MA: Boston Review; London: Verso, 2020), 15.

93 UN Women, "Recognize care as a human right, urge leaders of the Global Alliance for Care," December 14, 2021, accessed July 22, 2022, https://www.unwomen.org/en/news-stories/news/2021/12/recognize-care-as-a-human-right-urge-leaders-of-the-global-alliance-for-care.

94 Gita Gopinath, "The Great Lockdown: Worst Economic Downturn since the Great Depression," *IMF blog. Insights and Analysis on Economics &Finance*, April 14, 2020, accessed July 22, 2022. https://blogs.imf.org/2020/04/14/the-great-lockdown-worst-economic-downturn-since-the-great-depression/.

95 See: Criado-Perez, Caroline. *Invisible Women: Exposing Data Bias in a World Designed for Men* (New York: Ballantine Books, 2020), 240.

96 See: Criado-Perez, 240.

97 Criado-Perez, 240.

98 Diane Coyle, *GDP. A Brief but Affectionate History* (Princeton, NJ and Oxford: Princeton University Press, 2015), 111.

99 Criado-Perez, 240.

100 Marilyn Waring, *Counting for Nothing: What Men Value and What Women are Worth* (Toronto: University of Toronto Press, 1999), 58.

101 Coyle, 107.

102 Waring, 58.

103 Coyle, 8.

104 Coyle, 17.

105 Coyle, 17.

106 For poster images of Rosy the Riveter and a Victory Garden see: Kim Sajet, "Rosie the Riveter and Uncle Sam: Two Portraits, Two Methods of Persuasion," *Smithsonian Magazine* (February 6, 2018), accessed July 22, 2022,

Smithsonian Magazine; Senator John Heinz History Center in Association with the Smithsonian Institution, All Out for Victory Gardens, April 20, 2020, accessed July 22, 2022, https://www.heinzhistorycenter.org/blog/western-pennsylvania-history/all-out-for-victory-gardens.

107 Jill Lewis, "Mobilising Working Women in Red Vienna: Käthe Leichter and the Vienna Arbeiterkammer," *L'homme: Europäische Zeitschrift für feministische Geschichtswissenschaft* 26 (2015): 159 and 155. *L'homme* has been published since 1990 as the first German-language journal for feminist historical studies. Since 2003, the Vienna-based journal is part of the *Eurozine* network. *Eurozine* is an online magazine and European network of more than 90 cultural journals in 35 countries. It was established in 1998.

108 Criado-Perez, 241–42.

109 Waring, 59.

110 Allida M. Black, "Fundamental Freedoms: Eleanor Roosevelt, the Holocaust, and the Universal Declaration of Human Rights" (video including transcript, 2015), accessed July 22, 2022. https://www.facinghistory.org/resource-library/video/fundamental-freedoms-eleanor-roosevelt-holocaust-and-universal-declaration (10.12.2018).

111 UN General Assembly, "Universal Declaration of Human Rights," (Paris 1948), accessed April 4, 2020. https://www.un.org/en/universal-declaration-human-rights/.

112 Eleanor Roosevelt, "Where do Human Rights Begin? Remarks at the United Nations, March 27, 1953," in *Courage in a Dangerous World. The Political Writings of Eleanor Roosevelt*, ed. Allida M. Black (New York: Columbia University Press 2000): 190.

113 Sylvia Winter, "Unsettling the Coloniality of Being/Power/Truth/Freedom: Towards the Human, After Man, Its Overrepresentation–An Argument," *New Centennial Review* 3, no. 3 (Fall 2003): 260. The *New Centennial Review* publishes comparative studies on the Americas that, in their own words, suggest possibilities for a different future. The journal is published three times a year by Michigan State University.

114 William Rogers Brubaker, "The French Revolution and the Invention of Citizenship," *French Politics and Society* 7, no. 3 (1989): 31.

115 Joan Wallach Scott, "French Universalism in the Nineties," in *Women and Citizenship*, ed. Marilyn Friedman (Oxford: Oxford University Press, 2005): 37.

116 Sylvia Wynter and Katherine McKittrick, "Unparalleled Catastrophe for Our Species? Or, to Give Humanness a Different Future: Conversations,"

in *Sylvia Wynter: On Being Human as Praxis*, ed. Katherine McKittrick (Durham, NC: Duke University Press, 2015), 23.
117   UN Women, *Beyond Covid-19*, 80.
118   UN Women, 80.
119   UN Women, 81.
120   UN Women, 81.
121   Elke Krasny, "Care Feminism for Living with an Infected Planet,", 2022.
122   UN Women, 81.
123   Anamika Misra, "Humanity's Catastrophe: Following Sylvia Wynter in the Age of Coronavirus," *Critical Legal Thinking*, April 10, 2020, accessed July 22, 2022, https://criticallegalthinking.com/2020/04/10/de-prioritising-humanity/. The blog *Critical Legal Thinking* was set up in 2009 in the week of the G20 meeting in London with law seen as one field of critical intervention.
124   Constitution of Ecuador, October 20, 2008, accessed July 22, 2022, https://www.constituteproject.org/constitution/Ecuador_2021?lang=en.
125   UN Women, "Recognize care as a human right," 2021.
126   Foro Generación Igualdad, "Global Alliance for Care: An Urgent Call to Action," June 28, 2021, accessed July 22, 2022, https://forogeneracionigualdad.mx/7740-2/?lang=en. The Equality Generation Forum is a civil-society centered global gathering for gender equality convened by UN Women and co-hosted by the governments of France and Mexico. The Forum began in Mexico City in March and gathered in Paris from June 30 to July 2, 2021. Its aim is to accelerate the implementation of gender equality, which, since the Fourth World Conference in Beijing has been slow. The forum is based on multilateralism and brings together civil society, governments, youth-led organizations, trade unions, international organizations, the private sector and the media.
127   Foro Generación Igualdad, 2021.
128   See: Hebbel am Ufer, Kongress der Sorge | Ein Vernetzungstag für Arbeitskämpfe und feministische Initiativen anlässlich des Tages der Pflege am 12.5. 2022, accessed July 2022, https://www.hebbel-am-ufer.de/service/presse/kongress-der-sorge/; Bündnis Sorgearbeit Fair teilen, accessed July 22, 2022, https://www.bmfsfj.de/resource/blob/160288/162f9f1a46f048f59d07d1d8ef704457/flyer-bundnis-sorgearbeit-englisch-data.pdf; Mehr für Care. Wirtschaften fürs Leben, accessed July 22, 2022, https://mehr-fuer-care.at

129 UN Women, "Recognize care as a human right, urge leaders of the Global Alliance for Care," December 14, 2021, accessed July 22, 2022, https://www.unwomen.org/en/news-stories/news/2021/12/recognize-care-as-a-human-right-urge-leaders-of-the-global-alliance-for-care.
130 UN Women, *Beyond Covid-19*, 2021, 10.
131 Gender & Covid-19, "Beyond Covid-19: A Feminist Plan for Sustainability and Social Justice," March 8, 2022, accessed July 22, 2022, https://www.genderandcovid-19.org/editorial/beyond-covid-19-a-feminist-plan-for-sustainability-and-social-justice/.
132 Magdalena Sepúlveda, "The recovery will be green and feminist or it won't be," *Social Europe*, May 11, 2022, accessed July 22, 2022, https://socialeurope.eu/the-recovery-will-be-green-and-feminist-or-it-wont-be. Social Europe is a European digital media publisher, which was founded by German social scientist Henning Meyer. It was published from London between 2005 and 2018 and is now based in Berlin.
133 Nicole Aschoff, "Covid-19 Should be a Wake-Up Call for Feminism," *The Jacobin* (April 15, 2020), accessed July 22, 2022, https://jacobin.com/2020/04/covid-19-coronavirus-pandemic-feminism. *The Jacobin* is a quarterly American political magazine based in New York. It was founded by American political writer Bashkar Sunkara in 2010 and is published by Remeike Forbes. It offers socialist perspectives on politics and economics.
134 Graham Huggan and Helen Tiffin, *Postcolonial Ecocriticism: Literature, Animals, Environment* (London: Routledge, 2010): 202, quoted in Cajetan Iheka, "Rights," in *The Cambridge Companion to Environmental Humanities*, eds. Jeffrey Jerome Cohen and Stephanie Foote (Cambridge: Cambridge University Press, 2021), 31. 26–38
135 Tronto, *Who Cares?*, 39.

Essay

João Costa
Health as a Social System
Luhmann's Theory Applied to Health Systems.
An Introduction

January 2023, 198 p., pb.
30,00 € (DE), 978-3-8376-6693-9
E-Book: available as free open access publication
PDF: ISBN 978-3-8394-6693-3

Markus Gabriel, Christoph Horn, Anna Katsman, Wilhelm Krull, Anna Luisa Lippold, Corine Pelluchon, Ingo Venzke
Towards a New Enlightenment –
The Case for Future-Oriented Humanities

2022, 80 p., pb.
18,00 € (DE), 978-3-8376-6570-3
E-Book: available as free open access publication
PDF: ISBN 978-3-8394-6570-7
ISBN 978-3-7328-6570-3

Anke Strüver, Sybille Bauriedl (eds.)
Platformization of Urban Life
Towards a Technocapitalist Transformation
of European Cities

2022, 304 p., pb.
29,50 € (DE), 978-3-8376-5964-1
E-Book: available as free open access publication
PDF: ISBN 978-3-8394-5964-5

All print, e-book and open access versions of the titles in our list
are available in our online shop www.transcript-publishing.com